This wide-ranging study presents an examination of the extraordinary diversity and range of satirical writing in contemporary Russian literature and will be of interest not only to Slavicists but also to those interested in genre theory. Through the close analysis of seminal satirical texts written by five Russian and émigré authors in the 70s and 80s, Karen Ryan-Hayes demonstrates that formal and thematic parody is pervasive and that it provides additional levels of meaning in contemporary Russian satire. Each work under examination is placed within the wider European literary context as well as within the Russian tradition and is representative of a different subgenre of satire. The author focuses on a variety of these genres and modes and offers practical criticism on each text. The writers under discussion have enjoyed a positive reception in the West and their works demonstrate the variety and vitality of Russian and Soviet satire.

CAMBRIDGE STUDIES IN RUSSIAN LITERATURE

CONTEMPORARY RUSSIAN SATIRE

CAMBRIDGE STUDIES IN RUSSIAN
LITERATURE

General editor MALCOLM JONES

Editorial board: ANTHONY CROSS, CARYL EMERSON,
HENRY GIFFORD, BARBARA HELDT, G. S. SMITH,
VICTOR TERRAS

Recent titles in this series include
The Brothers Karamazov and the poetics of memory
DIANE OENNING THOMPSON

Andrei Platonov
THOMAS SEIFRID

Nabokov's early fiction
JULIAN W. CONNOLLY

Iurii Trifonov
DAVID GILLESPIE

Mikhail Zoshchenko
LINDA HART SCATTON

Andrei Bitov
ELLEN CHANCES

Nikolai Zabolotsky
DARRA GOLDSTEIN

Nietzsche and Soviet Culture
edited by BERNICE GLATZER ROSENTHAL

Wagner and Russia
ROSAMUND BARTLETT

*Russian literature and empire: Conquest of the
Caucasus from Pushkin to Tolstoy*
SUSAN LAYTON

*Jews in Russian Literature after the October Revolution:
writers and artists between hope and apostasy*
EFRAIM SICHER

For a complete list of books in the series,
see the end of this volume

CONTEMPORARY RUSSIAN SATIRE

A genre study

KAREN L. RYAN-HAYES

Published by the Press Syndicate of the University of Cambridge
The Pitt Building, Trumpington Street, Cambridge, CB2 1RP
40 West 20th Street, New York, NY 10011-4211, USA
10 Stamford Road, Oakleigh, Melbourne 3166, Australia

© Cambridge University Press 1995

First published 1995

Printed in Great Britain at the University Press, Cambridge

A catalogue record for this book is available from the British Library

Library of Congress cataloguing in publication data

Ryan-Hayes, Karen L.
Contemporary Russian Satire: a genre study/Karen L. Ryan-Hayes.
p.   cm. – (Cambridge studies in Russian literature)
Includes bibliographical references and index.
ISBN 0 521 47515 5 (hardback)
1. Russian literature – 20th century – History and Criticism.
2. Satire, Russian – History and criticism.
3. Russian wit and humor – History and criticism.
I. Title. II. Series.
PG3026.S3R94 1995
891.77′4409–dc20   95-2262   CIP

ISBN 0 521 47515 5 hardback

For Daniel

Contents

Acknowledgments		*page* x
Note on the translation		xi
	Introduction	1
1	Iskander's transparent allegory: *Rabbits and Boa Constrictors*	11
2	Beyond picaresque: Erofeev's *Moscow–Petushki*	58
3	Satire and the autobiographical mode: Limonov's *It's Me, Eddie*	101
4	The family chronicle revisited: Dovlatov's *Ours*	150
5	Dystopia redux: Voinovich and *Moscow 2042*	193
	Conclusion	239
Notes		244
Select bibliography		273
Index		284

Acknowledgments

I would like to acknowledge gratefully the assistance of several institutions and individuals in my work on the present study. Research for this book was supported in part by a grant from the International Research and Exchanges Board (IREX), with funds provided by the US Department of State. The American Council of Teachers of Russian (ACTR) facilitated my research on Iskander and Erofeev in Russia. A summer research grant and a semester leave from the University of Virginia enabled me to complete work on the manuscript. I am grateful to the late Galina Erofeeva for her insights into her husband's life and work. I thank those many friends and colleagues who read and commented upon the manuscript in its various permutations. While all of these institutions and individuals have contributed greatly to the realization of this study, none of them is responsible for the views expressed or for any of its shortcomings.

Note on the translation

In the case of critical sources in Russian, all English translations in the text and footnotes are mine. For quotations of the literary works examined, I have frequently used the published English translations listed in the bibliography (sometimes with slight changes). However, in many cases I have translated the passages myself in order to emphasize important stylistic, linguistic or thematic features. Thus all page references in citations refer to the original Russian texts listed in the bibliography.

Introduction

> Marina (with bitterness): I study satire.
> Miloserdov's son: Russian or foreign?
> Marina: Ours.
> Miloserdov's son: Nineteenth century?
> Marina: No, contemporary.
> Miloserdov's son: You have a marvelous profession. You study something that doesn't exist.
> (From the film *Garage* by El'dar Riazanov)

It is fitting to begin an examination of satire with a paradox and Russian literary history presents a fine one: although major works that might be classified as satire according to traditional genre definitions are rather rare in twentieth-century Russian literature, the satirical impulse permeates and reticulates throughout Russian prose of the modern period. Satire – understood as a manner of writing, a mode rather than a genre – offers critical and persuasive force that is central to much of contemporary Russian literature. In arguing for perceiving satire as a modality rather than a form, we lay the groundwork for a critical structure far more inclusive than that endorsed by Riazanov's character (quoted above). He is certainly right in noting that no contemporary writers have donned the mantles of Gogol' or Saltykov-Shchedrin, but he ignores the satirical and ironic spirit that in fact characterizes much of contemporary Russian writing.

Satirists of the post-Stalin era trace their lineage not only to nineteenth-century classics like Gogol' and Saltykov-Shchedrin, but to writers of the so-called "Golden Age" of Soviet satire that developed in the relatively liberal decade following the

Revolution. Vladimir Maiakovskii's plays *The Bedbug* (1928) and *The Bathhouse* (1930) helped to define Soviet satire; even in the post-Soviet period, the former is part of the permanent repertoire of Moscow's Theater of Satire. Mikhail Zoshchenko's innovations with *skaz* broke new ground in satiric characterization and effectively distilled the contradictions and excesses of the NEP period. Mikhail Bulgakov's *povesti* "Heart of a Dog" (written 1925) and "The Fatal Eggs" (1924) demonstrate his proclivity for fantasy and the absurd and prefigure his satirical *chef d'œuvre The Master and Margarita* (written 1940). Il'ia Il'f and Evgenii Petrov, masters of the feuilleton, also began their literary collaboration in the twenties and created the two picaresque novels that are regarded as the acme of Soviet satire, *The Twelve Chairs* (1928) and *The Golden Calf* (1931). The acceptance of socialist realism as Soviet literary doctrine in 1934, and especially its prescriptive corollaries of "typicality," "absence of conflict" and the positive hero, made the Russian satirist's position untenable. The fates of writers like Maiakovskii, Zoshchenko, Bulgakov and Il'f and Petrov range from tragic to dreary and need not be recounted here.

What might be termed (with some allowance for exaggeration) a "Silver Age" of Soviet satire occurred during the Thaw that followed Stalin's death in 1953. Not only were unorthodox works like *The Master and Margarita* and Iskander's *The Goatibex Constellation* published (the former in a heavily cut version 1966–67, the latter in 1966), but some of the best satirical works of the twenties were reissued during this period. The development of Russian satire in the post-Thaw contemporary period, i.e. the seventies and eighties, is the focus of the present study. This was not a propitious period for satire in the Soviet Union: censorship under Brezhnev was relatively rigid and writers and purveyors of *samizdat* and *tamizdat* literature were subject to prosecution. Indeed, all of the writers whose works are treated in this study experienced the consequences of official displeasure in the "period of stagnation." It is a measure of the power and resilience of satire that despite the hostility of the literary bureaucracy and the censor, works such as Iskander's *Rabbits and Boa Constrictors* and Erofeev's *Moscow–*

Petushki were nevertheless created. Recent changes in Russia – the dissolution of the Soviet Union and the restructuring of the cultural apparatus – have not obviated the central role of satire in literature. Indeed, the sweeping changes of the last decade have provided a clearer perspective on satire of the seventies and eighties, now that the Brezhnev era is receding into the past.

The specificity of Russian satire and the unique problems posed by Russian literary history present several challenges to the critic examining the satirical mode in its Russian context. In the first place, Russian and Soviet criticism tends to conflate satire and humor; a critical distinction is seldom made and the terms are usually used synonymously. The element of criticism that most Western theoreticians regard as a distinguishing feature of satire is presumed by most Russian sources to be present in humor as well. Russian literary criticism's insistence on relegating satire to a "low" status complicates the situation further. Following classical rhetoricians and eighteenth-century doctrine, Russian theoreticians and writers have ghettoized satire in special sections of journals and newspapers and in critical discourse. The bulk of Russian critical theory devoted to satire consists of manuals directing the aspiring satirist in the art of penning effective feuilletons, sketches, satirical essays and the like. Satire, unlike most other modes of literature, finds its object outside of art, in the social, political or moral life of the culture it treats. While Western literary traditions have often de-emphasized the didactic function of satire and viewed it as a forum for oppositionist commentary and mockery, Russian and Soviet criticism has emphasized the reformative nature of the mode. Theoreticians of Russian and Soviet satire have urged practitioners to capitalize on their opportunity to instruct their readers and to ameliorate the ills and excesses they pillory. This utilitarian, functional quality of satire that has often rendered it liminal in Western art has found special resonance in Russian and Soviet culture. Finally, the issue of censorship must be taken into consideration in any study of Russian satire. Lev Loseff follows Kenneth Burke in postulating censorship in Russia and the Soviet Union as (paradoxically) a factor that contributes positively to satirical writing. The artist's balancing aesthetic considerations against the possibility of reprisal has, according to Loseff, been instrumental in the creation of subtle and inventive satire.[1] Moreover, evading the censor may serve as a means of catharsis in a repressive society like the Soviet Union; breaking taboos in satire constitutes a literary carnival experience through which author and reader satisfy a need to transgress norms and come to terms with authority.[2] The role of satire is thus particularized critically, politically and psychologically in its Russian context and these factors necessarily shape this study of contemporary satirical literature.

One of the most prevalent and effective techniques used in contemporary Russian satire is parody of genre conventions. In demonstrating the importance of this literary procedure, it is essential to avoid confusing parody and satire and to that end, some clarification is in order. Parody, like satire, is better approached as a mode rather than a genre. It often supports satire, serving its ends of mockery and criticism, but it need not; parody is not subordinate to satire. With that caveat in place, we observe that in practice, the parodying of other genres is in itself a satiric convention.[3] The effectiveness of the device, as we shall see, depends on whether the satirist's target is susceptible to parodical treatment:

> Although we are accustomed to reading texts in which parody supports satire ... such a relation exists only when the subject matter of the parody relates closely to the subject matter of the satire. Only when the parodic target (particular *signa* and manners of expression) is a metonymy for the satiric target, that is only when a language represents its speakers, is parody supportive of satire.[4]

Joseph Dane's formulation focuses on language, but one can argue (as I shall) that the ideology, belief systems and behavior codes associated with particular genres also determine if parody of their conventions is effective in a given satire.

A crucial distinction between satire and parody is that the former posits extramural targets (politics, social mores, cultural institutions, etc.), while the latter refers to another artistic construct. Satire aims explicitly or implicitly at the exposure or improvement of a faulty *status quo* in life; parody, strictly speaking, is an aesthetic phenomenon. Thus parodic satire – satire that employs parody as a rhetorical means – has its point of reference outside of the text, but utilizes parody as a strategy to achieve its critical ends. As Linda Hutcheon notes, "Satire frequently uses parodic art forms for either expository or aggressive purposes when it desires textual differentiation as its vehicle."[5]

Standard descriptive or prescriptive definitions of parody are not particularly helpful in explicating the texts included in the present study. Gilbert Highet, for example, views parody as a subgenre of satire and divides it further into formal parody and material parody;[6] Fred Householder, focusing on classical examples, asserts that parody must be modeled on a specific work or author;[7] John Jump treats parody as a type of burlesque.[8] All of these theoreticians regard parody as an imitative form that utilizes exaggeration or distortion to discredit the original. Beyond this narrow basis of agreement, critical understandings of parody are extremely diverse. Indeed, Samuel Johnson's characterization of parody as "a kind of writing in which the words of an author or his thoughts are taken and by a slight change adapted to some new purpose"[9] is useful precisely because it is so open-ended.

A major critical reevaluation of parody has occurred in the modern period and the insights that have resulted are most apropos to a discussion of contemporary Russian parodic satire. The Russian Formalists, notably Viktor Shklovskii and Iurii Tynianov, view parody as a means of progress and evolution in literature. In "laying bare" the clichés that characterize a given work or genre, the parodist "disrealizes" literary norms. As the product of struggle with established, stale literary devices and genre conventions, parody has tremendous productive, creative potential: "The history of parody is most closely connected with the evolution of literature. The laying bare of convention, the disclosing of verbal behavior, of the verbal pose – this is the enormous evolutionary work accomplished by parody."[10]

Mikhail Bakhtin's writings on parody constitute a profound

reconsideration of our understanding of parody; theoreticians who have followed Bakhtin inevitably elaborate upon or respond to his work. According to Bakhtin, parody is a double-voiced utterance designed to be interpreted as the expression of two speakers.[11] The parodic utterance, moreover, is intended to discredit the original: "... the voices here are not only detached and distanced, they are hostilely counterposed" (*Rabelais*, p. 160). Valentin Voloshinov, who treats narratology in terms of "authorial speech" (*avtorskaia rech'*) and "another's speech" (*chuzhaia rech'*), views parody as a refraction of the latter.[12] The author of parody uses another's speech act in pursuing his or her own ends and thus endows the parodic utterance with a new intention. We experience parody – if we are apprehending it fully – as "paired." O. M. Friedenberg asserts that unless we perceive its doubleness, it is not parody: "without chiaroscuro, without something to be contrasted to something else, it does not exist."[13] Hutcheon's definition of parody as "repetition with critical distance, which marks difference rather than similarity" (*Theory of Parody*, p. 6) restates Bakhtin's idea but redirects the focus away from the socially and politically subversive aspects of parody toward aesthetics.

In recent critical treatments of parody as a metaliterary form, the term has come to mean almost any use of another writer's style or the conventions of another genre. In this respect, parody itself serves as literary criticism, though it is not analytic in its procedure. The reflexivity that is a feature of parody is characteristic of what Margaret Rose calls the "modernist episteme" as a whole. She suggests that parody has thus become normative and is no longer necessarily anti-generic.[14] The present study is concerned with parody's function within satire rather than its progressive potential, but the broader scope of contemporary parody may be inferred from G. D. Kiremidjian's assertion that the widespread presence of parody (understood as a metaliterary form) in modern literature suggests that it expresses something fundamental about our age.[15]

As our understanding of parody expands and as we move from structure to utterance, it becomes more and more difficult to establish what techniques are characteristic of parody; even devices such as exaggeration and emphasis become problematic. Moreover, parody can operate within a text of virtually any length, so that the parameter of size is also destabilised. The comic effect that often results from parody is deemed a false indicator by Rose (*Parody//Meta-Fiction*, p. 21), and Gary Saul Morson concurs that the "functional shift" that occurs in recontextualization through parody "need not be in the direction of humor" (*Boundaries of Genre*, p. 111). Perhaps only incongruity remains as a distinguishing feature of parody. The critical distance established by the parodist is usually signaled by irony and as Hutcheon notes, "Irony's patent refusal of semantic univocality matches parody's refusal of structural unitextuality" (*Theory of Parody*, p. 54). However, incongruity and irony are so broad in their scope that they are of little use in delimiting parody. Because it is essentially parasitic and dependent on a model, parody – even within satire – discourages any rhetorical systematization of formal features.

The notion that the primary intent of parody is mockery, derision or ridicule of its model has been largely discredited by critics. In fact, parody need not criticize the original at all. Rose points out that the parodist's admiration of the model is often inseparable from a desire to reply to or modernize it (*Parody//Meta-Fiction*, p. 30). J. G. Riewald traces the change in our critical perception of parody's intent; he writes: "True parody is always critical, but, being inspired by a certain amount of sympathy, it does not make the reader devalue its original. It is this element of sympathy, admiration, or love even, that takes the sting out of what used to be called the *genus irritabile*."[16] This is not, moreover, a strictly modern development. Aristophanes may well have approved of Euripides' poetry and there are many other examples of "pure" or "absolute" parodies that do not imply dissatisfaction with the original. Friedenberg, in examining classical sources of parody, stresses the contiguity that underlies parodic texts and performances ("Origin of Parody," p. 275).

Recognizing that the intent of parody is not exclusively negative illuminates the curious dual nature of parody as both subversive and affirmative. Because it incorporates and thus legitimizes the original, parody may function as "the custodian of the artistic legacy" (Hutcheon, *Theory of Parody*, p. 75). Even as it recontextualizes the model, it reinforces its primacy, its claim to aesthetic or ideological significance. In the works included in the present study, we shall see that parody tends to serve the stable norms posited by the model explicitly or implicitly. Indeed, in recent Russian satirical literature, there is none of the "anarchy and randomness" (*ibid.*, p. 80) that are associated with metafiction as a whole. Satire – even when it uses parody in experimental, productive ways – does not question the moral and ethical norms against which the target is measured. Instead, genre norms and individual texts are recast through parody so as to satirize social, political or moral aspects of contemporary culture.

Just as the intent of parody is variable, the resulting tone ranges from scathing and sarcastic to playfully ironic. Where on this tonal scale a particular parody (or parodic passage within a work) will fall is conditioned by the parodist's point of view *vis-à-vis* the model. The extent to which the parodist disagrees with or disapproves of the original may usually be inferred from tone. While we must certainly avoid the so-called intentional fallacy, it seems that satire presents a special case in which it is virtually impossible to proceed without making inferences about authorial intention.[17] The reader must decode the encoded intent and assign what Morson calls "semantic authority" correctly, i.e. to the second voice. We must understand with whom we are to agree in order for the parody to be effective (*Boundaries of Genre*, p. 109).

Given the extent to which satire pervades modern Russian literature, it is inevitable that a single critical study should be selective in its scope. Many important contemporary satirists are not treated here: Vasilii Aksenov, Iuz Aleshkovskii, Aleksandr Zinoviev, Andrei Siniavskii, Sasha Sokolov and others are not included. The works chosen for this study are, however, seminal on both historical and aesthetic grounds and taken together, constitute a representative corpus. The five works examined represent a common attempt to adapt and transcend genre canon through use of parody. Each of the satirists treated here – Iskander, Erofeev, Limonov, Dovlatov and Voinovich – writes within a recognizable genre tradition. Having adopted genres with established conventions, they all proceed to subvert, mock, modernize or respond in some other manner to the forms chosen. Generic parody thus supports and enhances satire of Russian and Soviet culture under Brezhnev.

The authors treated in the present study also represent the diversity of contemporary Russian satire. Iskander was formerly claimed as a "Soviet" writer and has been successful in both the Soviet and post-Soviet eras. Erofeev, though he never left the Soviet Union, was an iconoclast and never sought the official sanction of the Soviet Writers' Union. Limonov, Dovlatov and Voinovich were all to some extent dissident writers under the Soviet regime and emigrated to the West. The range of satiric tonalities expressed in the texts examined is predictably broad, from gentle and mocking (Horatian) to harsh and caustic (Juvenalian). Moreover, the prose styles of these works vary widely, from relatively conservative (e.g. Dovlatov and Voinovich) to experimental (e.g. Erofeev). Finally, the individual texts are not necessarily the best known or the most typical of these authors' works. Rather, they are selected to illustrate a technique that is artistically and ideationally effective and that unites disparate strains in Russian satire.

The evidence supplied by even a cursory reading of recent Russian prose suggests that the satirical impulse is a major motive force among contemporary writers. In light of this wealth of satirical literature, the dearth of criticism focusing on the praxis of Russian satire is striking. There are, of course, important exceptions. Richard Chapple's *Soviet Satire of the Twenties* is thorough, but limited in its scope; Peter Henry's two-volume *Anthology of Soviet Satire* includes an excellent historical introduction to Russian and Soviet satire. Russian critical contributions are more numerous, but these works remain for the most part untranslated. They include Ja. El'sberg's *The Heritage of Gogol' and Shchedrin and Soviet Satire*; L. Ershov's *Satirical Genres of Russian Soviet Literature*; V. Frolov's *The Muse of Flaming Satire*. Also very valuable to the student of Russian satire is E. K. Ozmitel''s comprehensive (if dated) bibliographical guide *Soviet Satire: Seminars*.

The present study is intended to fill a gap in Western criticism on Russian satire. It is my aim to characterize contemporary Russian satire through close reading of five texts written in the seventies and eighties. In each of the five chapters that follow, I place the text treated within the generic traditions – both Russian and Western – in which it is written. I then demonstrate through textual explication how parody functions as a device that supports satire. Since parody is intertwined with other elements (both formal and thematic), I consider related issues such as narratology and stylistics that contribute to satirical efficacy. Stated in the broadest terms, the goal of this study is to explore the extraordinary diversity and range of the satiric modality in contemporary Russian literature.

The chapters that constitute this study are arranged to reflect the chronological development of generic norms that serve as the models for parody in recent Russian satire. Chapter 1 examines Iskander's *Rabbits and Boa Constrictors* as a parodic recontextualization of allegory. Chapter 2 is an examination of Erofeev's *Moscow–Petushki*, a text that parodies the conventions of the picaresque. A reading of Limonov's *It's Me, Eddie* as a parody of autobiography follows in chapter 3. Dovlatov's *Ours*, the subject of chapter 4, is treated as a parodic adaptation of the family chronicle, a popular nineteenth-century genre. In the fifth and final substantive chapter, I analyze Voinovich's *Moscow 2042* as a modern dystopia, a genre arguably written exclusively in our century, but with roots in earlier utopian literature.

CHAPTER I

Iskander's transparent allegory: Rabbits and Boa Constrictors

> Precisely because a vital life is always moving and changing, we need the orientation of something as hard as a diamond, and that is truth. It might not be the complete truth, but it can't be consciously distorted even for the sake of the grandest goal. Otherwise everything falls apart ... A sailor can't get his bearings from falling stars.
>
> Fazil' Iskander: *Rabbits and Boa Constrictors*

Fazil' Abdulovich Iskander is an extraordinary figure in contemporary Russian satire. Popular and successful as a Soviet writer, he seems to have been minimally affected by ideological pressure. He is regarded by readers and critics within the former Soviet Union and in the émigré diaspora as an enormously talented writer who managed to preserve his artistic integrity during the difficult years of the Brezhnev period. Beginning in the sixties and throughout the seventies and eighties, Iskander's poetry and prose appeared frequently in the Soviet press and in separate editions. His stories were staged, his poems were set to music, and he was awarded numerous state prizes for literature; his public readings attracted large crowds. Under the new conditions occasioned by *glasnost'*, he has continued to be one of the most widely read of contemporary Russian writers.

Iskander was born in 1929 and grew up in Sukhumi, the capital of the then Autonomous Soviet Republic of Abkhazia. Although tiny geographically, Abkhazia has a rich cultural tradition steeped in 2,500 years of history. Sukhumi, a port located on the Black Sea, was a cosmopolitan city during the years of Iskander's childhood. Iskander's youth was also shaped by summers spent in the mountain villages of Abkhazia with relatives who were hunters, grape growers and shepherds. Because he held an Iranian passport, Iskander's father was deported to Iran in 1938, and Iskander was raised for the most part by his mother and her extended family. Only in the late fifties he discovered that his father had been arrested upon his arrival in Iran and sent to a penal colony in the Persian Gulf, where he died in 1957.

After finishing school with a gold medal in 1948, Iskander went to Moscow, where he tried unsuccessfully to enroll in the Philosophy Faculty at Moscow University; he wryly recounts this episode in his autobiographical story "The Beginning." Instead, he began his studies at the State Library Institute and then transferred to the Gor'kii Literary Institute, from which he graduated in 1954. Iskander initially worked as a journalist, writing news articles, sketches and correspondence first for *Briansk Komsomolets* (1954–55) and then for *Kursk Pravda* (1955–56). Returning to his native Abkhazia, he worked as an editor for the state publishing house for several years until moving to Moscow in 1962. Since that time he has made Moscow his home, although he visits Abkhazia frequently. Natal'ia Ivanova, who has written extensively on Iskander's life and work, regards his permanent move to Moscow as a determining formative influence on his developing world view.[1]

The question of how to define Iskander's nationality as a writer has become less ideologically charged with the dissolution of the Soviet Union, but the issue of his outsider status remains of interest. When the notion of the "friendship of Soviet peoples" still held some currency, Iskander was sometimes categorized as an Abkhazian writer who writes in Russian. In fact, he has always considered himself a Russian writer. Russian is his second native language, and he asserts that "in the final analysis, to whom a writer belongs is determined by language. So I am a Russian writer, but a singer of Abkhazia."[2] Nevertheless, he concedes (in a typically colorful manner) that some aspects of Abkhazian speech may influence his Russian usage and affect his literary style:

Knowing Abkhazian does not hinder my creativity in Russian at all. I think that each language is in some ways richer and in some ways poorer than other languages. Abkhazian is the language of mountain people. Russian is the language of valley people. Perhaps, without noticing it myself, I bring into my Russian a certain extra energy which is needed to shout over the noise of mountain rivers and waterfalls. Maybe one fine day my Russian readers will say "Speak more quietly, we're not at a mill!" But while they remain silent, I speak as I do.[3]

Leaving aside the issue of language, it is certainly true that the history, religion, mythology and symbolism of Abkhazia pervade Iskander's work and make it quite unique.

The influence of Russian classical prose and poetry is also clearly discernible in Iskander's style and choice of themes. Like Tolstoi, he concentrates on fine points of the human psyche; like Pushkin, he suffuses even his satire with passion and warmth that is life-affirming.[4] Among modern writers, Iskander cites Iurii Dombrovskii as a kindred spirit (Vail' and Genis, "Beseda," 22).[5] He shares some characteristics with the Youth Prose writers with whom he came of age in the fifties; he was a frequent contributor to the journal *Iunost'* from its founding in 1956. Like Aksenov, Bitov and Voinovich, Iskander was enthusiastic about the work of Western writers such as Hemingway, Faulkner, Salinger and Màrquez, whose prose became accessible to Russian readers during Khrushchev's Thaw. He is, as Ivanova notes, "a true child of the Twentieth Congress" (*Smekh protiv strakha*, p. 5).

In spite of his liberal leanings, Iskander was never a political dissident. He became a member of the Soviet Writers' Union in 1957 and was permitted to travel abroad extensively (to Czechoslovakia, Western Germany, Poland, Greece and Cyprus) before it became commonplace for Soviet citizens to do so. Moreover, Iskander was able to publish his most ideologically outspoken works abroad without incurring severe consequences at home. The first part of his epic *Sandro of Chegem* appeared in the West in 1979 and the second volume followed two years later. *Rabbits and Boa Constrictors*, the work which this chapter treats, was published in 1982.[6] Iskander's apparent immunity from official wrath was the subject of considerable rumor and speculation in the late seventies and early eighties,[7] but there are several mitigating factors. Ivanova attributes his success despite apparent defiance of official strictures against publishing in the West to his humor; because his criticism was couched in terms of gentle satire, she suggests, he emerged unscathed (*Smekh protiv strakha*, p. 5).[8] It may also be the case that his status as a "national writer" gave him more latitude in such matters. And while the publication of his works abroad was a statement in itself, he did not make inflammatory political statements or otherwise incite official displeasure (as, for example, did Solzhenitsyn and Voinovich). Iskander's involvement in the Metropole affair of 1979, however, resulted in a *de facto* ban on his works in the Soviet Union for several years. The severity of the punishment probably derived from the fact that he not only contributed a highly unorthodox work to the *Metropole* collection ("Little Giant of the Big Sex"), but also served as an editor of the almanach.

Like so many of his compatriots, Iskander made his debut in literature as a poet. He began writing poetry as a schoolboy and published his first poems in the mid-fifties. His first collection of poems was issued in Sukhumi in 1957 and several volumes have followed, including *The Way* in 1987. Iskander's poems have also appeared frequently in newspapers, journals and almanachs in Abkhazia and in Moscow. Despite his productivity as a poet, Iskander is far better known in the West as a prose writer. Of course, this is due in part to the relative unpopularity of poetry in the West and to the special difficulties posed by translation of verse. Yet even to Russian readers, Iskander's poems may seem conventional and less exceptional than his prose.[9] Somewhat romantic, they treat in more concise, distilled form many of the same themes Iskander develops in his prose writing.

Iskander's first story, "The First Thing," appeared in 1956 and he has published prose prolifically since that time. Literally hundreds of short stories, sketches, feuilletons and articles by Iskander have been published in the Soviet Union. His first collection of stories, *Forbidden Fruit*, came out in 1966. A *povest'* that brought him considerable notoriety, *The Goatibex Constellation*, appeared the same year. Aleksandr Tvardovskii, then editor of *Novyi mir*, not only published the tale, but also nominated it for a State Prize in 1966 and again in 1968. A remarkable satire of Lysenko's genetics and Khrushchev's agricultural campaigns, it was harshly criticized for showing the Soviet Union in a bad light and did not win either time. A series of largely autobiographical stories that feature a young protagonist named Chik dates from the seventies. Although not intended exclusively for young readers, Iskander's *Chik* stories established his reputation as a children's writer. However, not all of these were deemed ideologically sound; "School Waltz, or the Energy of Shame" appeared only in 1987.[10]

Iskander is probably best known both in his homeland and in the West as the chronicler of Chegem, a fictitious village in Abkhazia peopled by semi-mythical characters. The first collection of stories that comprise *Sandro of Chegem* was published in a heavily cut version in *Novyi mir* in 1972. In fact, only about a third of the text survived the censor's red pencil. Ivanova regards this as a turning-point in Iskander's career, a difficult compromise on his part intended to bring at least some portion of the book to its intended readers (*Smekh protiv strakha*, p. 17). Using tiny Chegem as a microcosm of the world, Iskander continues to add to the cycle, developing and intertwining characters and events in family and tribal history.[11] These stories gave Iskander a second "I"; the author is frequently confused with the narrator of his *Sandro* cycle (as he was earlier confused with the narrator of his *Chik* stories).

Like many Soviet writers, Iskander initially devoted himself to publicistic writing at the beginning of the *glasnost'* period. He wrote widely on social problems and became actively involved in the public debate surrounding political reforms. In 1989, he was elected People's Deputy of Abkhazia. With the dissolution of the Soviet Union shortly thereafter, his voice became one of moderation and temperance, as he urged restraint of growing nationalist passions in his homeland.

In the increasingly liberal atmosphere of the late eighties, the publication of those of Iskander's works that had previously appeared only in the West constituted major landmarks of *glasnost'*. Previously banned chapters of *Sandro of Chegem* appeared in literary journals; in 1989 the cycle was published in its entirety. One of the most striking of these chapters is the *povest'* "The Feasts of Belshazzar," in which Stalin is satirically portrayed as a cruel, demonic tyrant. *Rabbits and Boa Constrictors* was printed in 1987 in *Iunost'*, an example of what one critic sees as the rejuvenation of Russian satire.[12] In addition, several plays by Iskander were staged in the *glasnost'* period; the *Metropole* story "Little Giant of the Big Sex" was adapted and produced by an experimental theater in Moscow in 1988. Iskander continues to travel and perform widely, giving readings and participating in conferences in Europe and the United States.

Rabbits and Boa Constrictors, the *povest'* considered in this chapter, occupies a unique place in Iskander's *œuvre*. It is not part of a larger cycle, as are the *Chik* stories and the *Sandro* tales. No familiar characters have migrated into this work from other stories, as they are wont to do in Iskander's literary universe. Finally, although it may well stem from personal experience, this work is clearly not autobiographical.

Characterized by some critics as angry, negative and caustic,[13] this tale represents a shift in tonality that is in keeping with the general development of his prose style. Humor serves in his early stories as an antidote to hypocrisy, and satirical elements in these stories are of the Horatian variety. However, Iskander has never been at ease with the role of a humorist, and has become increasingly gloomy in recent years. A distinction noted by one commentator is that his later work is still "funny" (*smeshnaia*), but no longer "cheerful" (*veselaia*) (Lebedev, "... I smekh," 7). This is particularly true of *Rabbits and Boa Constrictors*, where Iskander's satire has taken on a distinctly Juvenalian cast. The moral, didactic strain that has always been discernible in Iskander's art is much more pronounced in this tale; humor has been decisively subordinated to satirical criticism. Nevertheless, it still surfaces from time to time, as though Iskander himself could not suppress his laughter at the irony that shapes the cruel life he allegorizes.

In *Rabbits and Boa Constrictors*, Iskander makes use of a literary tradition that finds little favor among contemporary writers or readers, that of allegory. Derived from Greek *allos* ("other"), allegory was originally understood as a rhetorical figure by which the speaker or writer said one thing and meant another. In literature, allegory came to mean saying not only something *other*, but also something *above* or *beyond* the direct meaning of the words used. The directionality of interpretation, that is, is often upward (to the more elevated) or outward (to the more general).

The term refers to both a specific genre and a mode of writing. Allegory in its broadest sense may be found in virtually all literature and art; it is, according to Angus Fletcher, the "fundamental process of encoding our speech."[14] Defining allegory so capaciously has often resulted, however, in inexact, impressionistic usage. At the other extreme, allegory as a genre either belongs to or is reminiscent of a small body of works written in the Middle Ages and the Renaissance periods. In this narrower sense, an allegory is a text that is allusive in its entirety, usually through the agency of personification.

Allegory was developed in ancient Alexandria as a means of interpreting Homer and was later adapted to biblical hermeneutics. In the medieval Church, allegory served as a tool of exegesis whereby the personae and events of the Old Testament were understood as foreshadowing the coming of Christ.[15] The allegorical level was one of four levels of analysis delineated by biblical scholars to complement the literal, the tropological (concerning the moral lesson to be drawn) and the anagogical (or prophetic).

Classical allegories include William Langland's fourteenth-century poem *Piers Plowman*, Edmund Spenser's six-volume poem *The Faerie Queen* (1590–96), Guillaume de Lorris' *Le Roman de la Rose* (1230) and probably the best known example, Dante's *Divine Comedy*. Historical allegorical interpretation, by which the critic "attempts to read the significance of a literary work in terms of its original or assumed original significance," developed during the Renaissance.[16] The four levels of exegesis were simplified in historical interpretation; all three symbolic levels were subsumed by the allegorical. This process of streamlining was furthered by neoclassical writers, who stressed allegory's potential to achieve clarity and serve as a model of rationality. To ensure that neoclassical allegories were accessible, critics attempted to codify rules governing the form and censured works that did not conform to these standards.

Theoreticians of allegory are careful to distinguish allegory from symbolism, but this is largely a historical issue. The Romantics, especially Blake and Coleridge, insisted on articulating the distinction in an effort to free their work from moralism and rationalism. As Northrop Frye points out, the Romantics' approach to the symbol was indeed innovative and the theoretical contrasts posited by these poets are valid.[17] However, the distinction took on a qualitative denotation in their critical writings; allegory was regarded by the Romantics as inferior to symbolism because it is explicit in its intention.

Although allegories in the modern period are rare, allegory has not become extinct as a literary procedure. What has occurred is a significant change in the value system that underlies this essentially didactic form. Unlike classical allegories of the Middle Ages and the Renaissance, modern allegories are not readily decipherable in terms of a stable hierarchy of moral values such as that provided by the Church. Instead, ambiguity is a consistent feature of modern allegory. William Empson views allegory as one of the major literary vehicles for expressing ambiguity, for "what is said is valid in, refers to, several different topics, several universes of discourse, several modes of judgment or of feeling."[18] Ambiguity, of course, is not synonymous with obscurity;[19] although definitive decoding eludes the reader of modern allegories, there are generally markers that facilitate interpretation.

Common generic features allow us to speak of allegory beyond the confines of a corpus that is temporally limited. One of these is extensive use of personification, including personified abstractions.[20] A second characteristic of allegory is its incorporation of authorial commentary and interpretation. Whereas authorial intrusion may be problematic in other literary forms, it is a determining feature of allegory. A third formal quality of allegory is a sustained, contrapuntal relationship between the tenor and the vehicle, i.e. what is expressed and what is meant. The primary or literal level consistently points to the secondary or abstract level, though these levels remain distinct and parallel. Moreover, the primary level is often considered subordinate to the secondary level: "In allegorical novels, then, the 'significance' exercises a close control over the plot, imagery, tone, and characters. Every element is theoretically there for its significance. The surface tends to exist for the sake of the signification or significations. The theme controls in a relatively close way the story. As we read, we sense this control" (Bloomfield, "Allegory as Interpretation," 310). Ideally, however, the primary and secondary levels of an allegory interact and enrich one another. Furthermore, the literal level must have textual integrity of its own; exegesis should not be *required* for it to make sense.

Several possible motivations – not mutually exclusive – underlie the writing of allegory. In the first place, allegorical procedure may be aesthetically productive; a straightforward explication of the author's belief may be clumsy or dull, while allegory gives vigor to the ideas set forth. Iskander, speaking of poetic images, describes a mechanism that is also operative in allegory: "The further an object lies from another object, the more pleasurable is our recognition of their similarity" (Anisimov and Bondariuk, "Korotko," 37). An allegorist may choose to rely on the general reader to draw the connections between the literal and abstract levels, or alternately expect to be understood fully by only a subgroup of *cognoscenti*. An extreme case is the allegorist who deliberately writes enigmatically in order to express mystical or occult experiences. Probably the most common motivation for writing allegory (and the most interesting from our perspective) is security. Writing under conditions of ideological censorship, the allegorist conceals a heretical tenor beneath an orthodox vehicle and presumes that a political or religious authority will not grasp the secondary meaning of the work.

Despite the absence of a stable hierarchy of values in modern allegory, it retains a didactic quality. Allegory is used to express the truth as the author perceives it, and since truth is often unpleasant and inconvenient, the reading public (as well as the censor) may be hostile to the allegorist's moral purpose. Allegorical form may make an object lesson more palatable, but it may also draw charges of crudity. Indeed, the unfashionableness of allegory derives from its moralistic, discursive qualities. As Gay Clifford notes:

> The fact that the structure of the fiction is dominated or preceded by the ideological structure causes considerable problems to any modern reader of allegory. It tends to make the critic sound defensive, if not about the values themselves, at least of their dominant role, since it has become something of a commonplace that a writer ought to conceal moral purpose and work almost subliminally to persuade.[21]

Allegory is often dismissed as dry and pedantic by readers to whom the conventions of didactic writing are unfamiliar. Qualitative judgments aside, the purpose of moral instruction sets allegory quite apart from mimetic literature.

Just as comedy is juxtaposed to tragedy, allegory is often contrasted with satire. Yet these modes share several important features and in some instances overlap: good allegory is indirect, as is satire; both are concerned with economy of means through intensification; both seek to convey the general by demonstrating the particular.[22] In considering the relationship between allegory and satire, the most problematic issue is didacticism. That satire always has a didactic function is far from universally accepted. Wyndham Lewis, for example, asserts that great satire is never moral in its intent.[23] It is certainly true that the degree of explicitness of satire's moral lesson varies tremendously. Those critics and satirists who claim didacticism as one of the mode's consistent features argue that the instructive aspect of a work need only be implicit, understood through inversion of what is demonstrated negatively. The Russian satirical tradition, however, tends to be relatively overt in its didactic purpose. Whether Horatian or Juvenalian, Russian satirists have endorsed the precept of

Iskander's transparent allegory

"teaching while delighting,"[24] and moral judgment is usually rendered quite explicitly in Russian satire.

Another aspect of this problem is the directionality of the moral lessons offered by allegory and satire. Satire criticizes vices and shortcomings by exposing them; it aims at reproof through downward explication. Allegory, on the other hand, is often conceived of as elevating and uplifting. According to this point of view, it instructs through demonstration of the potential for moral improvement. Although this holds true for much of classical allegory, the directionality of modern allegorical interpretation is less uniform (Leyburn, *Satiric Allegory*, pp. 4–5). Indeed, some works of classical allegory (e.g. *The Divine Comedy*) as well as many modern allegories are concerned with examining evil more centrally than with exhorting readers to achieve goodness.

This view of satire and allegory as proximate modes in terms of intention and procedure is consistent with Iskander's ideas about the function of literature. In an interview with the émigré critics Vail' and Genis, he speaks in almost mystical terms about literature: "... literature poses a most difficult task for itself: to consolidate consciousness, to introduce harmony – regardless of how difficult or sometimes unlikely this might seem" (Vail' and Genis, "Beseda," 20). Satire, he elaborates in another interview, aspires to the creation of harmony on the level of reason: "Indeed, when we mock madness and stupidity, this is also an attempt to reach harmony, to overcome chaos."[25] Moreover, the satirist is motivated by love for the people he satirizes, though this love is "insulted" (*oskorblennaia*) (Anisimov and Bondariuk, "Korotko," 40).

Allegory – especially the forms of the fairy tale (*skazka*) and the beast fable (*basnia*) – has a long and rich history in Russian literature. Use of the fairy tale for allegorical, didactic purposes may be traced to the eighteenth century, when examples of the genre began to appear in literary journals.[26] The tradition was weakened with the rise of Romanticism, but the 1830s saw a revival of allegorical genres concurrent with renewed interest in folklore. Fairy tales were written by Pushkin, Dal', Polevoi, Odoevskii and other less well known figures. In this period of relatively rigid censorship, the allegorical potential of fairy tales and fables was recognized by astute writers and readers. The 1860s saw the publication of many allegorical works by Saltykov-Shchedrin, Minaev and others. Saltykov-Shchedrin's works in particular are extraordinary; although they are essentially publicistic, they are artistically sophisticated and are still read as examples of classical Russian satire. Along with Garshin and Tolstoi, Saltykov-Shchedrin continued to produce satiric fairy tales and fables during the next two decades. Indeed, these genres played a central role as vehicles of propaganda until the 1905 Revolution. Writers such as Dem'ian Bednyi and Maiakovskii continued to write "underground" allegorical works to further the cause of revolution until 1917.[27]

The term "Aesopian language" (*ezopovskii iazyk*) was originally used by Saltykov-Shchedrin to refer to a variety of allegorical techniques. Although it initially described a phenomenon limited temporally and geographically (to Russia in the 1860s), it had taken on broader connotations for Russian literature by the beginning of the twentieth century. During the Soviet period, the term was associated only with prerevolutionary literature. A. Kviatkovskii's *Poeticheskii slovar'*, for example, defines the term thus: "In the prerevolutionary period in Russia revolutionary writers used Aesopian language in order to get their works through the obstacles presented by the tsarist censorship."[28] Nevertheless, allegory in general and Aesopian language in particular have had a strong tradition in Soviet literary culture. As literary censorship alternately constricted and relaxed over the seventy-odd years of Soviet rule, writers and readers learned to "read between the lines," to find ways to evade the often obtuse sensibilities of the censor.

Iskander's *Rabbits and Boa Constrictors* has been read productively as an allegory. In fact, it was presented to readers of *Iunost'* as an allegorical rendering of Soviet history. The illustrator of the tale represented the boas with a snake in a military service jacket, who has his left hand inside the placket and his right hand behind his back; the depiction immediately recalls Stalin's typical dress and posture. The rabbit in the illustration is wearing spectacles, the unmistakable appurtenance of the Russian *intelligent*. His suit jacket and cuffed pants complete the visual portrayal.

Critics have reinforced an allegorical reading of the text, though they differ as to the particularity of the target. Deming Brown calls the tale "an elaborately figurative commentary on Soviet society and its institutions, ideology, and psychology."[29] Mark Lipovetskii and Ivanova find Iskander's portrayal of hypocritical demogoguery, institutionalized distrust and the power of denunciation all too familiar.[30] Allegorical works are read most fully within the cultural context of the era that gave rise to them, and Iskander's *povest'* is certainly an evocative expression of the disillusionment and cynicism widespread during the Brezhnev era.

A somewhat broader interpretation of the work regards it as an allegorical treatment of social hierarchy and its by-products of tyranny and philistinism. Sergei Ivanov, a proponent of this point of view, elaborates in a review of *Rabbits and Boa Constrictors*:

> I am least of all inclined to see in *Rabbits and Boa Constrictors* a calque of some concrete social arrangement. Sometimes the author approaches the reality we know, sometimes he departs from it. Primarily he examines a world where the strong "work over" the weak (or the weak work over the weaker) and the most important factors that permit this to happen.[31]

While commentators like Ivanov agree that one target of Iskander's satirical allegory is Soviet society, they tend to see its focus as more encompassing. According to this reading, the tale is an exposé of dictatorship in general. Iskander himself supports this interpretation, calling his work "an attempt to show in a very abstract form what power is based on" (Ivanova, *Smekh protiv strakha*, p. 19). Far from being only a critical reexamination of the past, *Rabbits and Boa Constrictors* thus has relevance for the present and – as a prophetic warning – for the future.

An essential element of any but the most naive allegory is

indirection. Given that it conveys one thing in terms of another, there must be a gap to be bridged; the reader must resolve a disparity between what is said and what is meant. Iskander challenges this convention by creating an allegory that consists almost entirely of markers and no screens.[32] Laura Beraha notes that *The Goatibex Constellation* is characterized by mimimalization of the role of screens and that *Rabbits and Boa Constrictors* extends this technique, pushing "pseudo-Aesopianism" to an extreme.[33] Other critics have commented on the transparent quality of Iskander's allegory in this work, often seeing this as a lapse of artistic control. Iuliia Troll', for example, writes that the book "despite its allegorical character is completely devoid of camouflage."[34]

It is certainly true that the Aesopian context of *Rabbits and Boa Constrictors* is apparent and encourages instant decoding. While one may debate the symbolic significance of specific details, the decoding process that clarifies the allegorical meaning is largely incorporated into the text. Citing a representative passage, Troll' draws a conclusion that is applicable to the work as a whole: "This citation, as they say, needs no commentary, for there is no hint in it, but only an open text" (*ibid.*, 303). The presence of an allegorical subtext is felt, but is for the most part merely conventional.

The transparency of Iskander's allegorical procedure in this text can be explained on one level by the fact that it was written "for the drawer." It is overtly anti-Soviet and vociferously seditious because the author had no hope or intention of evading the censor. It follows from this reasoning that Iskander retains the form of an allegorical tale on aesthetic grounds. In his discussion of the "underground" fairy tale of the late nineteenth century, V. Osmolovskii notes that "allegory in the underground fairy-tale is not a means of masking as is often the case in the legal fairy tale, but a means of preserving fairy tale coloring, of strengthening the effect" ("Zhanr sotsial'no-didakticheskoi skazki," 71). The dissident quality of *Rabbits and Boa Constrictors* may similarly have been a definitive factor leading the author to retain some of the generic conventions of allegory while dispensing with indirection.

A more compelling explanation for Iskander's use of Aesopian conventions in this work involves both aesthetic and philosophical issues. In subverting some of the generic norms of allegory, he directs his irony toward the method itself. What we have in *Rabbits and Boa Constrictors* is *mise-en-abyme*, an allegory within an allegory, for the subtext is really connected with the role of the allegorical mode (especially Aesopian language) in Soviet literary culture. Beraha acknowledges that the impetus for Iskander's strategy is parodic, but she calls the parody "truncated, incomplete" ("Compilation," p. 220). To appreciate fully the sophistication of the formal parody in this work, we must, I believe, consider it in conjunction with the thematic satire accomplished concurrently.

Through allegory that is subject to instant decoding, Iskander satirizes the moral and ethical behavior of the Soviet intelligentsia in particular and of Soviet society in general. By contemplating ironically the literary mode given widespread currency in Soviet culture – indeed perfected as an art form by that culture – he creates a work of exceptional vigor and force. The traditions of allegory are turned in upon themselves, making Iskander's exposé trenchant and biting. I would argue that parody is far from truncated in this satire, but rather constitutes the warp and the woof of the textual fabric. It is on the one hand formal, as Iskander allegorizes the contemporary practice of Aesopian language as a game with the censor; and it is on the other hand thematic, as it enhances his satire of Soviet realia.

In spite of a long tradition, Aesopian language has long been regarded with disdain in Russian and Soviet literary culture. From Saltykov-Shchedrin to Rozanov to Solzhenitsyn, Russian critics have asserted that Aesopian practice reduces a literary work's aesthetic value. Aesopian language is denigrated as "slave's language" (*rabskii iazyk*) in the tradition of Juvenal, and Aesopian works are condemned by their detractors as servile. As Loseff points out, however, the prestige of allegorical writing has been subject to significant historical shifts. Both critics and sophisticated readers have learned to value the merits of allegorical literature during periods of "profound social stagnation," notably in the 1880s and 1890s and in the Brezhnev era. Censorship has actually contributed to the creative process in Russia, he reasons, in that it forced writers to veil their messages imaginatively. The resulting works are more vigorous, more forceful because the reader is more psychologically engaged in decoding their intended meaning. On a deep level, Aesopian literature facilitates a cathartic experience for the astute reader; he or she "celebrates" the experience of fully comprehending an allegorical text in a manner that transcends intellectual analysis (*Beneficence of Censorship*, pp. 222–23).

In the ebb and flow scenario depicted by Loseff, periods of vitality and richness in allegorical literature are followed by periods of disillusionment and dissatisfaction with this mode. Aesopian language falls out of favor when it becomes the norm for a large proportion of both writers and readers. This helps to explain the rise of dissident, *samizdat* literature in the Soviet Union and the increasing popularity of *tamizdat* in the eighties (*ibid.*, pp. 228–29).

Rabbits and Boa Constrictors also represents a reaction to the saturation of contemporary Russian literature with allegory. In this work, Iskander addresses the function of censorship in the creative process and the Aesopian tradition in Soviet culture. He suggests that Aesopian writing and reading have become deeply ingrained in modern Russian literature. Using the text itself as a vehicle, he shows that the encoding (and decoding) of ideas has become a consistent feature of *belles-lettres* in the Soviet context. Iskander seems to acknowledge that censorship is always a factor in the creative process, but far from viewing it as beneficial, he condemns it as debilitating and destructive.

Beraha has noted in regard to Iskander's work as a whole: "Iskander's pseudo-Aesopianisms, then, are two-voiced but unidirectional: they toy with the duality of meaning (the subtext to be read between the lines), not to deny Aesopianism outright, but to poke fun at the very need for circumlocution" ("Compilation," p. 221). There is an interesting parallel treatment of allegory in his story "School Waltz, or the Energy of Shame" that sheds light on the development of this motif in

Rabbits and Boa Constrictors. The narrator of the story, remembering his first experiences in school as a child, recalls a notebook he had with an illustration of Pushkin's *The Lay of the Wise Oleg* on the cover. He was told by his classmates that the illustration, properly analyzed and deciphered, contained forbidden expressions, and so he studied it laboriously to tease out the hidden illicit messages. His efforts were not successful and from the perspective of the present, he sees them as rather ridiculous.[35] This incident is, I believe, very significant for our understanding of the text at hand; always searching for concealed meaning at the expense of the surface text may well lead to triviality and banality. Iskander despises the cat-and-mouse game played by Soviet authors and censors and sees no benefit at all in the tradition. In *Rabbits and Boa Constrictors*, he actively rebels against the need to be subtle and to provide screens. Rejecting the convention of assuring one's safety through opacity or obscurity, he proceeds openly, mocking and satirizing the convention itself. At the same time, Iskander investigates the Aesopian tradition philosophically, looking for its roots in Russian culture and examining its psychological and spiritual effects on Russian writers and readers.

Reading *Rabbits and Boa Constrictors* as a parodical allegory discloses a profound indictment of the core of Soviet culture. Like his satirical predecessors Gogol′ and Saltykov-Shchedrin, Iskander is horrified at what he observes around him in his native land. Not only does he mock the institutions and traditions of Soviet life, but he compels the reader to look within to discover the sources of evil. One of the goals of satire, according to Iskander, is to facilitate the self-criticism crucial to the health of any society: "... the consciousness of our shortcomings in the form of irony, humor, satire – I think that is what is needed to bring about a renewal of artistic life" (Shklovskii, "Potrebnost′," 33). Acknowledging internal ills, he insists, allows a culture to move to a higher plane of civilization.

All of the allegorical traditions adopted and refined by the Russian intelligentsia, such as Aesopian language, evading the censor and reading between the lines detract from this transcendent goal. Iskander objects strongly to the voyeuristic quality of Aesopian art. While the writer risks discovery and punishment, the reader is entertained. Because Aesopian practice has permeated Soviet culture thoroughly, there is no question of imparting new information; indeed, this method rests on the assumption of joint possession of information, ideas and convictions by the author and reader (Loseff, *Beneficence of Censorship*, p. 219). The game is thus circular, and the level upon which it is played is horizontal, not vertical.

In *Rabbits and Boa Constrictors*, Iskander attempts to show how power is supported by those who submit to it. By engaging in Aesopian practices and concealing criticism or opposition beneath the veil of allegory, the Russian intelligentsia is helping to sustain the *status quo*. This kind of complicity has resulted in the distortion of literature; its function and its aesthetic properties have been corrupted. Iskander speaks as a member of his generation and as a representative of the Russian intelligentsia, and his sense of outrage is palpable. This, I believe, is the subtextual motivation that underlies his parody of the allegorical mode.

The tale that constitutes the literal level of an allegory is generally a well-established *fabula*. This *fabula* serves as a basis upon which the allegorical writer fashions a particular re-creation. In doing so, he may reasonably presume that his audience will be familiar with the tale and will be able to draw parallels with the antecedent. Edwin Honig postulates that this "twice-told" quality of allegory enhances its power to persuade:

> We find the allegorical quality in a twice-told tale written in rhetorical, or figurative, language and expressing a vital belief. In recognizing that when these components come together they form the allegorical quality, we are on the way to understanding allegory as literature... Rhetorical language is the most appropriate one for telling the story because such a language produces self-reflective images – that is, its figurative character makes possible the retelling of the old story simultaneously with the telling of the new one. The belief expressed in the tale is the whole idea supporting the parabolic way of telling and the reason for the retelling; the belief binds the one with the other, as a resolution and its hypothesis are bound together. The relating of the

new and the old in the reflective nature of both language and theme typifies allegorical narration. The tale, the rhetoric, and the belief work together in what might be called a metaphor of purpose.[36] Iskander parodies this convention in *Rabbits and Boa Constrictors* very cleverly. Having set up the expectation that this work will proceed like a fairy tale, he dispenses with the thematic conventions almost immediately. Instead of recreating on the pattern of a familiar *fabula*, he creates a literary work altogether new. Indeed, the genre Iskander claims for the work – a "philosophical fairy tale" – is rather misleading. In spite of this subtitle, *Rabbits and Boa Constrictors* resembles a fairy tale only slightly.

The world Iskander creates in this text is not completely fantastic, yet it relies heavily on *ostranenie* and exoticism for its satirical effect. As in any allegory, the setting is an important factor in determining the significance of what occurs. Iskander starts out in a traditional manner, using verbal shorthand to provide visual and atmospheric background. He establishes within two lines that his tale is far removed in time and place: "All this happened long, long ago in a land quite far to the south. To be brief, Africa."[37] That Iskander so quickly specifies Africa as the setting subverts the convention of abstraction associated with allegory. In addition, Africa has a complex of connotations for the Russian reader. The jungle is a metaphor for pre-civilization, for social and moral primitivism. Moreover, a land "quite far to the south" is an obvious screen, for its apparent difference from Russia will not convince anyone inclined to an allegorical interpretation. Finally, his setting may be an allusion to Kornei Chukovskii's "Doctor Aibolit," known to virtually every Russian child.[38] This connection with Chukovskii strengthens our expectation of allegorical significance in the present text, for Chukovskii's verse tales for children are widely interpreted as Aesopian.

In beast fables, animal characters have ready-made signification. They serve as traditional symbols of specific human qualities and their relationships represent the interactions of these qualities. Additional ironic impact is achieved through the narrative decentering that occurs, for the point of view used in animal stories "itself is an allegory of man's assumption that he is the center of the universe, with all other beings created for his benefit" (Leyburn, *Satiric Allegory*, p. 59). Iskander has often used animal characters in his works and has effectively exploited this technique of decentering.[39] An extended application of the device may be found in "Story of a Mule," one of the *povesti* that comprise *Sandro of Chegem*. This tale is narrated entirely from the point of view of a mule, who observes the foibles, weaknesses and ethical shortcomings of the world around him.

In using beasts as full-fledged characters in allegory, it is important to maintain a balance between their animal natures and their human qualities. The reader must simultaneously perceive them as animals and humans for satire to be operative. Seeing animal characters consistently as animals may actually help to accentuate their human traits, for these will stand out in greater relief. As vehicles of allegory, animal characters should have just enough incongruity to emphasize likeness with the satirical target. Iskander both adopts and flouts this convention. His rabbits use their paws as hands and hang criminals by their ears as punishment. Taking this one step further, the boa constrictors "seize" one of their number and "drag" him off to be stomped on by elephants (*Kroliki i udavy*, p. 13). Not only are Iskander's characters endowed with improbable physical capabilities, but they are psychologically complex individuals. Whereas allegorical beast characters represent only one human trait at a time (Leyburn, *Satiric Allegory*, p. 61), the personae of *Rabbits and Boa Constrictors* have fully developed personalities and act out complicated ethical dilemmas.

Iskander's choice of boa constrictors as one of the main sociopolitical groups in his allegory rests on the firm tradition of snakes as symbols of evil. The boas are devoid of conscience; their souls are located "at the bottoms of their stomachs" (*Kroliki i udavy*, p. 96). Asked to define the concept of a vow of silence, the Great Python's grand vizier quickly replies "A nap in the afternoon" (*ibid.*, p. 97). In particular, Iskander plays upon the biblical aspect of the snake as the embodiment of evil; the following dialogue occurs between the King of the Rabbits and the dissident Ponderer:

"Then tell me," the King leapt up, "why did God create boa constrictors?" "I don't know," Ponderer replied. "Perhaps He was in a bad mood. But maybe He created boas so we could understand just what baseness means, just as He created cabbage, so we could know what bliss is." (*Ibid.*, p. 29)

It is quite possible to interpret the boa constrictors as conservative, Stalinist figures. Certainly the Great Python resembles Stalin in his speech and his behavior. He urges constant vigilance and commands unquestioning loyalty. Even though the boa Squinter is unconscious when the anthem of the Great Python is sung, he raises his head through an involuntary reflex. It is also significant in this regard that the leader of the boas is a python. He is ethnically an outsider, as was Stalin (a Georgian). When he dies (or is killed), he is replaced by a boa who also has Stalinist features, the Great Hermit. Shortly after he reveals the technique of smothering to the boas, there is a rash of tangling and knotting as they enthusiastically practice the new method. The Great Hermit then delivers a speech entitled "Smothering Is Not an End in Itself," strongly reminiscent of Stalin's 1930 article "Dizzy with Success."

Cruelty is developed to an extreme among the boas. They have no compassion or sense of ethics either in regard to other species (rabbits, monkeys, natives) or in regard to one another. Paranoia is institutionalized in their society and – it is implied – surveillance is a constant feature of their lives. After Squinter tells the story of how he lost his eye to the young boa, they realize that they have been overheard by a rabbit (who turns out to be Ponderer). Their first reaction is to destroy one another as dangerous witnesses, but they are restrained by fear. In fact, the young boa hesitates to denounce Squinter only because he fears for himself:

"All this has turned out rather badly," the young boa hissed. "Most likely I'll have to denounce you before the Great Python for the way you slandered him here." "Please don't," Squinter begged, "you know how much he dislikes me..." "But what if this is discovered?" the young boa replied. "We'll hope no one finds out," Squinter answered. "That's fine for you," the young boa said, "you've already lived your life, but I have all of mine before me... No, I'll probably denounce you..." "But then you'll probably suffer too." "Oh, why is that?" "Because I started to run off at the mouth, so you were obliged to rebuff me," Squinter reminded him about the age-old custom the boas had adopted. As a matter of fact, the young boa thought, there is such a custom. He was perplexed. He couldn't figure out at all which alternative was more advantageous for him: to denounce Squinter or not. (*Ibid.*, p. 18)

Furthermore, the boas have perfected a punishment whereby they are compelled to swallow themselves. Starved for several days, an offending boa is offered its own tail and, as Richard Chapple puts it, "sanity falls victim to appetite."[40] This frenzy of self-destruction through which predator becomes prey is grotesquely reminiscent of the Stalinist purges of the thirties.

The use of boa constrictors as characters permits Iskander to develop the topos of transformation extensively. This motif is treated on two levels, both of which are satirical. A parodic restatement of Marx's ideas about social evolution is implied in the boas' reasoning about the process of digestion. When the young boa finally swallows Ponderer, he is elated, imagining that the rabbit's mental acuity will become his own. He thinks "After I digest him, when his body becomes my body, his mind will have no place to go, and it will become my mind..." (*Kroliki i udavy*, p. 81). The answer to the Great Python's riddle that poses the question "When can a rabbit become a boa?" is an elaboration of this idea: "'...a rabbit that has been swallowed by a boa can become a boa... because a rabbit processed and digested by a boa is thus transformed into the boa. That means boas are actually rabbits at the highest stage of their development. In other words, we are former rabbits and they are future boa constrictors'" (*ibid.*, p. 14).[41] Swallowing and assimilation are rationalized as a sort of "fraternal assistance" rendered to neighboring species in the interest of their own cultural advancement. A second, equally vivid image of transformation is that which takes place among the boas as they shift from hypnotizing to smothering the rabbits. The boas achieve a higher level of social development, Iskander ironically suggests, when they perfect a quicker, more effective method of killing.

On the level of parody, the motif of transformation has additional significance in *Rabbits and Boa Constrictors*. Transformation and especially metamorphosis are frequent topoi in allegory. The use of these motifs has a didactic basis, for showing the transformation of a character is an effective way of demonstrating a belief in the possibility of reform (Clifford, *Transformations*, pp. 29–30). Iskander focuses parodically on the notion of transformation in order to intensify his satiric exposé. Both kinds of transformation in this text – physical (through digestion) and social (through evolution) – illustrate the struggle between two opposing natures. Perhaps in his graphic descriptions of smothering, swallowing and digestion, Iskander alludes to Dante's evocation of metamorphosis in *The Inferno*. In a famous passage in the fifteenth canto, the sinner's human nature is subsumed and joined with that of the serpents that entwine him:

> The two heads had already fused to one
> and features from each flowed and blended into
> one face where two were lost in one another;
>
> two arms of each were four blurred strips of flesh;
> and thighs with legs, then stomach and the chest
> sprouted limbs that human eyes have never seen.
>
> Each former likeness now was blotted out:
> both, and neither one it seemed – this picture
> of deformity. And then it sneaked off slowly.[42]

Iskander too relies on the powerful image of snakes physically enveloping and consuming their victims. As in Dante's model, the process is a mutual, reciprocal one; the rabbits and the boas in fact comprise one whole, living symbiotically. Although swallowing and digestion is the most visceral expression of this fluidity in their natures, the principle of symbiosis actually governs all aspects of their lives. Their mutual dependence creates what Ivanova calls "a special sort of monstrous coexistence" ("Smekh protiv strakha," 9). This satirical image suggests the symbiotic relationship fostered by the Soviet system between the state (ostensibly oppressive) and the people (ostensibly oppressed).[43]

Rabbits, the other species central to Iskander's allegorical vision, are traditionally guileless and peaceful. To some extent, the rabbits in this text themselves promote this stereotype. Advocating a fatalistic acceptance of their lot, the King says "'...life is life. Since God created rabbits, then he must have had rabbits in mind!'" (*Kroliki i udavy*, p. 27). The ironic twist that Iskander adds is that these rabbits are not simply victims; they are complicit in their victimization and in some cases actively do evil to one another. They have been widely interpreted as Khrushchevites or, more generally, liberals in contrast to the Stalinist or conservative boas. Certainly their kingdom is more benign than that of the boas, but it is still an autocracy and the trappings of democracy it displays – elections, debates, freedom of dissent – are largely illusory. Moreover, the King is a problematic Khrushchev figure. Iskander endows him with a "rather coarse brand of humor" (*ibid.*, p. 140) that suggests Khrushchev, but some of the rabbits are sycophantic in a manner that recalls the clichés of Stalin's regime: "'Sire, you're a genius!' the Wise Old Rabbit exclaimed. 'Why do you need me, the scientists and scholars? Why do you need the Chief of the Guards, when you are everything?'" (*ibid.*). An even more telling detail is the nostalgia experienced by some of the rabbits for the past. Echoing the boas, one of the oldest rabbits sighs "there was order" (*ibid.*, p. 146).[44] In short, liberalism and democracy constitute an extremely thin veneer on the surface of the society of the rabbits.

The compliance of the rabbits is maintained through the myth of cauliflower, which will become available and plentiful in the future. When this happens, they are told, their life will "be transformed into one continuous holiday of fertility and gluttony" (*ibid.*, p. 19). Rumblings of discontent are silenced by the King's invocation of this symbol of paradise; discipline and sacrifice are necessary, he insists, to achieve this goal. On one level, the ideal of cauliflower clearly represents the dream of realizing communism in Soviet culture. Iskander has characterized the influence of the collective vision in an interview: "The entire ethic and philosophy of our power lay in the cult of the future: we'll just suffer a little more, be patient a bit longer in order to achieve justice and plenty" (Ivanova, *Smekh protiv strakha*, p. 273). It is significant that Iskander chooses the image of an ordinary vegetable to represent the grandiose theories of Marx and Engels. By replacing an abstract idea with a concrete image that is earthy and edible, he accomplishes satirical diminution of his target very effectively. Moreover, he implies that the myth is essentially false, a Machiavellian ruse; when the *cognoscenti* rabbits (the King's courtiers) gather, there is no pretense of devotion to the ideal of cauliflower. As Sharpie discovers and naively observes after his admission to the ranks of the elite: "...here, evidently, speaking about [cauliflower] wasn't considered good form" (*Kroliki i udavy*, p. 39).

The system of privileges that underlies the hierarchical society of the rabbits corrupts them. While the rabbits (in contrast to the boas) do have consciences and profess some ethical standards, they too are ultimately at the mercy of their physical appetites. The Table to which the rabbits are admitted or to which they aspire to be admitted is an apt symbol of privilege; self-interest is effectively embodied in the base images of produce. Furthermore, Iskander ironically undercuts the rabbits' pretensions to more elevated goals: "The rabbits sometimes overheard [the Poet] speaking, comparing the love for vegetables to the love for the higher destiny, and every time they were amazed because they clearly felt this love for vegetables in their souls, but the love for the higher destiny they felt only vaguely – actually they didn't feel it at all" (*ibid.*, p. 45). As Sharpie learns, a high price must be paid for the privilege of being admitted to the Table. Considerations of honor and self-respect are eroded by the temptations of comfort. The historical parallel for Iskander's satire can be found in the trade-off established under Stalin. As Iskander has said in an interview, "Stalin gave his henchmen all the privileges but one – the privilege of sleeping normally and peacefully planning one's life."[45] Iskander's satirical brush, however, is much broader and he implicitly paints the Soviet intelligentsia as a whole with the stain of moral compromise.

The rabbits live by stealing from the natives' gardens and they are accustomed to rationalizing their "base little deeds" by comparing them to the "tremendous baseness" of the boas (*Kroliki i udavy*, p. 69). Viewed relativistically, the rabbits do indeed stand on a higher moral plane than the boas; they are not naturally evil. As uneasy as they feel about stealing, however, they continue to pilfer from the natives, for their appetite is more strongly developed than their sense of ethics. Moreover, they are loath to confront difficult moral problems. They disagree with Ponderer's rational conclusions about the ineffectiveness of hypnosis because losing their status as victims of the boas would mean abdicating their right to steal from the natives' gardens. They resist Ponderer's insistence that they confront this issue since "for the rabbits, the most desirable decision at a difficult moment was the decision not to make a decision" (*ibid.*, p. 35).

Surveillance is highly refined among the rabbits, for they (like the boas) do not trust one another. The chief function of the standing army maintained by the King is not to fight external enemies or to guard the borders of the kingdom, but to control the rabbits themselves. The King has commissioned spies to sit among Those Admitted to the Table to ferret out deviations from the official line and to quash potential conspiracies. In the line of duty, these spies try to blend in by eating as much as possible, which, Iskander notes wryly, "in fact agreed with their natural inclinations" (*ibid.*, p. 38). The allegorical significance of this passage – the satirical exposé of the waste and corruption endemic in the Soviet security system – is quite clear.

Iskander goes beyond this surface allegory to examine the psychology of paranoia, tracing the sources of the distrust that pervades the rabbits' kingdom. Following the King's reasoning at each step, he shows how the surveillance system evolved and demonstrates the complications entailed in building a society based on suspicion:

> After all, if you introduce a law about secret surveillance, it should apply to everyone equally, the King thought. After all, if you tried to divide all the rabbits in the service who were under surveillance into those who had to be shadowed and those who didn't, this could evoke crude and mistaken notions in the guards' minds about the possibility

that there were rabbits who were trusted in everything and rabbits who weren't trusted at all. In fact, things were a good bit more complicated, and the truth was dangerously subject to modulation. (*Ibid.*, p. 48)

It is tempting to see an allegorical treatment of Stalinism in this analysis, but Iskander's satire cuts deeper; the King, after all, is not essentially a Stalinesque figure. We must read the King's rationalization (couched in quasi-indirect discourse) that the truth is protean as a highly ironic attack. Soviet leaders' tendency to view morality in a relativistic manner and the Russian people's readiness to accept this practice have led, according to Iskander, to serious ethical distortions.

Iskander's most damning indictment of the rabbits' society is the image he develops of their "submission reflex." The King has learned to play upon his subjects' natural proclivity for compliance. He has designed an exercise in which he directs them alternately to sit down and stand up; by distracting their attention from substantive problems and reducing their actions to repetitive motions, he keeps them docile. Moreover, he cleverly times an election to take place during one such exercise so that the rabbits, preoccupied with their sitting and standing, unwittingly leap up to reelect their king. On one level, Iskander allegorically charges the Soviet leadership with misleading the people and suppressing dissent. It is significant, however, that the subjects (with the exceptions of Ponderer and Yearner) are quite willing to be duped. Their aquiescence is also a key element in the established dynamics of hypnosis as it is practiced by the boas. They must agree to be hypnotized for the hypnosis to work; as Ponderer formulates his discovery to Squinter and the young boa, "'your hypnosis is our fear. Our fear is your hypnosis'" (*ibid.*, p. 17).[46] The image of burrows is apt in regard to the rabbits' tendency to withdraw from unpleasant or uncomfortable realities. As Irina Vasiuchenko notes: "Not for nothing does Ponderer forsake his burrow for his beloved green hill: from there everything is visible, there he can meditate well."[47] The rabbits' "submission reflex" allegorically represents the mindset of the Soviet intelligentsia and more generally that of the Soviet people. Thus Iskander delves beneath a superficial scheme of good and evil to examine the psychological sources of tyranny.

The marmosets play a dual role in Iskander's allegory, one that is both generically traditional and parodical. On the one hand, they serve as objective commentators on the behavior of the boas and the rabbits. Although they are peripheral to the plot, they help to interpret the allegorical significance of other characters' actions. While swinging through the jungle, the mother marmoset generalizes and offers moral summations by way of instructing her daughter about life. However, the marmosets are also implicated in the evil done by the boas and the rabbits. They act reprehensibly by failing to warn Ponderer of the King's treachery. The daughter marmoset, still naive and impressionable, begs to be allowed to save Ponderer, but her mother answers "'It's not really worth getting involved ... well, you know, it's probably too late...'" (*Kroliki i udavy*, p. 65). Caution and self-preservation are false values in Iskander's allegorical scheme, for the marmosets facilitate evil by abstaining.[48] He enhances the irony of their serving as moral judges by having the mother marmoset elaborate on her swinging instructions to her daughter. She emphasizes that one must not be afraid to fall, that taking risks is necessary; when confronted with a moral dilemma that holds some danger, however, she hypocritically counsels cowardice. Moreover, in denouncing Sharpie later at the rabbits' special meeting, the mother marmoset exaggerates her own heroism. She includes the detail of having spit in Sharpie's face in her retelling, although this remained only an intention in reality. In the final analysis, the marmosets' self-interest outweighs their moral outrage, for they too might have to give up stealing the natives' corn under the new system envisioned by Ponderer. Morally distancing oneself and finding solace in philosophy – favorite occupations of the Russian intelligentsia – are exposed by Iskander as illusory havens.

The only human characters in *Rabbits and Boa Constrictors* are the natives, who are not individuated at all. Their role is so minor that they do not even merit mention in the title. It is fully consistent with Iskander's choice of the beast fable as a satirical vehicle that his human characters should not be delineated in any detail; humans are typically excluded or given only peripheral status in examples of this genre (Leyburn, *Satiric Allegory*, pp. 60–61). What we do learn of the natives suggests that they do not stand appreciably higher on Iskander's moral ladder than either the boas or the rabbits. Indeed, since they are denied psychological characterization, they seem bestial. Iskander notes in passing that the natives' minds "didn't differ much from those of the boas" (*Kroliki i udavy*, p. 109). Their behavior is actually learned from the boas, whose social etiquette is somewhat more highly evolved: "By the way, the natives later adopted the boas' custom of exchanging insults in the broad sense, in order to conceal their own measure of vileness (if we're talking about villains), or of baseness (as is the case here), when dealing with a bastard" (*ibid*., pp. 11–12). They turn to the boas for help in their internecine wars and make pacts with the boas to thwart their common enemy, the rabbits.[49] To conclude from this representation of humans that Iskander is misanthropic is overly simplistic. Rather he uses the natives (and their relationships with the boas and the rabbits) as an additional example to illustrate the dangers of complicity with evil in the name of self-interest.

Treachery pervades this tale and Iskander continually circles back to focus on betrayal, duplicity and denunciation as cancers within the body of society. In regard to Iskander's work as a whole, Ivanova notes that treachery is "one of the main, global ideological symbols of our reality, the most repugnant one for Iskander" (*Smekh protiv strakha*, p. 11). In an early story called "Forbidden Fruit" (1963), he treats this theme through the evocation of a vivid childhood memory. In self-righteous indignation and because he hopes to curry favor with his parents, the narrator reveals that his sister has eaten pork. His father responds by striking him in disgust and the older, wiser narrator concludes: "... the lesson was not wasted. It taught me for the rest of my life that no lofty principle can justify meanness and treachery, and that all treachery is the hairy caterpillar that grows from a small envy, no matter under what high principles it may be concealed."[50] In a *povest'* called "Old Khasan's Pipe"

(1987), he returns to the theme of betrayal and examines its ramifications for society. He has said in an interview that this story is particulary important in his *œuvre* in that it expresses criticism of the people as unworthy of their best representatives (Vail' and Genis, "Beseda," 20); honor and loyalty are impossible in a society driven by denunciation. Yet another example of Iskander's treatment of the theme of treachery is his poem "Mozart and Salieri," in which he distills the essence of betrayal in the relationship between these paradigmatic figures.[51]

In *Rabbits and Boa Constrictors*, Iskander exposes the extent to which betrayal and denunciation permeate Soviet society; as allegory, the tale indicts various social strata for selling their souls to succeed. On a more profound level, he investigates the psychology of treachery. He is concerned not only with demonstrating this evil through allegory, but with comprehending its motivation. In complying with the King's request that he compose a denunciation of Ponderer, the Poet reasons that he can dispel any suspicions about himself in this way. Sharpie, who agrees to betray Ponderer to assure his Admission to the Table, insists on slight changes in the musical denunciation the Poet has composed. The King, a connoisseur of betrayal, understands instantly that "Sharpie was trying to outwit him and at the same time he had rather successfully outwitted his own conscience" (*Kroliki i udavy*, p. 41). It is important to Sharpie that he maintain his perception of himself as a liberal and a free-thinker making only minimal concessions to authority, but these concessions turn out to be pivotal. In fact, he is quite eager to cooperate with those in power to improve his own situation. Both Sharpie and the Poet are representative of the Soviet intelligentsia, the focus of Iskander's most caustic satire. As Ivanova notes, "Iskander's view is skeptical and his evaluation of the essence and the actions of the 'intelligentsia' is deeply pessimistic" ("Bestiarii," 109). If we extrapolate from this particularized satire, however, we see that all of the rabbits are implicated in Iskander's scenario of collaboration with tyranny. Even if they do not actively engage in denunciation or betrayal, they insist on remaining willfully ignorant of the truth, burrowing deep in their holes and refusing to acknowledge their leader's propensity for evil.

Iskander argues cogently in this text that betrayal is indefensible under any circumstances, regardless of the motivation of the traitor. In *Rabbits and Boa Constrictors* he frames this message within a parodical allegory, calling attention simultaneously to the seriousness of the satirical indictment and the simplicity of the protreptic prescription. By having his rabbit characters enact a betrayal (actually several betrayals) and experience the pangs of conscience that accompany it, he shows how treachery feeds on itself and corrupts the very core of society. When Sharpie is betrayed by the King and the Poet, he must confront the insidious nature of his own crime:

And like any traitor who is betrayed, he was stunned by the vulgarity of the way he had been betrayed. He couldn't understand that only the person being betrayed can sense the vulgarity of any betrayal. The one responsible for the treachery can't feel it, with the same force at any rate. Thus the betrayed traitor, recalling his own feelings at the time when he was carrying out his own treacherous act, and comparing them with his own feelings about when he himself is being betrayed, thinks with complete sincerity: still, I didn't sink that low. (*Kroliki i udavy*, p. 85)

The degeneration of a society, understood in an ethical sense, occurs when those who commit crimes of treachery begin to justify them as a consequence of natural law. Sounding rather like Solzhenitsyn, Sharpie preaches to his sole disciple: "'That's when the betrayal of the ideal begins, that's when the lie, from which there is no exit, starts'" (*ibid.*, pp. 71–72).

Moreover, parallels between Ponderer and Christ on the one hand, and Sharpie and Judas on the other[52] elevate the betrayal in *Rabbits and Boa Constrictors* to the level of sin. In his exile, Sharpie has the opportunity to philosophize about the ethical ramifications of treachery and concludes that any attempt at rationalization is futile. He realizes that rabbits are "warm-blooded and cleanly by nature" (*Kroliki i udavy*, p. 104), that their souls are like pure white tablecloths. Iskander's images in this case are double-edged. They are effective in terms of the surface allegory he constructs – the rabbits remain rabbits and the simile of the tablecloth emphasizes their unalterable preoccupation with food. Yet the notion of cleanliness and the image of the tablecloth have religious significance as well, for they are suggestive of the last supper and the Eucharist (a symbolic rite of purification). The extended metaphor that Iskander then uses to illustrate the moral effect of treachery is particularly effective, as the images contrast graphically with those of cleanliness and purity:

"What about the treachery? I knew that it wouldn't help to decorate my snow-white tablecloth, but I thought I could tear off a piece of it, the part spoiled by the treachery, and I'd spread the rest out, so that I could enjoy the blessings of life. And so what happened? Whoops! The whole tablecloth fell into the shit!..."
"And so now what happened? I have to eat alone on a shitty tablecloth! It turns out that treachery smears the whole tablecloth with its shit, not just a part of it, as I'd thought." (*Ibid.*)

Iskander's insistence that tyranny is a symbiotic relationship constitutes a significant reevaluation of the scenario proposed by many dissident writers. It is true that the rabbit King is a despot, but he finds many subjects willing to support his despotism. He has made a practice of accomplishing his acts of betrayal through other rabbits and, of course, the boas, thus keeping his own reputation untarnished. There are echoes of the Grand Inquisitor in Iskander's portrayal of the King, though these are filtered through the lens of parody. Admitting to Sharpie that there is no smaller elite among Those Admitted to the Table, he rationalizes perpetuating this myth on the grounds that it provides a goal, "something to aspire to." He himself is under no illusions: "'If I don't understand something, then this condition remains forever'" (*ibid.*, p. 43). Iskander injects an ironic bit of self-exposure into the King's speech to lighten the serious philosophical allusion; he is, after all, a furry animal and his depth of comprehension is limited by the dim-wittedness innate to his species.

Spies play a key role in supporting tyranny among the rabbits, but they are only nominal guardians of the regime. Iskander demonstrates that they are omnipresent, but they are also laughably inept. Charged with capturing the little bunny who insistently requests cauliflower, the secret police perform like Keystone Cops, bungling the job comedically. They manage to capture a squirrel, but are stymied at the prospect of suspending him by his tiny ears to facilitate interrogation. More damning is Iskander's charge that the secret police are utterly amoral, performing whatever heinous task their superiors set. Confronted with evidence of his perfidious behavior, a member of the secret police defends himself straightforwardly:

> By the way, Ponderer's widow found herself in the same company some time later and she again met the rabbit who worked in the Royal Guards. She told him that he (such a responsible rabbit) had repeated such irresponsible nonsense about the King and the Queen then. "It was necessary," the member of the Royal Guards replied, without even blinking. (*Ibid.*, pp. 121–22)[53]

Ponderer's widow and the other rabbits listening to this exchange accept his reasoning unquestioningly, even gladly: "... they'd sensed the mystical sweetness in the firm significance of his words: Of course, what more is there to say..." (*ibid.*, p. 122). The implication of their acquiescence in this instance is that the real enforcers of the *status quo* under a tyrannical system are the citizens themselves. Once again, Iskander charges that failure to oppose evil actively is tantamount to complicity.

In order to strengthen his satirical attack on the mindset that supports tyranny, Iskander engages in a secondary parody of Evgenii Shvarts' play *The Dragon*. The boas pay homage to the "Great Dragon," their progenitor, and their anthem includes a line that identifies them as "Descendants of the Dragon." As in Shvarts' model, myths about the omnipotence of the leader are perpetuated to support tyranny in Iskander's text. The Great Python became the leader of the boas by performing the extraordinary feat of swallowing an adult native. Although the native was drunk, the Great Python endorses a version of the story wherein he hypnotized him; eventually he begins to believe this version himself. Just as Shvarts' Dragon comes to believe in the hyperbolic tales of glory invented about him, the Great Python accepts this altered, more attractive "truth" because "he'd seen a sleeping native only once, and he'd heard about how he'd hypnotized this one hundreds of times, first from his own mouth, and later from others" (*ibid.*, p. 94). Iskander's parodic allusions to *The Dragon* are significant in light of the moral precepts he posits. Like Shvarts, he focuses through his satire on the dragon within ordinary people; the Russian people's tendency to submit to and even to support tyranny must be eradicated. The ending of *Rabbits and Boa Constrictors*, however, is far more pessimistic than that of *The Dragon*, and there is no Lancelot figure left to carry on the struggle against the metaphorical dragons of Iskander's jungle. Iskander has stated that the only viable alternative he sees for his country is the rule of law (Veselaia, "Esli ostanovimsia," 16), but his parodic dialogue with Shvarts suggests that little progress has been made toward that goal in the decades separating *The Dragon* and *Rabbits and Boa Constrictors*.

I have suggested that the Soviet intelligentsia – particularly the creative intelligentsia – bears the brunt of Iskander's satiric attack. The Poet is a paradigmatic figure who represents Soviet literature as a whole; it is significant that poetry is the instrument of betrayal in the text. The centrality of the Poet's role in the tale (his story occupies an entire chapter) is not surprising, given Iskander's own concerns. Simultaneously a comic and tragic figure, the Poet is torn between his striving to rebel and his desire to gain privilege and prestige. His life is a series of ethical compromises by which he silences the voice of his conscience and barters his creative talent to acquire a comfortable position. Iskander couches his story in quasi-indirect discourse to express the angst that accompanies his decisions and to show that corruption is a gradual process. The Poet reasons that he cannot abandon the court because this would ruin his son's budding career; it would destroy his daughters' chances to make a good match; it would prevent his being buried in the Royal Pantheon; it would mean deprivation of the court produce allotment. It is only toward the end of his life that he realizes that his family was not really a significant obstacle to his acting according to his conscience, but that "The obstacle was in the Poet himself" (*Kroliki i udavy*, p. 56). He finds some small consolation in drinking the fermented elderberry juice that is used for ink by the rabbits. Having once chanced to drink some, he discovered that "the soothing bitterness of the elderberry juice somehow aided his creative thinking" (*ibid.*, p. 123). Iskander transparently alludes to the prevalence of alcoholism among Soviet literati. In general, his treatment of the theme of literature certainly constitutes an exposé of "the servile work produced under the worst influence of socialist realism" (Chapple, "Fazil Iskander's *Rabbits and Boa Constrictors*," 43). Yet his satirical scope is broader, for he examines the internal ethical conflicts of the Soviet creative intelligentsia in a manner that transcends a particular historical period.

Iskander's satiric characterization of the Poet has been interpreted as an *ad hominem* attack on Maksim Gor'kii. In particular, his description of the Poet's inner conflicts is strongly reminiscent of Vladislav Khodasevich's memoiristic account of Gor'kii (Troll', "*Kroliki i udavy*," 303). Gor'kii, it would seem, represents for Iskander an especially egregious example of complicity for the sake of status and privilege. Focusing on Gor'kii's ambiguous, duplicitous character is consonant with Iskander's attack on Aesopian practice in this text. Although Gor'kii may have found some release of his subversive tendencies in Aesopian art, Iskander suggests, his behavior was nevertheless reprehensible.

It is possible, as I have noted, to read *Rabbits and Boa Constrictors* as an allegory of Christ's betrayal and crucifixion. However, the most powerful vehicle of satire used by Iskander in this respect is not allusion, but parody. Even as he establishes parallels with the Gospels, he renders them ridiculous and effects diminution of the behavior and thoughts of the characters he describes. The Trinity, for example, is debased and made utterly corporeal; the rabbits' Trinity is green beans, cabbage and peas. The intangible ideal to which they aspire is cauliflower, only a distant echo of spiritual salvation. Their shrine is an oak tree that is considered sacred "although the carrot oak's acorns aren't edible" (*Kroliki i udavy*, p. 32) and one of their number has achieved the status of Wise Old Rabbit (a sort of prophet) by being hit on the head with an acorn from this tree. By making the rabbits' idols and rituals base, Iskander satirizes the dogmatic, superstitious aspects of the Russian Orthodox Church.

A theological parallel that is treated very seriously, on the other hand, is the concept of martyrdom. Ponderer agrees to be swallowed by the young boa because he has been disillusioned by the rabbits' betrayal and because he loves them and hopes to save them. Yearner plays the role of disciple, specifically of Peter. He follows in Ponderer's steps, amplifying and popularizing his doctrine. Indeed, Ponderer explicitly charges him with this task shortly before his death: "'... now you know everything about hypnosis, and you can repeat everything...'" (*ibid.*, p. 79). Iskander's treatment of Ponderer as a Christ figure demonstrates that martyrdom is not an appropriate response to the social ills he exposes. As Vasiuchenko notes, "Ponderer proves the truth that means salvation for his fellow rabbits at the expense of his life, but they remain captive to the fatal lie that he has disproved" ("Dom nad propast'iu," 202). The truth that Ponderer reveals to the rabbits is an uncomfortable and inconvenient one; it means having to work and having to give up stealing produce from the natives. Unwilling to accept responsibility for their actions, the rabbits reject Ponderer's proposal with the plaintive and childish response "'Oo-oo-oh... Bor-ing...'" (*Kroliki i udavy*, p. 35).

Iskander's satirical point is that making martyrs of those who tell the truth – regardless of how willing they are to assume the role – is senseless. An act that appears to be sacrifice, moreover, may be motivated by faintheartedness, discouragement or the need to accommodate the existence of baseness. Seen in this light, Iskander's satire in *Rabbits and Boa Constrictors* is a virulent attack on some of the most deeply held of Russian cultural traditions. This interpretation is supported by both textual and extratextual evidence. In a rare exercise of free will and independence, Yearner does not vote for the King at the rabbits' election. Genuinely devoted to the truth at the expense of his own well-being, he has achieved freedom from tyranny and the "submission reflex." Another key to Iskander's stance may be found in his poem "A Biblical Fable" (*Put'*, p. 120). Having posed the question of why

Christ did not perform a miracle to prevent Judas' treachery, he answers that, in essence, his sacrifice was necessary to demonstrate the importance of man's free will. Only by refusing to compromise the truth, by steadfastly resisting the urge to lie "even for the sake of the grandest goal" (*Kroliki i udavy*, p. 68), by actively opposing evil, can Russia free herself from the past. This exercise of free will that Iskander seems to endorse includes the realm of art. Aesopian language, he argues explicitly through the character of the Poet and implicitly through his generic parody, is indeed "slave's language."

An allegorical convention readily adopted by Iskander in *Rabbits and Boa Constrictors* is strict narrative control. The authorial narrator's manipulation of the text is overt and indeed is often emphasized. His omniscience is a consistent feature of the narrative and a fairy tale-like frame underscores his traditional function of storyteller. The tale ends with a lengthy frame passage in which the narrator objectifies his stance: "And that's all I've heard about the rather sad history of relations between rabbits and boa constrictors. If someone knows any interesting details that I've omitted, I'd be happy to receive them. It's best to send a letter, okay to telephone, and even better to keep them to youself – I'm sick of this topic" (*ibid.*, p. 146). Within the body of the text, the narrator is privy to his characters' thoughts as well as their actions and unfailingly relates these to the reader. This allows him to comment ironically on the motives of both the boas and the rabbits, to reveal their hypocrisy, baseness and greed. For example, he traces the series of rationalizations performed by the Poet as he capitulates to the authorities and pinpoints the motive of self-preservation that underlies his behavior: "He thought that the King was exaggerating the danger, but apparently where there's smoke there's fire, and after all, they weren't arresting the Poet" (*ibid.*, p. 51).

From his omniscient vantage point, Iskander's narrator investigates and exposes the psychology of groups as well as that of individuals. To the rabbits' direct assertions that Ponderer's widow will certainly receive a generous allotment of produce, the narrator adds that "the rabbits answered her with totally liberal decisiveness, and the less decisiveness each one had shown in supporting her husband during the meeting, the more liberally and decisively he answered" (*ibid.*, p. 36). In another passage, the narrator examines the psychology that motivates applause; his satirical analysis has obvious connections with the behavior of Soviet citizens at mass meetings:

> It's interesting to note that each rabbit intended that his applause personally apply to the marvelous union of rabbits and produce. At the same time, he thought that others were not only applauding this union, but the King's speech as well. And since all of them thought that way, and each one gave some thought to admitting that the egotistical narrowness of his own applause was at least unattractive, they clapped for all they were worth, in order to conceal the egotistical narrowness of their own applause, and to merge with the common enthusiasm. (*Ibid.*, pp. 27–28)

Beraha terms this narrative procedure in Iskander's work a "three-tiered awareness" whereby we observe the character act on one level, overhear his thoughts on a second level and learn the author's judgment of both on a third level. Moreover, this technique may be traced to Tolstoi and hence to Sterne ("Compilation," p. 177). In the case of *Rabbits and Boa Constrictors*, it is both psychologically revealing and satirically effective, for Iskander's beast characters (with the exceptions of Ponderer and Yearner) are petty and hypocritical.

Not only does Iskander's narrator frequently engage in overt obtrusion into the text, but he also toys with his control of the narrative and emphasizes its artifice by discussing his role with the perceived reader. He apologizes for wandering too far afield in a digression and scolds himself for facile treatment of his characters: "But we've digressed again, and we should be talking about the lives of the Poet and the King in an orderly way. Besides, this whole story is basically much sadder, and we really should tone it down correspondingly" (*Kroliki i udavy*, p. 46). Even as he establishes a clear connection between the boas and the rabbits' King in their tendency to exploit the rabbits' weak will, he anticipates an allegorical reading and ironically rejects it. The rabbits, he notes, "were impressionable by their very nature, and the boas took advantage of that, as did the King himself, though we don't want to draw any parallels between them" (*ibid.*, p. 26).

Iskander openly flouts narrative conventions of restraint and concealment in such asides. In general, as Beraha observes, this "rejection of literary sophistication must in a literary context be read as a post- or even supra-literary sophistication" ("Compilation," p. 184). Keeping in mind the allegorical nature of this text, we may also see the obtrusion of authorial commentary as generically motivated. Writing about *Gulliver's Travels* and *Brave New World*, Clifford suggests that "our awareness of the allegorical element in these works derives very much from the thread of commentary coming from an outsider observing the action" (*Transformations*, p. 25); the same may be said of *Rabbits and Boa Constrictors*. In order for allegory to be successful, we must know the point of view of the author, and Iskander leaves no doubt as to where he stands on the issues he allegorizes. Critics less inclined than Beraha to see innovation in Iskander's narrative praxis object to his didacticism. Such objections exemplify what Frye postulates as a modern prejudice against allegory stemming from its limiting the freedom of critical interpretation (*Anatomy of Criticism*, p. 90). It is interesting in this regard that Iskander justifies his narrative style on the basis of maximizing authorial freedom. In an interview, he discusses his frequent obtrusions into his texts:

I strive – unconsciously and consciously – toward complete inner freedom. This freedom, to the extent that it is realized, gives the author outlets into the narration. I would say that an abundance of freedom is in no way a hinderance. That's why I "climb in." Of course, there is the opinion that such authorial interference destroys the illusion of the independent course of life ... However, it seems to me the presence of the author does not bother the reader at all. I believe that the more there is in a work that is involuntary and spontaneous, the greater will be its contribution to the formation of the reader's inner freedom. (Shklovskii, "Potrebnost'," 33)

By exaggerating and parodying the generic convention of authorial intrusion, Iskander molds his own allegory to address the specific spiritual needs of contemporary Russian society.

Although the allegorist plays the part of a judge, it is important that he or she give the impression of being an impartial, fair observer. Indeed, one of the criticisms leveled at *Rabbits and Boa Constrictors* upon its publication in Russia was that the author displayed cold-blooded impartiality. One reviewer complained that "the author views his characters as if from the opposite bank, they are 'other' for him" (Kazintsev, "Ochishchenie," 189). He is charged with demonstrating a lack of sympathy for his compatriots in his stark analysis of tyranny. To an extent, this observation is justified, but it displays a misunderstanding of the intention of the allegorist. The fact that Iskander makes his characters animals establishes the authorial narrator's superiority. They are pitiable at times, but the narrator neither expresses sympathy himself, nor does he elicit the reader's sympathy. He is primarily concerned with demonstrating evil and its manifestations in the totalitarian state and he reveals his judgments through the filter of irony.

While sympathy, then, is precluded, the narrator's attitude toward his characters ranges from mockery to sardonic ridicule. He pokes fun at the Wise Old Rabbit's pretension to erudition, noting that his assertion that he is "an old, wise rabbit... was partly right, because since he had received the post, he had managed to grow older" (*Kroliki i udavy*, p. 33). He describes the Poet's creations as "if not exactly divine, then at least righteous ... rhythms" (*ibid.*, p. 53). His ironic comment on Sharpie's behavior has more serious critical implications; when Sharpie asks whether the Poet has knowingly contributed to the King's treachery, the narrator comments acidly: "It was easier for him if he wasn't the only one participating in Ponderer's betrayal" (*ibid.*, p. 42). Occasionally the narrator gives vent to moral indignation. To the Wise Old Rabbit's assurance that Sharpie will survive quite well in exile, he adds "The old egotist, who was looking at the suffering rabbit and recalling that he could suffer too, demanded sympathy for himself, as if he were the one suffering" (*ibid.*, p. 92). In general, the narrator's asides become more caustic and more judgmental as the plot moves toward its denouement and the consequences of Ponderer's betrayal are played out.

Another function of the allegorist parodically exaggerated by Iskander is that of moral interpreter of the tale he relates. That is, he frequently pauses to generalize and draw abstract truths from the particular actions and words of his characters. He overtly urges the reader to apply his didactic conclusions to life, as he moves blithely from generalization to universality. Mocking the young boa's sincerity in vowing silence, he notes "as all of us who take oaths do, he mistook the intensity of his curiosity for fiery loyalty to the vow" (*ibid.*, p. 3). Iskander's generalizations often sound aphoristic; he formulates the psychology of betrayal concisely: "whoever ponders this question ultimately, and most certainly, goes ahead with the denunciation, because each thought aspires toward the accomplishment of the possibilities it contains" (*ibid.*, p. 19). The rabbits avoid complicated ethical decisions because they "were inclined to think that today's awkwardness was more unbearable than tomorrow's treachery" (*ibid.*, p. 41). His truisms sometimes take on the quality of moral precepts, as for example his adage "bravery too often results from a feeling of not treasuring life, while cowardice always results from a false estimation of its worth" (*ibid.*, p. 101). Although these encapsulated moral lessons may strike the reader as preachy or facile, they are quite in keeping, on the one hand, with the nature of the text as allegory and, on the other hand, with Iskander's penchant for simple, universal truths.

In examining Iskander's narrative praxis, Benedikt Sarnov compares him to a documentary filmmaker and finds that his "slow-motion" method of narration with multiple authorial intrusions, abundant use of detail and extended philosophical musings serves his purpose well. He suggests that this technique enables Iskander "to see what in the ordinary, normal course of events would be either incredibly difficult or else impossible to discern" ("Mir Fazilia Iskandera," p. 20). Intensive discussion of the significance of certain details and careful analysis of characters' motivations by the narrator are features characteristic of Iskander's *œuvre* as a whole. Nevertheless, the degree of authorial control and manipulation observable in *Rabbits and Boa Constrictors* transcends that found in all but his purely publicistic works. In short, a technique that Iskander has found congenial and effective in much of his prose (both satiric and non-satiric) becomes aggressively overstated and hyperbolic in his parody of the allegorical mode. His procedure is self-referential, of course, but also serves his satiric goal, for the didactic points he makes have a protreptic function.

Digressions – often lengthy and sometimes comprising entire chapters – complicate the structure of this text. They function to enrich the meaning of Iskander's allegory, for they contribute additional insights, further examples or historical background. They are generally confined within obvious frames. A brief digression relating the story of the Wise Old Rabbit is introduced by Iskander thus: "The story of this rabbit's rise in stature is not without interest" (*Kroliki i udavy*, p. 32). A longer digression that comprises all of the fourth chapter begins with an authorial intrusion: "Now we're going to divert our attention from the plot and tell a story about how the Poet and the King of the rabbits got along" (*ibid.*, p. 45). The narrator's tone in such asides tends to be especially chatty and confidential, sometimes playfully apologetic for his failure to proceed straightforwardly:

And [Squinter] continued his amazing story. Now since he often interrupted his story, sometimes busying himself with the proper movement of the rabbit through his bowels, at other times suspecting that someone was overhearing what he was saying – which the young boa didn't agree with at all, because apprehensions about someone else's secret always seem exaggerated – we'll tell the story a little more quickly. (*Ibid.*, p. 4)

The irony embedded in this frame is that the narrator himself is continually veering into digressions, so that his gentle admonition is wryly self-mocking.

In keeping with the nature of this tale as allegory, there is also clearly discernible linear progression. While the symbols evoked in allegory may be static (e.g. boas are evil, Sharpie is ambition, Poet is moral turpitude), allegory itself is kinetic; it consists of the movement and interaction of the symbols created (Clifford, *Transformations*, p. 12; Leyburn, *Satiric Allegory*, p. 4). In fact, major transformations occur within the framework of this tale. The rabbits discover that hypnosis is ineffective, the boas change their hunting tactics, the Great Python dies and is replaced by the Great Hermit and a new *status quo* is established. Although attempts at real reform ultimately fail, the plot is dynamic.

As I have noted, there is as a general rule no firm hierarchy of values to guide the progress of the characters in modern allegories. Progress is nevertheless retained as a conventional structural device. The expectation of ascension (anagogy) or descension (katagogy) may be frustrated, but the impression of movement remains a generic feature (Clifford, *Transformations*, pp. 16, 34). Iskander goes a step further and reestablishes a scale of moral values through his parody of the mode. Unlike the hierarchy of values guiding the medieval allegorist, these are not borrowed wholesale from the Church. Rather, they are personal and particularized, reflecting the author's own ethical convictions about the spiritual malaise affecting Russia. The ending of *Rabbits and Boa Constrictors* invokes these values explicitly. Iskander asserts the need for a spiritual reformation and exhorts his reader to acknowledge the positive value of truth.

Given that the characters represent specific vices and failings, the narrative structure allows Iskander to express abstract patterns and connections through their interactions. As in most allegorical works, the relationships between characters represent the clash of opposite ideals or the power struggle between opposing moral forces. Encounters thus take the narrative shape of verbal confrontation (dialogue), combat or imprisonment (*ibid.*, p. 19). Iskander's characters discuss the major themes of the tale in many different groupings: the boas among themselves, the rabbits in their meetings and in smaller groups, and the boas and rabbits together. It is significant that both species engage in large-scale debate concerning the events that transpire. These debates are ritualized; they adhere to the forms characteristic of the two societies. Thus the boas engage in very limited discussion and unfailingly yield to the will of their autocratic leader, while the rabbits fulfil the roles assigned to them in their pseudo-democracy. The values that they discuss – freedom, truth and individual responsibility – are the larger themes of Iskander's allegory and may fruitfully be "cross-referenced to the more comprehensive meaning of the whole" (*ibid.*, p. 26).

The boas and rabbits also engage in physical and mental combat. There are numerous scenes of swallowing and suffocation, but there is also the prolonged episode of Ponderer's mocking resistance to the young boa's hypnosis. Swallowing constitutes a form of imprisonment in Iskander's text, and there is one instance in which a rabbit continues to resist the power of evil from within the body of the boa.[54] In interpreting such encounters as emblematic of the clash of moral forces, it is important to appreciate the degree to which Iskander debases the convention he adopts. The images of swallowing, digesting and smothering are calculated to evoke a visceral reaction on the part of the reader. Rendered graphically, the clashes become at once more brutal and more profound.

The stylistic peculiarities of Iskander's prose make a significant contribution to the satirical effect of this work. All of his characters are given symbolically meaningful names in accordance with allegorical practice. These names denote abstractions and broad, generalized traits and offer keys to the characters' speech and behavior. Ponderer (*Zadumavshiisia*) deciphers the mystery of hypnosis and articulates the fallacious nature of the relationship between the boas and the rabbits. Sharpie (*Nakhodchivyi*) is indeed bright, but puts his mental acuity at the service of his ambition; his name is appropriately tinged with irony. Yearner (*Vozzhazhdavshii Znat' Istinu*) "thirsts" for enlightenment and truth at the feet of his teacher, Ponderer. By endowing his characters with such clearly allegorical monikers and by making these intentionally awkward, Iskander parodies the conventions he adopts. As Beraha observes, Iskander's cast of characters in *Rabbits and Boa Constrictors* "pushes the convention of speaking-names to a bald-faced extreme" ("Compilation," p. 214). This is also true of his names for groups, such as Those Admitted to the Table

(*Dopushchennye k Stolu*) and Those Aspiring to Be Admitted to the Table (*Stremiashchiesia Byt' Dopushchennymi k Stolu*).

Iskander's sarcasm is still more overt in the names he bestows on other characters. The Wise Old Rabbit (*Staryi Mudryi Krolik*), as he shows, is really only old; the Great Hermit (*Velikii Pustynnik*) is not a holy ascetic, but rather an unwilling political exile. Squinter (*Kosoi*) is named inaccurately, for "he was actually one-eyed and not squint-eyed" (*Kroliki i udavy*, p. 1). Even as he applies this device, Iskander suggests that such a procedure of abstraction must be flawed. The simplification of human nature to a single trait is inherently reductive and – by extension – an allegorical procedure that relies on such emblematic representations must be read cautiously and skeptically.

In general, the style Iskander develops in *Rabbits and Boa Constrictors* is colloquial, at times tending to substandard and vulgar. Honig notes that allegory is traditionally rendered in a "middle" style wherein "'high' and 'low' are combined for a unified effect" (Honig, *Dark Conceit*, p. 15). Iskander balances his colloquialisms with exotic, unfamiliar terms associated with the setting (references to liana, marmosets, coconuts, etc.) and the formal, rhetorical speeches of the Great Python, Great Hermit and Rabbit King. Furthermore, he satirizes the peculiarities of Soviet speech. The boas use clichés strongly reminiscent of the Stalin era, such as the adages repeated by the Great Python: "'Whisper when you hiss; don't forget that the enemy is within us...'" (*Kroliki i udavy*, p. 7)[55] and "'Any boa who harbors a talking rabbit is not the kind of boa we need'" (*ibid.*, p. 13).[56] The image of hissing in the first example is especially evocative; the figurative snakes of the Stalinist milieu become the literal snakes of Iskander's allegorical jungle. Vasiuchenko finds this aspect of Iskander's style as effective as the substance of the plot: "The murky official turns of speech, beloved by the characters, spread like a cancer through the living, supple fabric of Iskander's prose. In my opinion, this is even more striking than the evil described in the tale" ("Dom nad propast'iu," 202).

Iskander also satirizes the Soviet penchant for euphemisms to replace direct language. The boas refer to "processing" (*obrabotka*) the rabbits they swallow; the rabbits speak delicately of "collecting surplus" (*otbiranie izlishkov*) instead of stealing produce from the natives. Iskander's most scathing satire is reserved for the distortion of the concept of victory. Ponderer instructs Yearner:

> "Remember this aphorism: victory is the truth of scoundrels. Whenever they talk a lot about victory, they've either forgotten the truth or they're hiding from it. Just recall how the boas love to talk about their daily victories over the rabbits, and remember how our hypocritical King announces the impending victory of the rabbits with each casual decrease in the number of rabbits swallowed by the boas, and calls every rise in the number of rabbits lost a temporary success for the boas." (*Kroliki i udavy*, p. 70)

Ponderer's diatribe is consistent with the larger themes of the work, for the use of euphemisms and clichés are for Iskander means of distorting and concealing the truth.

Rabbits and Boa Constrictors has been criticized as mere sneering and Iskander has been accused of pointing out the faults of contemporary Russian culture without offering any solutions in this work. Some theoreticians of modern allegory suggest that in times when values have become "objective, realistic, and material" (Bloom, "The Allegorical Principle," 190), we cannot expect to find firm moral parameters girding allegorical works. There are, however, several factors that mitigate a completely pessimistic reading of this tale. While admitting that the prospects for internal reform are not good, Ponderer insists that the rabbits must admit their own (relatively minor) baseness and cease stealing from the natives. "It's our difficult task," he tells Yearner, "to shatter this consciousness" (*Kroliki i udavy*, p. 69). Recovering the values obscured by the Sovietization of Russian society is the positive goal Iskander sets in his allegory. One of the first steps to achieving this end, he suggests through his own satirical practice, is to reject all forms of obfuscation such as Aesopian language, and to respect the truth in art. Speaking of his predecessors Voltaire and Gogol', Iskander notes that their didactic purpose accounts for the astringent tone of their work: "This plan for the humanization of man... This is the source of the gloomy and sometimes even bilious expressions that we see on the faces in the portraits of great satirists" (Anisimov and Bondariuk, "Korotko," 40). Iskander's own desire as an artist and a citizen for the humanization of Russian society helps to explain his choice of allegory as a vehicle of moral instruction; it also helps to clarify his parodic caricature of the mode. Aesopian literature is, he implies, like the rabbits' pilfering. If the great baseness of the boas is to be overcome, the mindset that admits the pragmatic efficacy of petty baseness must first be reformed.

CHAPTER 2

Beyond picaresque: Erofeev's Moscow–Petushki

> Oh, the ephemeral. Oh, vanity. Oh, that most infamous and shameful of times in the life of my people – the time from the closing of the liquor stores until dawn!
> Venedikt Erofeev: *Moscow–Petushki*

Prior to *glasnost'*, Venedikt Erofeev was known only to a limited circle of *cognoscenti* as the mysterious author of the *samizdat* work *Moscow–Petushki*. Very little information was available about him and his biography was the stuff of rumor and hearsay. With *glasnost'*, numerous publications devoted to Erofeev and to his works have appeared and the background of *Moscow–Petushki* can be reliably reconstructed. Erofeev was born in 1938 in Zapoliar'e, in the Murmansk region. He grew up and received his primary education in Kirovsk, a city on the Kol'skii Peninsula north of the Arctic Circle. His sister recalls that even as a young child he resisted conforming to Soviet social norms, refusing to become a Young Pioneer or a member of the Komsomol.[1] In 1946, his father was arrested under the infamous Article 58 (dissemination of anti-Soviet propaganda), and both Venedikt and his brother were put in a children's home in Kirovsk, where they remained until his father's release in 1954.[2] After completing the tenth grade with a gold medal for academic excellence, Erofeev crossed the Arctic Circle for the first time – like his eminent predecessor Lomonosov – on his way to Moscow.

Erofeev's start in the capital was auspicious; he enrolled in the Philological Division of Moscow State University in 1955 with a major in Russian language and literature. However, after only three semesters, he was expelled, either because of his participation in a student play which met with the disapproval of university authorities, or because of his failure to attend military preparation classes.³ Most likely, his expulsion was the result of a combination of these (and perhaps other) factors, for his contemporaries recall his behavior in this period as consistently unconventional, bordering on scandalous. Following his departure from MGU, Erofeev enrolled in various institutes; these endeavors were, it seems, pragmatic, for student status gave him the right to remain in Moscow or its environs. One of his more extended stays was at the Vladimir Pedagogical Institute, where he studied in the Philological Division. He was again expelled, this time either for writing satirical poems or because he was found in possession of a Bible.⁴ More significantly, he became associated with a circle of semi-dissident young writers and artists in Vladimir, with whom he would remain in close contact for the rest of his life.

In the course of the sixties and seventies, Erofeev worked at a series of odd and mostly menial jobs. In addition to holding positions as a glassware inspector, stoker, watchman and construction worker, he was employed for quite lengthy periods laying telephone cable and repairing telephone lines. This work took him to many different areas of the Soviet Union, as did his subsequent affiliation with biological and geophysical research expeditions.

Erofeev's first wife, Valentina Zimakova, had been a student at the Vladimir Pedagogical Institute during his stay there; she bore him a son in 1966. By all accounts, Erofeev was deeply devoted to the child, and often travelled to Myshlino, a settlement near Petushki, where his wife was teaching in the late sixties and early seventies. (These facts suggest, of course, interesting autobiographical parallels with the tale told by Venichka, the unfortunate protagonist of *Moscow–Petushki*.) His second wife, Galina Erofeeva, was active in preserving and publishing his unfinished works and notebooks.

After Erofeev was diagnosed with cancer of the throat in the mid-eighties, he underwent a radical operation that left him virtually unable to speak. Although he was invited to Paris to undergo treatment (and to work at the University of Paris), he was denied permission to travel to France.[5] His death in May of 1990 at the age of 52 was noted in both émigré and Soviet newspapers; obituaries appeared in publications as diverse as *Russkaia mysl'* and *Literaturnaia gazeta*.

It is likely that Erofeev will be regarded by future generations as the author of a single book, his satirical and philosophical *chef-d'œuvre, Moscow–Petushki*. By the author's own account, the work was written over the course of two months in 1970 while he was working on telephone lines and living in a train car. Moreover, it was written for a small group of the author's friends who would recognize themselves in the tale. The manuscript disappeared briefly within a week of its completion, but was recovered in the Vladimir region.[6] While it was disseminated in *samizdat* within the Soviet Union, the text found its way to the West, where it was published in *tamizdat*. *Moscow–Petushki* first appeared in a short-lived Israeli émigré journal, *AMI*, in 1973. It was subsequently published in Paris (in French and in Russian) as a separate edition. An English translation, entitled *Moscow to the End of the Line*, came out in 1980;[7] it has been translated into several other languages (including German, Polish and Italian) as well. In Erofeev's homeland, *Moscow–Petushki* was first published serially – in a substantially shortened version – in the journal *Trezvost' i kul'tura (Sobriety and Culture)* in 1988 and 1989. The nearly complete text appeared in an anthology put out by the independent publishing concern Vest' in 1989. The publishing house Prometei issued a separate edition, what Erofeev's friend Vladimir Murav'ev calls "the first authentic text" of the work, that same year (Frolova *et al.*, "Neskol'ko monologov," 91).

Several other works by Erofeev are extant, but for the most part, these remain unpublished; others have simply been lost. His first literary effort, a "lyrical diary" entitled *Notes of a Psychopath*, was written while he was a student at MGU and has never been published (*ibid.*). Several critics make reference to a novel about student life written in the early sixties, possibly called *Notes of a Happy Neurasthenic* (Kasack, *Dictionary of Russian Literature*, p. 471; Gaiser-Shnitman, *Venedikt Erofeev*, p. 20). *Good News*, another novel written in this period, vanished somewhere in the Tula region after being read by a small group of Erofeev's acquaintances. In the late sixties, Erofeev composed several anthologies of verse for his son. His intention, according to Svetlana Gaiser-Shnitman, was to provide him with examples of various verse constructions (Gaiser-Shnitman, *Venedikt Erofeev*, p. 21). Aside from some early attempts at verse under the influence of Severianin, these unpublished pieces were Erofeev's only experiments with poetry. A third novel, tentatively entitled *Dmitrii Shostakovich*, was written in 1972, but disappeared when it was left in a bag with several bottles of vodka on a train.[8] "Vasilii Rozanov Through the Eyes of an Eccentric," a surrealistic philosophic and literary essay, was written in 1973 and published in 1978. In the mid-seventies, Erofeev again turned to writing for his son, this time composing textbooks on geography, history, philosophy, literature and so on. He also worked on several literary studies of Norwegian authors such as Hamsun and Ibsen, though these were not published. In 1988, he composed a piece called "My Little Leniniana," in which he collected and strategically arranged quotations from Lenin's essays, speeches and letters and interpolated his own wry comments; the work was published in *Kontinent*.

Toward the end of his life, Erofeev turned to writing plays, though he rarely attended the theater himself (Frolova *et al.*, "Neskol'ko monologov," 85). Of the trilogy he was working on in the eighties, only *Valpurgis Night, or the Steps of the Commander* was completed. This play was published in the West in 1985 and in the Soviet Union in 1989, and was staged at the Malaia Bronnaia Theater in Moscow. Erofeev envisioned *Valpurgis Night*, which takes place in a psychiatric ward and has as its hero a Jewish alcoholic, as the second work in the trilogy. The first, *Fanni Kaplan* or *Dissidents*, and the third were left unfinished at Erofeev's death.[9]

Erofeev was a paradoxical figure, introverted and eccentric. Although his formal education remained sketchy, he was extraordinarily erudite. History – especially Russian history – fascinated him. He knew Latin and German and loved classical music in a highly personal, emotional way. His biographers agree that depression and pessimism were certainly a part of his complex psychology, but he is also described as intellectually playful, even childlike in his apprehension of the absurdity of the world around him (Frolova *et al.*, "Neskol'ko monologov," 105). As even a cursory reading of *Moscow–Petushki* will suggest, Erofeev possessed a sound knowledge of Russian and world literature. He knew a great deal of Russian poetry by heart and read voraciously, keeping notebooks of ideas and turns of phrase that struck him as insightful or interesting.[10] Questioned about literary sources of influence on his own writing, he cited the works of Saltykov-Shchedrin, Gogol', the early Dostoevskii and Sterne, as well as the lesser known Sasha Chernyi and Vasilii Kniazev (Bolychev, "Venedikt Erofeev," 13; Frolova *et al.*, "Neskol'ko monologov," 113).

Religious faith was also an important component of Erofeev's world view. He read the Bible from an early age and a few years before his death, in 1987, was baptized a Catholic under the influence of Murav'ev.[11] By all accounts, Erofeev was also an alcoholic from his youth. His biographers tend to cast his drinking in the light of facilitating his genius and stress that his awe-inspiring feats of consumption did not noticeably affect his demeanor. Alcoholism, according to his friend Igor' Avdiev, was an integral part of Erofeev's character, a calling and a vocation (Frolova *et al.*, "Neskol'ko monologov," 109).[12] For most of his adult life, Erofeev had no fixed place of residence. His work as a cable fitter and lineman meant constantly moving; he evaded military registration (which would have meant documentation) and he never had a residence permit for Moscow until his second marriage. His entire biography is one of slipping through the cracks of the Soviet bureaucratic apparatus. He was, however, frequently denounced and apparently watched closely by the KGB (*ibid.*, 88). Like every other aspect of his life, his dissidence was of an unorthodox variety. He apprehended and elucidated the inhumanity of the Soviet state, but at the same time he required that milieu as the source of satiric inspiration. *Moscow–Petushki* in particular is very much the work of a specific time and place. Whether or not we see Erofeev the man as a victim of the Soviet regime, Erofeev the satirist lived in a symbiotic relationship with his surroundings; he was "in Soviet reality like a fish in water" (*ibid.*, 94).

Moscow–Petushki can fruitfully be read as a modern picaresque. In outlining the work's relationship to the picaresque tradition, our approach will not be – as much critical treatment of the picaresque has been – extrinsic or diachronic. The appearance of the picaresque as a stage in the development of the novel associated with the social and literary history of sixteenth- and seventeenth-century Spain is not of primary interest here. Nevertheless, there are interesting historical parallels between the Counter-Reformation, which gave rise to the picaresque, and the "period of stagnation," which was the background for the creation of *Moscow–Petushki*. Writing about the Spanish picaresque, N. Tomashevskii asserts: "The great merit of these writers is that in conditions of stagnation caused by the most severe reaction, they all were able to reflect the fall and disintegration of society, to express clearly their own disillusionment with society and their bitter anxiety for the future."[13] Tomashevskii's use of the word "stagnation" (*zastoi*) is certainly fortuitous, but his comments are applicable to Erofeev's work as well. The picaresque originally arose in conditions of class confusion, rampant poverty and hopelessness, during what Claudio Guillén calls "days of irony and discouragement."[14] The Soviet context, which parallels that of sixteenth-century Spain, is the freeze – political, intellectual and spiritual – that followed the Thaw of the late fifties and early sixties. Vail' and Genis refer to this period as the "Soviet Baroque" and note the characteristic rise of literary anti-heroes engaged in spiritual quests.[15]

The omnipresent threat of the Inquisition shaped the original picaresque narratives. Although *Moscow–Petushki* was ostensibly not written with considerations of the censorship in mind, the conditions of communist totalitarianism were operative in the context of Erofeev's work. It is interesting in this light that *Moscow–Petushki* was, like *Lazarillo de Tormes*, considered subversive. Andrei Zorin, reviewing two Soviet editions of Erofeev's works in 1989, wryly commented that the places of publication (a journal about alcoholism and a tiny independent publishing house) attest to the fact that "Erofeev's prose still burns the hands."[16] During the Counter-Reformation, the religious-philosophical system that had previously been regarded as eternal was subjected to skepticism and increasingly abandoned. So too, in the period of *zastoi*, was orthodox socialism discredited. The sacrifices of the past, including the Five-Year Plans, World War II and Stalinism, were questioned and the authority of the Party was implicitly challenged by the intelligentsia. The picaresque was employed to reflect the disillusionment and doubt characteristic of both periods.

Intriguing as these historical parallels are, viewing the picaresque as a narrative pattern or mode, i.e. synchronically or intrinsically, offers still more enlightening angles of analysis. Employing the poetics of the picaresque (formulated *a posteriori*) allows us to examine *Moscow–Petushki* against the background of a picaresque theme or "myth."[17] The picaresque, understood in this sense, generally features a rogue hero (the picaro), who is liminal and alienated from his society. He becomes a rogue through necessity, and remains essentially innocent and honest; in fact, he is often ultimately reformed or converted. The picaro's viewpoint is usually a filtering device, for picaresque narratives are generally rendered in the first person. This viewpoint tends to be reflective and philosophical, often revealing criticism of society. The hero typically wanders or travels, giving the picaresque narrative an episodic structure. Life is metaphorically presented as a pilgrimage through an unsympathetic, even hostile world. The picaro may, however, ascend vertically in society, exposing the peculiarities of its various strata. Events are not the primary focus of the picaresque mode; it is rather human behavior and relationships that concern the picaresque author. Several critics have postulated a connection between the picaresque and the medieval carnival tradition.[18] Like carnival, the picaresque may function cathartically, providing emotional release and amusement within a rigid hierarchical system.

Models of the picaresque germane to an analysis of *Moscow–Petushki* include both Western and Russian sources. Early examples of the picaresque (predecessors of the Spanish picaresque narratives) may be found in classical literature, notably Petronius' *Satiricon* and Apuleius' *Golden Ass*. The Spanish originals, such as the anonymous *Lazarillo de Tormes*, Alemán's *Guzmán de Alfarache* and Quevedo's *La vida del buscón*, were widely translated and imitated in other European literatures, and the social and historical contexts of these countries gave rise to interesting variations. The French picaresque, which reached its zenith in Lesage's *Gil Blas*, is relatively lighthearted; the German tradition, typified by Grimmelshausen's *Simplicissimus*, focuses more directly on the suffering of the lower classes; the English adaptation, which found its fullest expression in Defoe's *Moll Flanders* and *Colonel Jack*, tends to use the rags-to-riches motif.

The picaresque declined in European literatures after the eighteenth century. A notable exception is Dickens' works, in which the influence of the picaresque tradition is discernible. In American literature, Melville and Twain adapted the theme of the picaro to peculiarly New World conditions. It is the twentieth century, however, that has seen a true revival of the picaresque in Western literatures. Taken in the broadest sense, the picaresque encompasses the works of authors such as Gide, Pirandello, Brecht, Steinbeck and Orwell. Significantly for our understanding of Erofeev's work as picaresque, modern examples of this mode tend to express metaphysical despair and spiritual alienation. Unlike the heroes of the original models, modern picaros "do not, as a rule, themselves suffer anguish, but rather are vehicles for the communication of the author's own" (Blackburn, *Myth of the Picaro*, p. 24).[19]

The Russian literary tradition adopted the picaresque theme very early. Several seventeenth-century secular tales, such as the anonymous "Tale of Frol Skobeev," are picaresque in their structure and tone. The eighteenth century produced numerous translations and imitations of Western models. Among these, the most popular was *Gil Blas*; Lesage's work was translated, adapted and imitated widely from the middle of the eighteenth century, and in 1814 Vasilii Narezhnyi's *A Russian Gil Blas* appeared.[20] Probably the best example of an original Russian picaresque work dating from the eighteenth century is Mikhail Chulkov's "The Comely Cook, or the Adventures of a Depraved Woman." In the nineteenth century, Faddei Bulgarin's *Ivan Vyzhigin* incorporated elements of the picaresque, as did Gogol''s *Dead Souls*.[21] As was true in the West, the twentieth century has witnessed a revival of the picaresque in Russian literature. Kataev's *The Embezzlers*, Erenburg's *The Extraordinary Adventures of Julio Jurenito and His Disciples* and, of course, Il'f and Petrov's masterpieces *The Twelve Chairs* and *The Golden Calf* all show the influence of the picaresque mode.

The relationship between the picaresque and satire, which will be of central interest in our discussion of Erofeev's work, is a variable one. In examining this problem, Ulrich Wicks concludes that the chief difference is one of perspective; in the picaresque, the author's focus is on the observer (the picaro), while in satire proper, the focus is shifted to the satiric object or objects.[22] There is, however, often overlap between the picaresque and satiric modes, with more or less emphasis on satiric elements within picaresque structures. In extreme cases, satiric aspects may predominate, leading to some variant of the *satura*, the formless catch-all or rogue's gallery (Paulson, *Fictions of Satire*, p. 70).

Like the satiric mode, the picaresque is in theory not necessarily didactic, but is in practice often critical, polemical or tendentious. Didacticism was indeed a canonical feature of the original Spanish picaresque narratives, for they were intended to be morally instructive and corrective. This presents an interesting parallel with the Russian and Soviet literary traditions, which have always stressed the didactic function of literature. What can be said about the picaresque as a rule is that it unsettles the reader, compelling him to perceive the world around him in a new light. The picaro, both representative of and alienated from his society, unmasks the human foibles and social abuses he observes.

From the earliest period of its development, the picaresque served as one of its own objects of critical commentary; a self-reflexive, parodical impulse has virtually always been a feature of the picaresque mode. Most scholars of the picaresque agree that the original texts arose as parodical inversions of the medieval chivalric romances, but within only a few decades, these texts themselves gave rise to parodies.[23] It would seem that parody is inherent in the picaresque mode, for transformation and transgression of genre markers is extraordinarily common in examples of the picaresque. This dynamic of assimilating and surpassing (both to comment and to criticize) is operative in all stages of the development of the picaresque and is crucial to an understanding of *Moscow–Petushki* as satire.

As we have seen, parody involves revitalization of its model or models. It is in this sense a creative literary process, for it affirms the genre code at the same time that it deconstructs it.[24] This kind of parody may be an end in itself, a literary game, or it may be a point of departure, a means to an end. In the latter function, parody often becomes a vehicle of satire (or simply criticism). For Erofeev, parody serves both of these aims. Intertextual criticism of *Moscow–Petushki* has elaborated many of the allusions, reminiscences and references to other texts[25] and convincingly demonstrated that this is a densely polysemic work. In fact, intertextuality itself may be posited as an object of parody. *Moscow–Petushki* is on one level a pastiche of preexisting motifs and citations. One of Erofeev's achievements is a complex dialogue with earlier works and their authors. And even on this level, an urge to commentary and criticism is discernible; Erofeev is frequently ironic as he engages his literary and philosophic predecessors in dialogue.

The secondary level of parody in *Moscow–Petushki* effects social and political satire. Although this text is not simply or obviously didactic in its treatment of Soviet reality (and it is certainly not primarily a tract against alcoholism), Erofeev shows that conforming to the norms of a corrupt, brutal society while retaining one's humanity is impossible. More broadly stated, *Moscow–Petushki* poses the moral and philosophical problems that beset the author's generation as it satirically exposes the conditions that give rise to them. The paradoxical nature of the picaresque mode suits Erofeev's purposes, for any absolute truth – political, social or ethical – is illusory in the world he describes. Ambiguity, doubt, or what Julia Kristeva calls "nondisjunction"[26] prevails and constitutes a counterpoint to the firm basis of socialist truth. The triumph of deterministic influences, forces far stronger than the hero, gives this text a nihilistic tonality and links it with other parodic picaresques of the contemporary period.[27] Nevertheless, for all its satirical darkness and tragedy, this book is remarkably funny, and the laughter that it evokes is stubbornly life-affirming.

It is quite possible to see *Moscow–Petushki* in formal and thematic terms as parodic in respect to several other genres or modes. Models that have been suggested include the epic, the lyric and drama. Gaiser-Shnitman proposes the Menippean satire as a formal basis of parody (Gaiser-Shnitman, *Venedikt Erofeev*, pp. 257–65).[28] Examining the work as a parody of the picaresque, however, offers insights particularly relevant to our appreciation of its satirical aspects. Structural, thematic and stylistic similarities suggest a close relationship with the picaresque. The historical and social parallels we have pointed out encourage such a reading. In addition, the satiric impulse clearly underlies Erofeev's refracted view of Soviet society.

Venichka, the first-person narrator of *Moscow–Petushki*, is shaped by the model of the picaro and simultaneously transcends it, parodying the norms that it implies. We do not witness the process of Venichka's becoming a picaro, but he does explain or hint in digressions why and how this came about. The picaro narrator is typically an orphan. Venichka is deracinated in the sense that he has no coherent past, is of uncertain class background and would seem to be an orphan. He recalls experiencing nostalgia for his mother after having consumed a bottle of cologne:

It was like this: I drank a whole bottle of Lily of the Valley Silver, sat down and cried. Why was I crying? Because I recalled my Mama, that is, I recalled Mama and couldn't forget her. "Mama," I say. And I cry. And then again, "Mama!" I say, and once more I cry. Somebody else, a bit stupider, would've just sat there crying. But me? I grabbed a bottle of Lilac and drank it up. And what do you think? My tears dried up, I was overcome by idiotic laughter, and as for Mama – I even forgot her name.[29]

Through the terse, inexpressive monologue, Venichka stresses the banality of his emotion even as he recounts it and readily dismisses the memory. His orphanhood is of a more profound metaphysical variety; ejected from his Edenic Petushki and unable to make his way back, he is a spiritual outcast. The world in which he has been sentenced to exile, the Soviet Union of the sixties, offers him no values to live by. He is, as Guillén calls the modern picaro, "a godless Adam" ("Toward a Definition," 79). The loss of memory he so blithely accepts may be understood as the excision of the collective social and historical memory of the Soviet people. If we take Venichka as a representative of his generation (and such a reading is encouraged by his rhetorical asides to and about "my people"), then this is a generation of orphans, deprived of memory and, moreover, unable to regret the loss.

The picaresque hero grows and learns as he makes his way through society and sometimes accomplishes a vertical ascent in his fortunes. Venichka learns little and overtly rejects the opportunity to rise in the world: "I'll stay below and from below I'll spit on your whole social ladder. Right, spit on every rung of it. In order to climb it, you have to be a shithead without fear or reproach, you have to be a shitass forged from pure steel from head to toe. And this I'm not." (*Moskva–Petushki*, p.36). Achieving success would mean moral capitulation and loss of innocence, a quality that Venichka retains. He is quite aware, however, that this does him little good in practical terms; he laments ironically "My delicacy is indeed detrimental to me. It distorted my youth. My childhood and adolescence..." (*ibid.*, p. 28).[30] Whereas the traditional picaro often renounces his roguish ways to fit into society, Venichka resists any such reform, for the society he describes is itself utterly corrupt. As a parody of the picaro, Venichka proceeds in a downward spiral instead of an upward ascent; he is ultimately destroyed because of his failure or inability to conform.

The motivations that underlie the actions of the picaro are satirically adapted by Erofeev to the reality of contemporary Soviet society. Venichka, like the traditional rogue hero, leads a peripatetic existence, urged on by poverty and insecurity.

Ruminating on Peter's betrayal of Christ, he sympathizes with his weakness: "I know why he betrayed Him: because he was shivering from the cold, yes. He was still warming himself by the fire, together with them. But I don't have a fire, no, and I've been boozing for a week. And if they tortured me now, I would betray Him to the seven times seventieth time and more..." (*ibid.*, p. 118).[31] Hunger, which shapes the actions of the picaro, is replaced in *Moscow–Petushki* by thirst, specifically for alcohol to achieve oblivion. The traditional picaro must live by his wits and survives by exercising the power of his mind over external conditions. In Erofeev's world, by contrast, there is little scope for such triumphs of intellect. Venichka's strategy for obtaining some sherry in Kursk Station, for example, is pathetically obtuse and meets with failure and disgrace. When he is told that there is no sherry, he continues to ask plaintively, insisting that he will just wait until some appears; finally, the waiters grow impatient and physically eject him from the restaurant.

A low profession, such as that of a servant, is characteristic of the classical picaro. Venichka's job of laying cable (from which he has been fired) is indeed menial, but his servitude is of a more complex nature. He is not in bondage in a straightforward sense, for Soviet society has ostensibly obviated the very concept of the servant–master relationship. However, the spiritual subservience required of him is still more insidious. Traditional picaros could accept positions of servitude within the social system without betraying their essential freedom; Venichka must try to evade the demand that he surrender his in- dividuality, his uniqueness. His roommates rebuke him for not urinating and defecating in their presence, i.e. for his attempt to establish his right to privacy. The servant–master relationship is further parodied in the exchange between Venichka and Petr, his (or the Princess') valet. Petr is neither helpful nor obedient, refusing to give Venichka anything to drink and in fact attacking him before abandoning him for good. This entire scene is extremely confused and it is unclear who Petr is and if indeed he exists outside of Venichka's imagination. Given Venichka's earlier identification with the Apostle Peter, how- ever, it seems plausible that the valet (who appears only in this scene) is his own *alter ego*. Although a servant, Petr is stronger and more in control than his master, somewhat like Oblomov's Zakhar; these aspects of his personality desert Venichka entirely with Petr's flight (or, to extend the biblical parallel, his betrayal).

Like all picaro narrators, Venichka is the single most important character in the text. He effectively portrays himself as a rogue-errant, a delinquent in his behavior and his world view. Moreover, he is labeled as such by other characters. An unnamed old man on the train addresses him as "sweet vagabond" (*ibid.*, p. 98) and the valet Petr calls him "trickster" as he runs away (*ibid.*, p. 111).[32] What characterizes him as a rogue are human weaknesses, not criminal acts; he drinks, avoids work and is irresponsible. These would seem to be pardonable sins, but in the Soviet context they constitute subversive parasitism. His liminality is made complete by his alienation from his fellow workers; as he sums it up: "they fired ... me, who was considered, at the bottom, a fink and a collaborator and, at the top, a good-for-nothing with an unstable mind" (*ibid.*, p. 36). It is significant for the satirical impact of the text that Venichka is, for all his outcast status, representative of his time and place. In fact, all of the workers laying cable are inveterate drunkards and pilferers and the investigators who look into their abuses are equally irresponsible. These modes of behavior are pandemic in the world Erofeev describes.

Venichka's outsider stance provides him with a satirist's detachment. Alcoholic parasite that he is, he is markedly less corrupt morally than the society he observes: "I, who have partaken of so much in this world that I've lost count and the sequence of it all, I am soberer than anyone else in this world" (*ibid.*, p. 116). The duplicity and cruelty of the world never cease to confound him: "Is it really so difficult to open the door to someone and let him in to warm up for three minutes? I don't understand it. They, they're serious and understand it, but I'm a lightweight and I'll never understand it..." (*ibid.*, p. 117).

Several critics of the picaresque have noted the link between the picaro and what anthropologists call the "trickster" figure of folklore and mythology.[33] The picaro has retained, according to this view, the duality characteristic of the archetype. He is both subhuman and superhuman and demonstrates both bestial and divine traits. Perhaps more clearly than most rogue heroes, Venichka combines a profound spiritual essence with utter baseness. He communicates directly with both God and Satan (though both may be only aspects of his own psyche). Projecting this duality outward, he regards his lover sometimes as an almost divine entity, describing her in terms reminiscent of the "Song of Songs" and sometimes as a whore. Venichka as trickster is an agent of disorder and thus a subversive figure. He is, as Jung formulates it, "a collective shadow figure, an epitome of all the inferior traits of character in individuals" ("On the Psychology," p. 209). Embodying the least admirable traits of his countrymen, Venichka is simultaneously dissident and representative. As has been pointed out, Venichka also has saintly, Christ-like attributes (Paperno and Gasparov, "'Vstan' i idi'," 388).[34] This is not as contradictory as it might seem, for the trickster archetype has connections with Christ. Venichka combines these qualities as a parodic picaro and aspires to transcend the corruption of the world around him even while he remains a rogue; as trickster and as saint, as we shall see, he is defeated.

That the entire text of *Moscow–Petushki* is rendered in first-person narration means that the perception of the world we receive is filtered through Venichka's consciousness. His viewpoint is, of course, partial and prejudiced. Omission and selection are generic features of the picaresque and they are generally employed to the narrator's advantage. That is, the picaro attempts to win the reader's sympathy by presenting himself in the best possible light.[35] The limitations of Venichka's viewpoint ironically do not shape our apprehension of him in a positive way. His presentation of himself is indeed full of gaps and is certainly subjective, but he tends to expose his worst traits and concentrate on his own reprehensible behavior. The narrator's attitude toward himself is consistently ironic and he is as much a focus of satire as the world around him.

The first-person narration of *Moscow–Petushki* does strengthen the verisimilitude of Erofeev's account and would seem to bolster his claim to historical accuracy. An identification of the narrator, Venichka, with the author, Venedikt, is supported by his use of actual names of characters and references to recognizable places and events. All of this is, of course, conventional and the apparent authenticity of the text may be quite deceptive. As a rhetorical device of satire, however, Erofeev's narrative procedure is very effective. He minimizes the distance between the implied author and the implied reader and encourages the reader to associate himself with the confidential, garrulous narrator. Far from being a drawback of the picaresque or evidence of its primitiveness, this kind of narration may enhance a text's satirical efficacy. Barbara Babcock asserts that picaresque satire is saved from "dull and explicit social criticism or the typical self-righteousness of the satirist" precisely by the picaro's limited, equivocal perspective ("'Liberty's a Whore'," 107). This is most pertinent to *Moscow–Petushki*, for didacticism and moralizing are alien to Venichka's *Weltanschauung*.

Erofeev parodies the convention of confession that is inherent in the picaresque mode through his narrative technique. The element of confession is always somewhat problematic in the picaresque tradition, for confessional relies upon the trustworthiness of the narrator. In the picaresque, language itself may be a tool of deception or prevarication; the picaresque is formally confessional, but the picaresque narrative is paradoxically "the confession of a liar" (Guillén, "Toward a Definition," 92). Erofeev muddies the waters further by making the narrator wholly unreliable (though his intentions are honorable). The very possibility of veracity is called into question in this text. Dissembling and hypocrisy involve some degree of control, a firm grasp of the reality concealed behind the facade. Venichka's grip on reality progressively weakens, so that by the end of *Moscow–Petushki*, his intention to confess honestly tells us nothing about the actual relationship between his account and reality.

Since the picaro recounts the story of his life, the narration of picaresque texts is usually ulterior and retrospective. Venichka's account includes numerous digressions and flashbacks that are narrated simultaneously with the present time frame of his trip to Petushki. In fact, because all of the events of *Moscow–Petushki* may take place exclusively within the narrator's mind, it is impossible to ascertain their chronological relationships. Whereas the conventional picaro must claim to possess a perfect memory in order to recall his adventures and conversations accurately, Venichka does not even perceive the present clearly. Like most picaresque narrators, Venichka comments on the narrating process itself, but his qualifications are not the typical protestations of difficulties with remembering details. Following a reported dialogue about the relative worth of women, Venichka concludes: "They all observed a significant silence. Each thought his own thoughts, or they all thought the same thing, I don't know" (*Moskva–Petushki*, p. 70). Not only does the narrator not claim omniscience, he dismisses the possibility of knowing what other characters think.

Picaresque narration conventionally reflects the estrangement and alienation of the rogue hero through a split between the narrator's inner and outer "I." That is, the experiencing "I" (the "I" of the chronological past of the text) is distinguishable from the narrating "I" (the "I" of the present of the text). Erofeev introduces yet another level of estrangement in his parodic adaption, for Venichka's narrating "I" is itself subject to fracturing and disjuncture. To express the hero's extreme alienation, Erofeev uses the cliché of the heart–mind or emotion–reason dichotomy. These aspects of the narrating "I" take on quite absurdly independent personalities, arguing to support their conflicting opinions:

Yes, yes, on that day my heart struggled for a whole half hour with reason ... My heart said to me, "They've insulted you, they've treated you like shit. Go on and get drunk, Venichka. Get up and go get drunk as a skunk." This is what my beautiful heart said. But my reason? It grumbled and insisted, "You won't get up, Erofeev, you won't go anywhere and you won't drink a drop." While my heart responded, "Well, OK, Venichka, OK. You don't have to drink a lot, you don't have to get drunk as a skunk – drink 400 grams and let it go at that." (*Ibid.*, p. 37)

This splitting of Erofeev's narrating "I's" facilitates satire in *Moscow–Petushki*.[36] Whereas the focus of the picaresque narrator is usually outward, on society, Erofeev directs his critical lens inward, into the psyche of the hero. The self-analysis he carries out is not, as the above passage illustrates, profound or illuminating; rather it exposes the alienating and trivializing effect of Soviet society on the individual spirit.

The narratee is explicitly addressed frequently in the text, but the "you" the narrator posits is highly unstable. At times the narratee is a potentially sarcastic, disapproving observer of the narrator's actions: "Of course, you all nod your heads at that. I can even see from here, from the wet platform, how all of you scattered about my world are nodding your heads and getting ready to be ironic" (*Moskva–Petushki*, p. 24). Venichka has to convince his narratee of the value of his cocktail recipes; he urges the "you" of the text to listen and write them down carefully. Occasionally the narratee serves as a foil to Venichka, a contrast to his inclinations or behavior. The "you" seems to take on definite characteristics when Venichka asserts "If you took the chances I did, you'd either bust your gut or have a stroke. Or, actually, if at your age you took the chances I did, one fine morning you'd wake up dead" (*ibid.*, p. 50). To emphasize the strength of his faith in the ultimate triumph of the meek over the powerful, he draws his narratee into the debate: "I believe in that more firmly than you believe in anything" (*ibid.*, p. 117). What is consistent about this persona is that it is always an "other" in relation to Venichka. Whether sympathetic, interested, indifferent or hostile, it is part of the world in which Venichka is an outsider. In explaining his condition of spiritual illness, he says "Everything that you speak of, everything that occupies your time, is forever alien to me" (*ibid.*, p. 39). To emphasize this distance between them, Venichka always addresses the narratee as *vy*, either a collective "you" or an individual "you" who is not an intimate.

Venichka reports dialogues with many other interlocutors who also represent "others" in the text. Sometimes these voices are identified, as is the case with the angels, God, the narrator's little son and Satan. These verbal encounters become progressively more bizarre as his hallucinations increase and his perception of reality becomes more distorted. His conversation with Satan, for example, occurs late in the text and can very plausibly be interpreted as a product of Venichka's drunken imagination. The Princess and the valet Petr are equally problematic, for their exchanges with Venichka are almost wholly comprised of *non sequiturs*. Like his addresses to the unnamed narratee, these conversations provide insights into the narrator's own psyche; they are, whether recalled or imagined, primarily dialogues with himself. In fact, these characters seem to be further manifestations of the narrator's own spiritual disjuncture.[37] Venichka's addresses to the narratee and his dialogues are self-reflexive and give the text as a whole a curiously closed quality.

Erofeev subtitled *Moscow–Petushki* a *poema*,[38] which suggests interesting structural links with the picaresque. Two notable predecessors in this respect are Dante's *Divine Comedy* and Gogol''s *Dead Souls*. Both utilized the dual structural nature of the *poema* – its linearity and its circularity – to express philosophical criticism. An interesting thematic similarity also exists between Erofeev's text and Dante's and Gogol''s models. *Moscow–Petushki* too conveys a vision of hell and describes a journey through it.

An episodic, linear structure is characteristic of the picaresque. Lacking a well-defined plot, the picaresque narrative is rather based on a series of situations, the common link being the picaro-narrator. Especially in the modern picaresque, he typically encounters characters with whom temporary communion is possible (Lewis, *The Picaresque Saint*, p. 34), though no stable relations are established. This structure provides a series of frames for satirical portraits. Within these episodes or portraits, there is usually a confrontation, some scheme on the part of the narrator to satisfy a need, a complication and an extrication (Wicks, *Picaresque Narrative*, p. 55). Erofeev parodies this rhythm, for Venichka is defenseless, indeed helpless in his confrontations with the various knaves he encounters. The characters he meets are either largely or entirely mirror images or doubles of himself; thus there can be no extrication, but only frustrated attempts to flee the self.

As Alexander Blackburn has shown, it is shortsighted to dismiss the episodic structure of the picaresque as too primitive to allow for symbolic, moral or psychological coherence (*Myth of the Picaro*, p.18). And as a basis for parodic adaption, the episodic structure eminently suits Erofeev's satiric purposes. It reflects the chaos and fragmentation of the world around Venichka; the rapid pace of the text and the disjuncture between episodes enhance this effect. What Stuart Miller calls the "dance pattern" helps to account for the mysterious and seemingly haphazard appearance and disappearance of characters in the picaresque in general and in *Moscow–Petushki* in particular:

> If this pattern occurs often enough in a [picaresque] novel, it is possible to see the protagonist as moving blindly through a complicated dance in which, at irregular intervals, he dances with a previous partner again, and again leaves him. This strange pattern may either soften or exaggerate the effect of chaos developed by the episodic plot and other devices.[39]

The latter is true of Erofeev's text, for characters appear, disappear and reappear with startling unexpectedness and lack of logic.

The episodic structure in general and the dance pattern in particular are facilitated by the fact that most of the action of the narrative takes place on a train. Travelling or wandering is a conventional motif of the picaresque and in *Moscow–Petushki*, the reader is given fully recognizable space coordinates. Venichka's trip ostensibly takes place on the Moskovsko-Gor'kovskaia railroad line that runs from Moscow to Petushki and all of the place names are actual stops. The train bears its usual literary symbolic significance in that it represents life. (That the picaresque narrative is essentially a *vida* lends credence to this interpretation.) This is, however, a satirically distorted life (or partial life), for Venichka's train trip is a peculiarly unpleasant one "with its boorish passengers, suitcases, string bags and ticket controllers."[40]

The title of Erofeev's tale is reminiscent of Radishchev's

A Journey From St. Petersburg to Moscow, and it is possible to read the text as a parody of this work.[41] Perhaps the most significant trait that *Moscow–Petushki* shares with Radishchev's tale is its use of the travel motif as a means of posing broad philosophical questions. As is the case with Radishchev's narrative, exposure of social abuses is only part of the author's purpose; what goes on within the hero, his spiritual evolution, is more important. In light of these broad similarities, the ways in which Erofeev departs from Radishchev's model are interesting. Whereas Radishchev titles his chapters for the stations where action takes place, Erofeev gives his chapters titles that signify the space between stations. The convention of breaking time and space up into discrete pieces where the development of the hero occurs is retained;[42] here, however, the hero is a passive victim, conveyed helplessly from station to station. This drifting further characterizes Venichka as a picaresque hero. His consciousness determines the structural division of the text, but he appears to have no control over this process.

Like Sterne, another practitioner of the travel narrative, Erofeev sometimes inserts a chapter division in mid-sentence:

If you want to know everything, I'll tell you, but wait. I'll tie something on by Hammer and Sickle and
          MOSCOW – HAMMER AND SICKLE
then I'll tell everything, everything. Be patient. Aren't *I* being patient? (*Moskva–Petushki*, p. 25)

This device strengthens the effect of movement in the text and emphasizes the narrator's being swept along by external forces. The missing chapter is another convention of the travel narrative adopted and parodied by Erofeev. While its notable absence may heighten the sense of mystery (Paperno and Gasparov, "'Vstan' i idi'," 388), the author's stated reason for omitting it is rather banal. It was, he tells us in the foreword, so full of obscenities that readers of the first edition (one copy) were skipping to it without reading the first chapters. Mystery is thus undercut at the outset, for the author has exercised his prerogative to select only in order to cut out some particularly offensive language. The repetition of the official announcement that the train will not stop at Esino is also satirically significant.[43]

Beyond picaresque 79

The arbitrariness and the iron illogic of Soviet reality are emphasized in this unexplained warning. Causal, logical connections between episodes tend to be weak in the picaresque tradition, but in *Moscow–Petushki* they are often entirely absent. The unreliability of the picaresque narrator's memory may explain gaps in the chronology of the text. Erofeev takes this convention to an extreme; because Venichka is in various stages of inebriation throughout the course of the narrative, sudden shifts of focus and mood and uneven exposition are the norm. For example, the transition between an account of the Petushki revolution and a framing episode on the train is accomplished through the haze of the narrator's drunken confusion. One moment he is wandering about the countryside, having abandoned the revolution, and the next moment he is back on the train:

"Where is Petushki, anyhow?" I asked, going up to somebody's lighted veranda. Where did it come from, this veranda? Maybe it wasn't a veranda at all but a terrace, a mezzanine, or a wing? I don't really understand the difference and I'm forever getting them mixed up. I knocked and asked, "Where's Petushki, anyhow? Is it still far to Petushki?" And, in response, everyone on the veranda burst out laughing and didn't say anything. I got offended and knocked again – the neighing on the veranda started up again. Strange! If that wasn't enough, someone was neighing behind my back. I looked around; the passengers on the Moscow–Petushki train were sitting in their places with filthy smiles on their faces. What's this? So, I'm still on the train? (*Moskva–Petushki*, p. 97)

Venichka's exit from the train and his movement from the platform to the Kremlin are even more hallucinatory. The picaro's life is always controlled by fortune or accident; Erofeev utilizes the increasing inebriation and delusion of his narrator to enhance the role of blind chance. However, the particularly Soviet setting of *Moscow–Petushki* implies a satirical subtext. In Marxist parlance events are historically determined and cannot be merely the products of chance. Thus the society that guides the hand of fortune is rendered monstrous and threatening.

Interpolated digressions, adventures, anecdotes and flashbacks are characteristic of picaresque structure. To some extent,

Erofeev draws on this tradition and viewing the text in this light may help to explain its apparent formlessness. But it is the extreme self-consciousness, the parodic motivation underlying these devices that make them satirically effective. Classical picaresque narratives included moralistic monologues or sermons that were intended to placate the ecclesiastical censor. Erofeev too engages in moral or philosophical digressions, but these tend not to be instructive or didactic in a conventional way. They do posit ideals, but these usually serve the primary function of contrast with Venichka's rather squalid reality.[44] Moreover, they are frequently interlaced with trivial or scatological asides, undercutting their moralistic tone:

> We are mere trembling creatures while it is omnipotent. It – that is, the Right Hand of God which is raised above us all and before which only cretins and rogues do not bow their heads. He is incomprehensible and, therefore, He is. And thus, be perfect as your Heavenly Father is perfect... Yes. Drink more, eat less. This is the best method of avoiding self-conceit and superficial atheism. Take a look at a hiccuping atheist: he is distracted and dark of visage, he suffers and is ugly. Turn away from him, spit, and look at me when I begin to hiccup: a believer in predestination without any thought of rebellion, I believe in the fact that He is good and therefore I myself am good and pure. (*Moskva–Petushki*, p. 54)

Although some of Venichka's digressions are motivated by alcohol-induced delusions, others parody literary models. Before explaining the conductor's reference to Scheherazade, he informs the reader that he is going to make "a small digression" and that this will be chronologically parallel with the conductor's consumption of his fines, i.e. a large quantity of vodka (*ibid.*, p. 86). Prior to the passengers' telling their stories of exceptional love (which turn out to be absurdly banal), they concur that they are just like characters in Turgenev: "how marvelous it is that we're all so intelligent. We're just like in Turgenev – everyone sits around arguing about love" (*ibid.*, p. 72). The adventures that Venichka himself relates to his fellow passengers and to the reader are bizarre and implausible. These include his wanderings in Europe and the story of the unsuccessful Petushki revolution.

Erofeev's use of the travel motif also suggests a connection between *Moscow–Petushki* and the Russian literary tradition of the *stranstvie*, or story of spiritual wandering (Gaiser-Shnitman, *Venedikt Erofeev*, p. 261; Paperno and Gasparov, "'Vstan' i idi'," 387). A specific model for Erofeev's parody in this case may be found in the anonymous medieval "Tale of Grief-Misfortune." This is suggested by the presence in the text of angels who converse with and guide the hero. Venichka's angels, however, ultimately fail to lead him to a safe refuge and abandon him to be killed by satanic figures. Erofeev's parodic version includes many references to Grief, who almost takes on an individualized persona. Venichka recalls "I turned right, staggering a bit from the cold and from grief" (*Moskva–Petushki*, p. 17). He muses on the enigma of Kramskoi's painting *Inconsolable Grief* and reflects "is there anything on earth higher than that which is inconsolable?" (*ibid.*, p. 108). The poet Ol'ga Sedakova's remarks in this connection are illuminating: "Grief was a real passion of Venia's. He proposed writing this word with a capital letter, as in Tsvetaeva: Grief" (Frolova *et al.*, "Neskol'ko monologov," 100). The motif of drunkenness as the path to ruination is also reminiscent of the medieval moral tale. Yet in this respect too, the relationship is parodic. In Erofeev's depiction of Soviet reality of the *zastoi* period, there is no possibility of redemption, no escape from oblivion and death. There is no monastery – symbolically speaking, no haven of faith – to which Venichka can flee.

Several possibilities in addition to linearity have been suggested to explicate the structure of *Moscow–Petushki*. Vail' and Genis discuss the text as a "tragic end-game" developing through an exposition, complication and culmination.[45] Murav'ev views the composition as spiral[46] and Gaiser-Shnitman analyzes it as a triptych (*Venedikt Erofeev*, pp. 235–36). While all of these approaches have critical merit, the structure of the text is best seen in terms of picaresque parody as circular. Although this may seem paradoxical, the circularity of *Moscow–Petushki* does not contradict its episodic quality. Erofeev uses several devices to create the effect of a "vicious circle" which transcends the primary linear structure of the text. Thus on the one hand he uses a traditional picaresque structural principle and on the other hand links the episodes (especially the beginning and end) to comment creatively on that principle. The circularity of the text reinforces Erofeev's satiric conclusion that the world he describes is bleakly limiting and inescapable.

The circular, cyclical quality of the tale is enhanced, first of all, by a repetition of key events (or echoes of them). Images of expulsion, rejection, crucifixion and resurrection, for example, recur frequently. The repetition of these and other images suggests frustration of forward momentum, what has been called the "labor of Sisyphus" motif characteristic of the picaresque mode. On one level, Venichka is aboard a train speeding toward his destination; paradoxically, he is standing still, his senses dulled by alcohol and spiritual emptiness. He is, as one reviewer put it, "doomed eternally to repeat his journey, each time unaware of the fate awaiting him at the end of the line."[47] Directionality is ultimately irrelevant, because the circle is closed and there is no exit: "'Run, Venichka, any place at all, doesn't matter where. Run to the Kursk Station. To the left or the right or back, it doesn't matter where you end up. Run, Venichka, run...'" (*Moskva–Petushki*, p. 119). It is significant that the final three chapters bear dual titles, indicating that the narrator is located in Petushki and in Moscow simultaneously: "Petushki. Station Square," "Petushki. Sadovoe Circle," "Petushki. The Kremlin." There is no difference between the endpoints of Venichka's journey; his ideal of an Edenic haven was illusory. Indeed one may read the entire text as an extended hallucination and conclude that Venichka never leaves his entranceway at all.[48]

Moscow–Petushki ends with Venichka's brutal murder by four assailants. This ending emphasizes the absolute closure of the circle and constitutes yet another element of structural parody of the picaresque. Ending the picaresque narrative is always somewhat problematic, for by convention, the plot of the picaresque is not end-determined. The picaresque text is characteristically left open and death is usually excluded as a possible ending, since the picaro himself narrates his life story. Here Venichka recounts his own murder, becoming a victim of the social order he describes. Instead of triumphing over the constraints of a restrictive society, the hero is destroyed by it. The murder is carried out by figures who vaguely represent authority. All four have "classical profiles" and inspire convulsive shaking in Venichka: "All four stared at me intently and all four probably thought, 'The bum, what a coward, how transparent!' Oh, let them, let them think it, if only they'd let me go! Where, in what newspaper, have I seen their repulsive faces?" (*Moskva–Petushki*, p. 119). Moreover, the leader of the gang kills Venichka with an awl (perhaps a reference to Stalin, whose father was a shoemaker) (Gaiser-Shnitman, *Venedikt Erofeev*, p. 270).[49]

Whereas picaresque narratives often conclude with the conversion or reform of the hero, the ending of *Moscow–Petushki* implicitly denies the possibility of change. Instead, despair and resignation prevail. This darkly pessimistic tonality is enhanced by the parallel between Venichka's murder and the crucifixion. His resurrection (indeed several symbolic resurrections) through the agency of alcohol and the affections of his lover have been recounted earlier in the text. That these events occur in reverse order underscores the hopelessness of the hero's position. The angels who have accompanied him on his trip laugh and desert him at the moment when his murderers are approaching. Moreover, Venichka describes their laughter as something diabolical and obscene. Erofeev's final vision, then, is one of hell, and not even an implicit ideal can be reconstructed from this satirical wasteland.

As he is dying, Venichka has a vision of the letter *iu*. Certainly this image is linked with that of the hero's little son, who has learned to write this letter. E. A. Smirnova asserts that the ending thus contains a glimmer of hope and beauty ("Venedikt Erofeev," 65).[50] The *iu*, however, is horribly "thick" and red (*Moskva–Petushki*, p. 122), writ in the hero's own blood. Furthermore, his child never becomes more than an abstraction in the text; if he represents an ideal of purity and love, he remains completely intangible. The hope he holds out to Venichka for his own redemption is far too delicate and ephemeral to withstand reality. In addition, the *iu*, in Cyrillic script ю, presents a circular visual image. Thus Venichka's final vision in fact reinforces the closure of the text and the inescapability of this world of madness and despair.

The recurrence of imagery and allusions provides unity in the text and allows us to discuss the thematics of Erofeev's satire. Christian imagery permeates *Moscow–Petushki* and has been examined in depth by Smirnova, Paperno and Gasparov, and others. The theme of the Gospels gives the text a mystical dimension that parallels the physical setting. Erofeev explicitly links these levels, intertwining his accounts of quite ordinary events with allusions to events in the Gospels. Referring to his being fired from his job laying cable, he writes "My star, which had blazed forth for four weeks, passed from view. The crucifixion took place exactly thirty days after the ascension" (*ibid.*, p. 36). Venichka's persona blends with the image of Christ; he is persecuted and martyred at the hands of an uncomprehending and unforgiving society.[51] However, Erofeev's use of Christian imagery is double-edged and it is simplistic to presume that every allusion to the Gospels is evidence of Christian faith. The picaresque has had an ambiguous relationship to religion and indeed in modern examples of the mode, religion is often the target of satire (Babcock, "'Liberty's A Whore'," 103). Mixed as they are with pagan and secular images, the Christian images in *Moscow–Petushki* serve to broaden the resonance of the tragedy enacted, to emphasize the satirical effect of the text through incongruity.

The significance of the chronological reversal of images of crucifixion and resurrection was discussed in relation to the closure effected in the ending of the tale. A complex of associated images reinforces the pessimism of the ending, the implicit denial of the possibility of rebirth or eternal life. Paperno and Gasparov point out the symbolic similarity of the entranceways where Venichka wakes up and is eventually murdered (they appear to be the same) to a coffin ("'Vstan' i idi'," 393). Thus the resurrection that the narrator recounts in the text offers only temporary and illusory hope:

Take me, for example: twelve weeks ago I was in a coffin, I had been in a coffin for four years already, so that I had already stopped stinking. And they say to her, "Look, he's in a coffin. Resurrect him, if you can." And she walked up to the coffin, if only you had seen how she walked up to it ... She walked up to the coffin and she says, " *Talife cumi,*" which means, in the translation from the Ancient Kike-ish: "I say to you get up and walk." And what do you think? I got up and walked. And it's already three months that I've been walking around, muddled ... (*Moskva–Petushki,* p. 71)

Despite his being raised from the dead here, his subsequent death is final. The last lines of the book are "since then I have not regained consciousness, and I never will" (*ibid.,* p. 122). It is significant in this respect that Venichka's journey takes him from light to darkness; it becomes inexplicably dark as he approaches his destination. He resigns himself to this, concluding "there's no demanding light beyond the window if beyond the window it is dark" (*ibid.,* pp. 99–100).

Satanic images become more prevalent as Venichka nears the end of his journey. He actually encounters Satan, who tempts him to throw himself off the train. Mithridates, who threatens him with a knife, turns black and laughs horribly; it is, Venichka says "as if a thousand devils possessed him" (*ibid.,* p. 114). The angels, whom Venichka took for heavenly beings, turn out to be diabolical. Most importantly, as his four assailants climb the stairs to murder him, "God was silent" (*ibid.,* p. 121). He is deserted, left to disintegrate in a spiritual vacuum where chaos and disharmony rule. The displacement or expulsion of God – not necessarily a Christian God, but rather the embodiment of spiritual values – is the ultimate crime of this society.

A theme linked to the Christian motifs in *Moscow–Petushki* is that of the quest. Specific textual references suggest the centrality of the idea of the search for an ideal. Erofeev includes several allusions to Lohengrin, implicitly recalling the theme of the Holy Grail. These are, however, couched in farcical contexts. Ivan Kozlovskii, who sings in a voice that is "nauseous" in the restaurant at Kursk Station, mangles lines from Wagner's opera; the kolkhoz manager named Lohengrin regularly gets drunk, weeps and urinates on the floor. Erofeev intertwines references to the Grail with extremely low, scatological images, creating an effect of travesty. Similarly, numerous references to Goethe and to Faust suggest the theme of the quest for immortality (Paperno and Gasparov, "'Vstan' i idi'," 395). A Gogolian subtext may be discerned in Venichka's search for an elusive female figure connected in the hero's mind with tranquility. These images too are diminished and mixed freely with scatological elements.

Venichka's own quest may be read as a parodical inversion of the picaro hero's search for home. The quest motif is typical of the picaresque, though it is chiefly in modern examples of the mode that the quest becomes metaphysical. R. W. B. Lewis sees the search for meaning in life as characteristic of the contemporary picaresque and Wicks views the picaro's attempt to reach some safe haven as canonical (Lewis, *The Picaresque Saint*, p. 28; Wicks, *Picaresque Narrative*, p. 48). Venichka too is searching for something sacred, some ideal which may only be his own self. One may interpret the object of his search, the definition of "home", variably, but it is consistently frustrated. Certainly his quest involves the ideal of freedom, and that freedom from social convention he has achieved turns out to be deceptive; there is no possibility of real liberation within the society he depicts and he is punished for trying to evade its strictures. Companionship is another aspect of the modern picaro's quest and Venichka tries repeatedly to establish links with his fellow passengers. He muses:

Man should not be lonely – that's my opinion. Man should give of himself to people, even if they don't want to take. But if he is lonely anyway, he should go through the cars. He should find people and tell them: "Look, I'm lonely. I'll give of myself to the last drop (because I just drank up the last drop, ha-ha!) and you give of yourselves to me and, having given, tell me where are we going." (*Moskva–Petushki*, p. 107)

Venichka's search for an antidote to alienation in community is, however, in vain. His efforts go unrewarded and he himself realizes that there is no basis for a spiritual link with "the crowd": "And, indeed, what do these vain and repellent creatures have to do with me?" (*ibid.*, p. 18). Companionship is closely related to compassion for Venichka and he reiterates the importance of demonstrating and receiving compassion. He preaches "Love for the dust that is man, for every womb. And for the fruit of every womb – pity" (*ibid.*, p. 75). Yet as he approaches his destination, he realizes in utter despair that this ideal is impossible: "What's left to you? In the morning to moan, in the evening to cry, at night to grind your teeth. And who, who in the world cares about your heart? Who? Just go into any home in Petushki, at any threshold ask, 'What do you care about my heart?' Oh, my God..." (*ibid.*, p. 116). Venichka's quest is frustrated in an overt manner by the Sphinx who compels him to respond to a series of absurd riddles. Like the others whom Venichka encounters on his journey, the Sphinx may be a splinter figure of his own psyche, or in Jung's terms a "shadow."[52] Thus the connundrums it poses, the obstacles it places in Venichka's path, may be products of his own mind.

The object of Venichka's quest is symbolized by Petushki, his personal Eden "where the birds never cease singing, not by day or by night, where winter and summer the jasmine never ceases blooming" and where no one feels the burden of original sin (*Moskva–Petushki*, p. 37). Having been ejected from paradise, Venichka is trying to regain entry. As it turns out, there can be no reentry; Petushki may be only an illusion. Addressing himself, Venichka says "Once you had a heavenly paradise, you could have found out the time last Friday, but now your heavenly paradise is no more..." (*ibid.*, p. 116). The Sphinx mocks Venichka, laughing "'Nobody, in general, ha, ha, will end up in Petushki!'" (*ibid.*, p. 105). The realization that expulsion from paradise is a permanent condition is actually typical of the modern picaresque. This discovery underlies the picaro's alienation, and is a primary motivation for roguish behavior. In Erofeev's version, however, this discovery is fatal. Venichka's loneliness is an incurable condition. He denies that his soul has become coarsened by extreme alienation but he is unable to cry, to express his grief. What must inevitably follow under these circumstances is death and disintegration.

Another pervasive theme of *Moscow–Petushki* is alcohol. Erofeev tentatively entitled his work "The Drunkards" (Paperno and Gasparov, "'Vstan' i idi'," 391)[53] and the book has been interpreted, perhaps naively, as an anti-alcohol tract. Alcohol functions on several levels in the text. The drunkenness of the hero facilitates his spiritual quest; he compares his cocktail recipes to alchemy. Drinking also contributes to Venichka's increasing disorientation, and thus motivates the loose structure of the narrative. Moreover, it broadens the scope of action, allowing free movement to and from the plane of the fantastic.

Drunkenness is treated in the text as a Russian (and Soviet) national trait. In fact, abstaining is a negative characteristic in the eyes of the narrator: "All worthwhile people in Russia, all the necessary people, they all drank, they drank like pigs. But the superfluous, the muddle-headed ones, they didn't drink. Eugene Onegin, when he visited the Larins, the only thing he drank was bilberry juice, and that got him the trots" (*Moskva–Petushki*, p. 65). Venichka and his fellow passengers concur that alcoholism transcends class boundaries. The muzhik drinks from despair and the educated classes drink from grief and sympathy with the muzhik. However, the reasons for this state of affairs are not economic, but spiritual. Contemplating his recently purchased bottle of rosé, Venichka asks "But truly is *this* necessary to me? Truly is this what my soul is pained over? This is what people have given me in exchange for that over which my soul is pained" (*ibid.*, p. 25). One cannot *not* drink in this dismal, empty world. Furthermore, there is a special link between art and alcohol in Erofeev's universe. Drinking is, asserts Venichka, the legacy of Russian culture, born of desperation and guilt.

Erofeev's evocation of a world steeped in drunken oblivion has important satirical connections with the contemporary period of *zastoi*. The drinking binge represents modern Soviet life as a whole in *Moscow–Petushki*. As Mark Al'tshuller writes in relation to Erofeev's work, "in drunkenness is contained the entire spiritual world of Soviet man" ("'Moskva–Petushki'," 75). Venichka describes the work schedule of his team of cable linemen and recalls that once a piece of cable was unwound and placed in the ground in the morning, "we'd sit down and everyone would take his leisure in his own way. Everyone, after all, has his own dream and temperament" (*Moskva–Petushki*, p. 31). What this "leisure" consists of is drinking everything from vermouth to eau de cologne in order to escape into sleep and oblivion. This social satire is extended by Erofeev to the point that all of life is equated with a binge:

> For isn't the life of man a momentary booziness of the soul? And an eclipse of the soul as well? We are all as if drunk, only everybody in his own way: one person has drunk more, the next less. And it works differently on each: the one laughs in the face of this world, while the next cries on its bosom. One has already thrown up and feels better, while the next is only starting to feel like throwing up. (*Ibid.*, p. 116)

From the standpoint of the picaresque hero, to exist in this society means to drink, and the only alternatives that present themselves are those of degree.

In the context of the carnival tradition, drunkenness connotes social rebellion and Venichka does display revolutionary tendencies. However, the uprising he leads in Petushki is a travesty of a revolution; it fails because no one notices. Both its goal (opening the local liquor stores) and its outcome are paltry. A second function of alcohol that Erofeev's work shares with the carnivalesque is escapism. This too turns out to be a delusion on Venichka's part, for he is ultimately compelled to confront the Kremlin and is destroyed by its representatives. Alcohol is only a temporary – and finally unsuccessful – means of transcending or evading society's strictures. For all its Rabelaisian tone, *Moscow–Petushki* lacks the gaiety associated with rebellion or escape in the carnival tradition.

Drinking in Erofeev's text has ritualistic overtones and may suggest a travesty of the mass. Desacramentalization is a common feature of the picaresque mode and one that links it with the carnival tradition. The symbolic significance of the Eucharist makes Erofeev's satire particularly strong. The sacrament represents a renewal of man's link with God and drinking is for Venichka an attempt to reestablish a spiritual connection he has lost. However, the means of his sacramental drinking – rosé, vodka, beer, cologne, furniture polish, and so on – are foul and in any case, God has deserted him. Another aspect of the mass, the achievement of a sense of community, is also travestied by Erofeev. His attempts at "symposium"[54] end in failure; his fellow passengers steal his bottles and abandon him.

Love and sex are typically treated in naturalistic terms in the picaresque. In *Moscow–Petushki*, other characters' romantic or sexual experiences are indeed presented negatively. The Decembrist relates the story of a man who fell madly in love with Ol'ga Erdeli but was deluded by his friends into believing that a drunken old woman was actually the famous harpist. The woman with the black moustache recounts her affair with a Komsomol organizer and poet in an equally coarse and farcical way; he knocks her front teeth out and gives her a concussion as they drunkenly scream about their love. On the other hand, the narrator's own passion for "the whitish one" is described almost purely through abstract similes and metaphors. Although his account of their first sexual encounter is highly suggestive, it is far from naturalistic:

> She herself made my choice for me, sprawling back and stroking my cheek with her ankle. There was something of encouragement in this, something of a game, and something like a gentle slap. And something of the blowing of a kiss – there was that too. And, then, that turbid, that bitchy whiteness in her pupils, whiter than delirium and seventh heaven! And her stomach like the sky and the earth. (*Moskva–Petushki*, pp. 46–47)

Like the stories Venichka tells the conductor to distract him from demanding the train fare, his autobiographical account of his own passion is only superficially erotic. The unnamed object of his love is actually a parody of femininity, a stylized Mary Magdelene figure who in this case cannot or will not be saved from sin. For the purpose of picaresque satire, she must remain an abstraction because she is a focus of Venichka's quest. And she, like Petushki, is unattainable, an impossible construction of Venichka's alcohol-inspired idealism.

In regard to the element of social satire in *Moscow–Petushki*, it is significant that Erofeev satirizes not Russian, but Soviet society. Specifically, he exposes the replacement of genuine Russian culture with Soviet pseudo-culture. The claim of cultural continuity advanced by the Soviets is a prime target of his satire; he paraphrases Turgenev's famous lines about Russia to emphasize the vacuity of Soviet culture: "In days of doubt, in days of burdensome reflection, at the time of any trial or calamity, these eyes [of my people] will not blink. They don't give a damn..." (*ibid.*, p. 27). In an interview given shortly before his death, Erofeev expressed his conviction that the Russian intelligentsia had effectively been destroyed and was pessimistic about any attempt to revive it (Bolychev, "Venedikt Erofeev," 13). A thorough Russianness is the norm against which his satiric distortion is accomplished. Yet his relationship with Soviet contemporaneity is a symbiotic one. The many citations, references and allusions encoded in the text suggest that his picaresque alienation could only be expressed in terms of the social authority that he rejected. His trip to the West (though purely fictive) inspires only apathy and disillusionment.

The Soviet state is a satirical target insofar as it is atheistic and has deprived people of spirituality. Most evocative of Erofeev's ideological quarrel with the regime is his account of the brutality inflicted on Venichka by the statues in Vera Mukhina's monumental sculpture *Triumph of Socialism*. The two figures representing agriculture and industry attack Venichka with their hammer and sickle, exacting punishment for his heretical free-thinking. Lenin is a special target of Erofeev's satire; many of his quotations are embedded and travestied in the text. For the purpose of satirical diminution, it is crucial that the society's mentors and preceptors be exposed as false or corrupt. Lenin stands as the most potent symbol of Soviet ideology; undercutting his stature effectively indicts the ideological whole. The Kremlin is for Venichka a place of punishment synonymous with hell. Despite living for years in Moscow, he has managed never to see the Kremlin and when he finally confronts it, he concludes that it is an unholy place: "If He has left the earth forever but sees every one of us, He never once looked in this direction... And if He never left the earth, if He has passed through it barefoot in the guise of a slave, He went around this place and passed to the side..." (*Moskva–Petushki*, p. 119). His attackers smash his head against the Kremlin wall, so that it literally becomes an agent of his destruction; it too exacts retribution.

Related to the ideology of the state and similarly satirized by Erofeev are the values endorsed by Soviet culture. Labor, idealized and celebrated by the Party and the press, is rendered ridiculous. Working six or seven hours a day brings on terrible depression and requires one to drink from early morning to ease the psychological pain. Courage is likewise devalued by Erofeev. Guillén notes that ironic diminution of bravery is a common feature of the modern picaresque ("Toward a Definition," 106), and this has special significance in the Soviet context. Venichka yearns for "universal chicken-heartedness," the eradication of valorous enthusiasts (*Moskva–Petushki*, p. 21). He finds social or political activism offensive. In a society where the courage of revolutionaries, World War II combat soldiers and guerrillas, Stakhanovites and border guards is officially lionized, Venichka's sentiments are blatantly heretical.[55] Revolution, which occupies such a large place in the Soviet collective memory, is also satirically undercut by Erofeev in his account of the Petushki uprising. By employing similarly grandiose terms in his description of the event and including allusions to the same issues that occupied the Bolsheviks (the role of terror, the issuing of decrees, the unprecedented nature of the undertaking, and so on), he travesties his model.

Poshlost', or vulgarity, is a feature of Soviet society singled out for especially sharp satire in *Moscow–Petushki*. The picaresque traditionally stresses the mundane and the sordid; the picaro's concern with hunger and poverty is a common feature of the mode. In classical picaresque narratives, the picaro's goal was often simple survival, while in later examples he sometimes became a lover of material comforts and luxury. In illuminating this opposition between spirit and matter, the picaresque author often includes plentiful details of contemporary life concerning food, money and property. This has certainly been characteristic of the Russian picaresque tradition; Gogol' and Il'f and Petrov focus heavily on the material aspects of existence to emphasize the disparity between the life of the soul (or the ideologically correct mind, in the case of the latter) and the life of the body. In Erofeev's text too there is considerable emphasis on details about prices, kinds and quantities of food and drink. Venichka stresses the physical attributes and functions of his fellow passengers. His selective focus on the nastiness of other characters – their hideous appearances, their vomiting, their runny noses, their urinating and defecating – creates the impression that they are devoid of spiritual qualities.

More important than physical *poshlost'*, however, is philosophical *poshlost'*. Since the physical, tangible aspects of the world around him are offensive and offer no reason for living, Venichka looks to a higher realm (as does the classical picaro). In his exchanges with other characters on philosophical questions, however, he finds only banality and this philosophical vulgarity is distressing to him. He imitates and parodies the empty verbiage that he hears in formulating his own "philosophy," a hodgepodge of undigested clichés:

No, take now – to live and live. Living is not at all boring. Only Nikolai Gogol' was bored, and King Solomon. If we've already lived through thirty years, it's necessary to try to live another thirty, yes, yes. "Man is mortal." That's my opinion. But since we've already been born, there's nothing to be done about it, we have to live for a while... "Life is beautiful" – that's my opinion. (*Moskva–Petushki*, p. 49)

Philosophical and spiritual banality cause Venichka's great sorrow and compel him to attempt to escape into the oblivion of drink. For Venichka, philosophical *poshlost'* is dangerous, threatening and murderous to man individually and to culture as a whole.

Allusions to specific works of art and literature permeate the text of *Moscow–Petushki*. The sources of Erofeev's references range from the Bible, Aeschylus, Luther, Rabelais and Sterne to Gor'kii, Ostrovskii, Dostoevskii, Bulgakov, Blok and Pasternak. These have been analyzed by others (Gaiser-Shnitman, *Venedikt Erofeev*; Paperno and Gasparov, "'Vstan' i idi'"; Smirnova, "Venedikt Erofeev") and certainly more work remains to be done in this regard. Erofeev's allusions and citations have social, philosophical, political and religious resonance; what Gaiser-Shnitman calls the "literary incrustation" of the text gives it richness and density (*Venedikt Erofeev*, p. 269). There is also a satirical aspect to Erofeev's extensive borrowing (aside from his parodying specific models). His use of the ideas, images and words of others suggests the difficulty, even the impossibility of creating anything new within the confines of contemporary culture. *Moscow–Petushki* reads, at times, like one of Tom Stoppard's adaptations of Shakespeare in that the essential ideas are distilled out, the words are much the same, but their arrangement and their density are distorted. Lewis suggests that in the modern picaresque, art can serve as a sufficient basis for life or failing that, that a positive "sense of life" can nevertheless be found to underlie the picaresque vision (*The Picaresque Saint*, pp. 21, 27–28). Erofeev, in his parodic adaption of the picaresque mode, transcends the model proposed by Lewis to charge that in Soviet society, art cannot substitute for living reality and underneath the ugliness of reality lies a terrible spiritual vacuum.

Stylistics are the source of much of the satire in *Moscow–Petushki*. The speech of the narrator and that of the characters he describes is approximately the same; there is little individual differentiation. Moreover, this is not "real" speech, not the speech of actual people, but rather a stylized verbal creation of Erofeev.[56]

Elevated, stylistically "high" language, when used to discuss ordinary or "low" matters, functions to convert the terrible or the disgusting into the comical. In this respect, Erofeev borrows upon the *velirechie* tradition of Avvakum (Dunham, "Introduction," p. 9). Rabelais too is a notable practitioner of this technique of speaking of common human affairs in ornate, grandiose language; certainly the latter influenced Erofeev's style. The effects of this device vary considerably within the text. Comparisons are often wildly incongruous; Venichka concludes that he will never know how and where he drank up six roubles, "Just as we don't know to this day whether tsar Boris killed the tsarevich Dmitrii or the other way around"

(*Moskva–Petushki*, p. 17). Rhetorical exclamations combine epic grandeur with farce: "Oh, that most helpless and shameful of times in the life of my people, the time from dawn until the liquor stores open up!" (*ibid.*, p. 18). Passages of incongruously elevated language are sometimes extended for whole pages, for example in Venichka's examination of the science of hiccuping. The subject matter takes on an aura of philosophical seriousness when surrounded with inflated verbiage:

> They say that the leaders of the world proletariat, Karl Marx and Friedrich Engels, thoroughly studied the schema of social formulae and, on this basis, were able to foresee much. But here they would be powerless to foresee the least thing [i.e. the length of the intervals between hiccups]. You have entered, following your own whim, into the sphere of the inevitable – be at peace and be patient. (*Ibid.*, p. 53)

When we are reminded that the subject of this discourse is a rather graceless physiological function, the rhetoric dissolves into absurdity.

Erofeev culls individual words and phrases from widely disparate sources. His use of biblical language – either verbatim or adapted citations – creates a tragicomic effect when applied to the world of Soviet contemporaneity (Gaiser-Shnitman, *Venedikt Erofeev*, pp. 250–51, 266). Attempting to escape from his attackers at the end of the book, Venichka intones "Inscrutable are your ways..." and "Deliver me, Lord..." (*Moskva–Petushki*, p. 120) and describes the forbidding expanse beyond the Petushki Social Welfare Agency as "dark forever and ever and the resting place of departed souls" (*ibid.*, p. 119). In addition to biblical language, Erofeev employs the clichés, the specifically "Soviet" turns of speech peculiar to the milieu in which he lived and wrote. Pseudo-scientific language is used frequently and incongruously, reflecting its overuse in Soviet reality. Venichka confusedly quotes Hegel: "He'd say, 'There are no distinctions, except distinctions in degree, between various degrees and the absence of distinction'" and proceeds to "translate" this statement into ordinary language: "'Who doesn't drink these days?'" (*ibid.*, p. 110). Journalese and the language of Soviet propaganda are broadly parodied. In building on the ready-made cliché, Venichka reduces it to nonsense: "My tomorrow is bright. Our tomorrow is brighter than our yesterday and our today. But who'll see to it that our day after tomorrow won't be worse than our day before yesterday?" (*ibid.*, p. 39). By applying historical and political slogans to mundane events, Erofeev exposes their emptiness. Recounting the unsuccessful uprising in Petushki, for example, he writes: "The district is in flames, and the world is silent because it is holding its breath, perhaps, but why has no one extended his hand – not from the east, not from the west?" (*ibid.*, p. 95). The answer, of course, is that no one is paying any attention, and the pompous language itself becomes a target of ridicule. In general, Erofeev satirizes set forms of expression, the ossified formulae that strangle the creative use of language.

An aspect of *Moscow–Petushki* that many readers initially found troubling was its inclusion of vulgarisms and street language. To some extent, Erofeev's use of "substandard" lexicon, as some critics delicately put it, reflects the widespread vulgarization of the language that was taking place in the Thaw period. Smirnova suggests that a primary cause of this phenomenon was the return from prisons of large numbers of Soviet citizens who brought with them the influence of camp speech.[57] Indeed Erofeev's use of the vernacular strengthens the gritty realism of certain passages. However, vulgarisms are not used in a straightforwardly naturalistic manner in *Moscow–Petushki*. They are rather employed creatively to enrich the style of the whole. Often they serve the purpose of contrast, as in this dialogue concerning the execution of the Petushki rebellion:

"The calendar – what do you think? Should we replace it or leave it as it is?" "Oh, better leave it. As they say: don't poke around in shit or it'll start smelling." "You put it correctly, we'll leave it. In you I have a brilliant theoretician, Vadia, and that's good." (*Moskva–Petushki*, p. 49)

Erofeev uses a number of rhythmical techniques that give his *poema* an almost musical quality. One of these is the Gogolian *poliv*, the long, continuous stream of rhetoric interwoven with phonetic and semantic associations (Vail' and Genis, *Sovremennaia russkaia proza*, p. 43; Gaiser-Shnitman, *Venedikt Erofeev*, p. 253). Here the *poliv* becomes a drunken, stream-of-consciousness monologue, e.g. Venichka's musings on the desirability of "universal chicken-heartedness" (*Moskva–Petushki*, pp. 21–22) and his extended comparison of life to a drinking binge (*ibid.*, p. 116). Lyrical passages are occasionally interpolated in the text and these tend to stand out as incongruous.[58] Venichka describes his abandoning the Petushki rebellion in pastoral terms: "I went through meadowland and pastures, through sweetbrier thickets and herds of cattle; the grain bowed before me and cornflowers smiled" (*Moskva–Petushki*, p. 97). There is paradoxically nothing prior to or following this passage to motivate its lyricism and it strikes the reader as absurdly out of place.

The most frequent rhythmical device employed by Erofeev is the juxtaposition of stylistically diverse linguistic and cultural elements. These are, as Vail' and Genis note, recognizable units of various stylistic systems, but "as in the pictures of Salvador Dali, they are united according to absurd laws that breach the etiquette of common sense."[59] His use of heterogeneous styles in direct contrast eloquently expresses the chaos of his universe. His clashing of incongruous words and phrases reflects Venichka's attempt (which is ultimately unsuccessful) to link the planes of his narrative. Struggling to empathize with his fellow workers, he counsels himself:

Are you familiar with the dialectic of the heart of these four shitasses? If you were familiar with it, then you would understand better what "Nightingale Garden" and Freshen-up have in common and why "Nightingale Garden" is incompatible with both blackjack and vermouth, while both Moshe Dayan and Abba Eban are quite compatible with them. (*Moskva–Petushki*, p. 33)

These contrasts intensify the paradoxes which underlie Erofeev's world view. The effects range from the wryly humorous ("Next payday they'll beat the shit out of me, according to the laws of good and beauty" [*ibid.*, p. 36]) to the tragic ("Oh, shameful beings! You have transformed my earth into the shittiest hell, and you force us to hide tears from people and to put laughter up for show" [*ibid.*, p. 108]).

Realism, with all its burden of critical ambiguity, has always had a problematic relationship to the picaresque. The milieux of picaresque narratives do tend to be historically specific and recognizable, and this is the case with Erofeev's *Moscow–Petushki* as well. However, the background is not described in conventionally realistic terms, but evoked through a system of associations and allusions. This allows Erofeev to create instead of a naturalistic exposé of the period of *zastoi*, a "realistic grotesque"[60] that is far more effective (and entertaining) satirically.

The characters Venichka encounters are metamorphized and only marginally resemble real human beings. They are, as T. E. Little writes of Gogol''s picaresque characters, "born of imagination rather than observation" ("*Dead Souls*," p. 123). Yet if Gogol''s imagination created distorted, sometimes subhuman caricatures, Erofeev's fancy produces surreal monsters:

> But the grandfather – he looked at me even more intensely, as if into the muzzle of a gun. And with such blue, swollen eyes that from both of these eyes moisture flowed – as from two drowned men – straight into his boots. And he was like a man condemned to be shot, with a deathly pallor on his bald head. And his whole physiognomy was pockmarked as if he had been shot point-blank. In the middle of his shot face dangled a swollen, bluish nose that swayed like a victim of hanging. (*Moskva–Petushki*, pp. 60–61)

Inanimate objects or abstract qualities predominate in Erofeev's characterizations, taking the place of multiple concrete details. Alternately, he employs synecdoche to an extreme degree, allowing a single feature to swallow up the character. The man with the black moustache, for example, has no other features. Erofeev pushes this device even further, making the man speak grotesquely "through his moustache, and through the sandwich in his moustache" (*ibid.*, p. 68).

The characters in *Moscow–Petushki* tend to be enantiomorphs, or mirror images of one another. However, the mirror Erofeev uses is a highly distorting one; his doubles share some feature or features, but these are reflected grotesquely.[61] Black Moustache and the girl in the beret are, strangely enough, the doubles who resemble one another most closely: "they are amazingly similar – he is wearing a jacket and she is wearing a jacket; he has a brown beret and a moustache and she has a moustache and a brown beret" (*Moskva–Petushki*, p. 60).⁶² The detail of the woman's moustache is, of course, bizarre, an example of Erofeev's tendency to focus on a single physical trait in characterization. (It may also be a parodic exaggeration of Tolstoi's repeated references to Princess Bolkonskaia's downy upper lip in *War and Peace*.) The grandfather and grandson are also distorted mirror images of one another: "The grandson is two heads taller than his grandfather and feebleminded probably from birth. The grandfather is two heads shorter but feebleminded, too" (*ibid*.). Both lick their lips and behave in a similar manner. The characters Venichka calls Herzen and the Decembrist (earlier "Stupid-Stupid" and "Smart-Smart") are doubles, but inverse images. Since all of these characters may be products of Venichka's imagination, it is possible to regard them as representing different aspects of his own psyche.⁶³ The passengers' discussion of the idea of the mirror image curve that explains the equilibrium of nature is most apropos to this interpretation. Venichka dismisses the idea of balance and harmony in nature as "silly" and seems to second the man with the black moustache in his judgment of "Stupid, stupid nature" (*Moskva–Petushki*, p. 69). The ruling principle of Venichka's inner and outer worlds is rather disharmony, chaos and distortion.

While realism is far from the norm in the picaresque and Erofeev all but disregards its precepts, he does retain and adapt the picaresque's emphasis on the brutal, the ugly and the cruel. His heavy use of scatological elements has already been noted. In addition, he compresses the bleakness and horror of the society he describes into several specific incidents (Wicks, *Picaresque Narrative*, pp. 65–66). The attack of the figures from Mukhina's sculpture and Venichka's death at the hands of the four hooligans are eloquent expressions of senseless brutality, but he includes two other reminiscences that serve this purpose as well. The account of the two little boys who were crushed to death on the train is grotesque: "They lay as they fell between cars; their little hands, turning blue, still clutched their tickets" (*Moskva–Petushki*, p. 85). We know from Venichka's references to his own small son that this child represents purity and vulnerability for him; thus the death of the two nameless boys suggests the mindless destruction of innocence and goodness by "the herd" of passengers, citizens of this society. His reminiscence of the man cut in two by the train is still more appalling in its grotesque naturalism:

The train pulled away but he – that half of him – remained standing there, and on his face there was a sort of perplexity and his mouth half open. A lot of people couldn't stand to look at it and turned away, pale, with a deathly weariness in their hearts. But some children ran up to him, three or four children, they had picked up a lighted cigarette butt from somewhere and stuck it in his dead half-open mouth. And the cigarette butt continued to smoke and the children ran around and laughed at their joke. (*Ibid.*, p. 121)

Even more terrible than the senseless death of children is the spiritual brutalization that leads them to laugh at death. The scene – another parodical adaption, this time of the famous scene from *Anna Karenina* – reflects the surrealism of Venichka's world. The children's laughter, like that of the heavenly angels who abandon Venichka, is truly that of the void.

CHAPTER 3

Satire and the autobiographical mode: Limonov's It's Me, Eddie

> I have a little wisdom, and I know: A thing that is likened to childhood cannot be a lie.
>
> Eduard Limonov: *It's Me, Eddie*

Eduard Limonov is an extremist writer whose satire borders on vituperation. His pseudo-autobiographical *It's Me, Eddie* aroused a storm of controversy that has not been entirely quelled after more than a decade. Critical discourse on Limonov's work tends to superlatives and hyperbole. *It's Me, Eddie* has been lauded as "the quintessential novel of the third wave emigration"[1] and reviled as pornographic slander. However one regards the subject matter and the tone of the book, it is an ingenious adaptation of the autobiographical novel to the satirical impulse.

Born auspiciously on Soviet Army Day, 1943 in Derzhinsk, Eduard Savenko was named after the poet Eduard Bagritskii. The son of a career NKVD officer and an educated homemaker, he grew up in the Ukrainian industrial city of Kharkov. According to his own account, he became a petty criminal at the age of sixteen. His experiences as a thief and adolescent hooligan constitute the basis of his Kharkov cycle of autobiographical works, including *Memoirs of a Russian Punk* and *Young Rascal*. He began writing what he has called "very bad" poetry at thirteen[2] and as a young man moved in the bohemian literary circles of Kharkov. It was in this period that he adopted Limonov, with its connotations of acidity and bitterness, as a *nom de plume*.

Limonov's move to Moscow in 1967 (without benefit of a residence permit) brought him into contact with a more numerous and more sophisticated artistic counterculture. He rejected and was in turn rejected by the dissident intelligentsia of the capital and instead allied himself with the "Concrete" group of poets that included Genrikh Sapgir. These "boys of the sixties," as he calls them (Iakushkin, "Eto on, Edichka," 16), were devotees of the modernist poet Arsenii Tarkovskii. Since literature was not a paying proposition for Limonov in this period, he supported himself by sewing clothing for friends and acquaintances and by selling typescript volumes of his poetry for five roubles apiece. (The latter occupation was a radical departure from *samizdat* practices of the sixties and seventies, when payment was not expected for circulated material.) To complete his image as an eccentric provocateur, Limonov married the poet Elena Shchapova in an Orthodox wedding ceremony. She subsequently figures both as "Elena the Beautiful" in his 1974 poem "We Are the National Hero" and as his nemesis in *It's Me, Eddie*.

In 1974, Limonov emigrated and eventually settled in New York. The details of his departure from the Soviet Union are somewhat hazy, but in essence, he was provided by the Soviet authorities with false papers in return for his agreeing to leave. Residing in Moscow without a residence permit, he attracted unfavorable attention by staging a "big and noisy wedding" and was subsequently summoned and urged to cooperate with the security organs.[3] Although neither he nor Shchapova are Jewish, he was issued an Israeli visa and his "forced departure"[4] was expedited by the KGB. With the advent of *glasnost'* and the selective publication of his work in his homeland, his unwillingness to leave the Soviet Union has paradoxically been emphasized.[5]

Arriving in New York, Limonov found temporary haven as a journalist and proofreader for the émigré paper *Novoe russkoe slovo*. In the course of a year, he contributed about twenty articles, many of which were interviews published under the rubric "The Third Emigration – Who Are They?" The last of his articles, a piece called "Disillusionment," earned Limonov considerable infamy. Expressing his disenchantment with the West and indicting American propaganda for enticing Russians to emigrate, he voiced sentiments seldom heard openly in either

Satire and the autobiographical mode 103

the American or the émigré press. He wrote, in part: "It must be admitted that for a great many émigrés who in the USSR did not suffer persecution and did not spend time in the camps or psychiatric hospitals, emigration sometimes seems like a tragic mistake, a personal failure."[6] The article was quickly reprinted by both *Literaturnaia gazeta* and *Nedelia*, establishing Limonov's reputation as politically pro-Soviet and giving rise to rumors about his working for the KGB. In the fall of 1975, Limonov collaborated in writing an open letter to Andrei Sakharov protesting America's treatment of Russian émigrés and the decimation of the Soviet intelligentsia. Although the letter was published only in the *London Times* (it had been submitted initially to the *New York Times*), it contributed significantly to Limonov's *enfant terrible* image. His organization of a demonstration against the *New York Times* the following spring added fuel to the fire.

As he increasingly distanced himself from the émigré community, Limonov nevertheless continued to write and publish his poetry in émigré journals. His works appeared in *Apollon*, *Grani*, *Ekho*, *Kovcheg* and other literary publications in the diaspora. In 1979 a separate volume of his poetry entitled *Russkoe* appeared. Although he took the unprecedented step of submitting some poems to *Novyi mir*, they were not printed; his reputation as unpredictable and politically suspect, however, gained considerably. He explains his reasoning in making this gesture in *It's Me, Eddie*:

> The letter to the editors of *Novyi mir* was written out of mischief and my love of scandal. Although I was almost positive they would not print my poems, I did not deny myself the pleasure of having some fun at the expense of both camps. My conscience was clear. Solzhenitsyn, while living in the USSR, had published his books here in the West; his conscience hadn't bothered him, in point of fact he had thought only of his own career as a writer, not of the consequences or influence of his books. So why couldn't I, while living here, publish my poems over there in the USSR? Both governments had made good use of me, at last I could use them too.[7]

Limonov completed *It's Me, Eddie*, his first major prose work, and submitted the manuscript for publication in 1977. The first chapter appeared in 1977 in the Israeli émigré journal *Nedelia* and an abridged version of the book was published in *Kovcheg* in 1979. The manuscript was rejected, by Limonov's account, by about thirty-five American publishing houses before it finally appeared in book form in France in 1980. In interviews, Limonov has charged that American publishers refused to print the book because of its sharp criticism of the United States and because it is not unambiguously anti-Soviet.[8] It was printed in full in the original Russian by Index Publishers of New York only in 1982; an English translation by Random House followed the next year.

It's Me, Eddie was an almost immediate *succès de scandale*, arousing passionate polemics among its Russian readers (and among those who had merely read about the book). Limonov's heavy use of obscenities (*mat*), his inclusion of numerous explicitly erotic scenes and his avowal of leftist political tendencies made the book explosively controversial. Emigré readers' reactions tended toward outrage, fury and disgust. Journals which printed interviews or articles about Limonov, such as *Kovcheg* and *Al'manakh Panorama*, received stormy letters of protest and threats to discontinue subscriptions from readers.[9] Soviet commentators seized on the book as an exposé of the travails of émigré life and a warning to those who would abandon Russia for the West. Leonid Pochivalov, for example, in a long article published in *Literaturnaia gazeta*, treats *It's Me, Eddie* as a cautionary tale of the misfortune awaiting many émigrés.[10] More moderate reactions were expressed by editors and critics who recognized the implicit threat of censorship in readers' outraged protests. To the suggestion allegedly made by Vladimir Maksimov, editor of *Kontinent*, that *It's Me, Eddie*, should not even be a topic of commentary or critical discussion, Nikolai Bokov responded: "It is known from the history and practice of Soviet journalism that silence is the strongest weapon against literature... they are proposing that we remain silent about the most important problems, which are posed for the first time in this work."[11] Perhaps the most curious response to the work has been Elena Shchapova's book *It's Me, Elena*. Consisting largely of photographs of Shchapova in various stages of artistic undress, it was conceived as a rebuttal to Limonov's portrait of her in *It's Me, Eddie*.

Since writing *It's Me, Eddie*, Limonov has turned increasingly to prose and has published five more "autobiographical novels." A number of his short stories have appeared in literary journals and miscellanies, and these complement his longer works thematically.[12] With *glasnost'*, publication of his works in the Soviet Union became possible as well. A lengthy and sympathetic interview with Limonov appeared in *Moskovskie novosti* in August of 1989, signaling his debut in Soviet literature. His *povest'* "Ours Was a Great Epoch," about growing up in Kharkov as the son of an NKVD officer, was printed in *Znamia* in November 1989 and occasioned a positive review in *Literaturnaia gazeta* the next month.[13] His short story "The Beautiful Woman Who Inspired the Poet" appeared in the journal *Iunost'* in 1991. In an interview that was published together with this story, Limonov indicated that he would like to be published more fully in the Soviet Union, but that the traditional linguistic and cultural taboos of Russian literature continue to present obstacles (Maliugin, "Eduard Limonov," 36–37). Since the dissolution of the Soviet Union, this question has become moot. Limonov has been extremely visible and vocal in the publicistic media within Russia in recent years. He resides in Paris, where he moved in 1980, but travels frequently to Russia. He has continued to court controversy, perfunctorily fighting with the Serbs in Bosnia and publicly endorsing the extremist views of Vladimir Zhirinovskii (before becoming disenchanted and devoting an entire book – *Limonov Against Zhirinovskii* – to their falling out). At present, his books may be found between glitzy, suggestive covers alongside popular works of soft-core pornography in Moscow bookshops.

The critical response to Limonov's work that has appeared since *It's Me, Eddie* has been relatively muted. He is, of course, quite young and it is far too early to judge the corpus of his writing as a whole. Nevertheless, in his attempt to recast his autobiographical hero in the time frame following that of *It's Me, Eddie* (in *His Butler's Story*) and prior to it (in *Memoir of a Russian Punk* and *Young Rascal*), there is much that strikes the reader as artificial and forced. The remarks made by the émigré critics Vail′ and Genis in 1982 immediately upon publication of *It's Me, Eddie* are worth noting in this regard:

> Limonov has written talented confessional prose in a desperate attempt to take physical, bodily cognition of oneself to the extreme limit. Such prose is written once in life and can neither be repeated nor rewritten. Only knowledge and experience, not invention or fantasy, give inspiration to writing in which "everything is permitted" [*vsedozvolennost′*]. And therefore it is still not clear whether Eduard Limonov is a writer; but his book, of course, is literature. (*Sovremennaia russkaia proza*, p. 168)

Any discussion of this book is complicated by what can be called the phenomenon of Limonov; intentionally obscuring the line between art and life, he has cultivated an authorial persona who is an outcast and iconoclast. He has expressed unwillingness to be consigned to the "depressing literary ghetto" of émigré literature which is, he insists, manipulated by Western politics and distorted by commercial censorship ("Limonov o sebe," p. 220).[14] Furthermore, Limonov denies knowing or being influenced by Russian literary tradition and asserts that he is better acquainted with American literature.[15] Even after he lost his *persona non grata* status in the Soviet Union, he rejected the appellation of Soviet writer, whose image for him was that of "some fat bourgeois uncle [*diadia*] who makes a career in literature" (Iakushkin, "Eto on, Edichka," 16). Like the Futurists, the Oberiuty and other avant-garde artists of the twentieth century, Limonov resists classification by nationality and aspires to transcend traditional literary classification schemes. In addition, Limonov's public statements connected with politics, art and social issues seem calculated to be outrageous and offensive, guaranteeing him a certain distance from all political and literary camps.[16] He encourages confusion of his authorial persona with his created narrative persona, Edichka, and appears to thrive on the controversy and polemics that surround him.[17]

Critical interest in the autobiographical mode among literary scholars, social historians, anthropologists and others has burgeoned in the last few decades. To some extent, this is the result of broadening the scope of *belles-lettres*; autobiography as an aesthetic act has recently come under the same sort of critical scrutiny previously reserved for fiction and poetry. However, breaking down traditional genre distinctions has also made approaching the autobiographical text problematic. The expectations we can reasonably bring to an autobiography have been destabilized. Given this uncertainty about what constitutes an autobiography, how an autobiography can or should be read, how autobiography differs from other literary modes and so on, it is possible to conclude that all literature is essentially autobiographical (if not autobiography).[18] A crisis of form that may eventually lead to the disappearance of autobiography is discerned by Roy Pascal:

> I do not think one can evade the conclusion that the supreme task of autobiography is not fulfilled in modern autobiography... I have already suggested that the lack of great autobiography in certain earlier periods may be ascribed to the fact that certain social periods are unpropitious to autobiography, in particular those in which social life is so violent and unpredictable that personal life itself is subject to the violent caprice of external events. This is true to some extent today, particularly in the autobiographies of men and women tossed about by fearful events. But what more profoundly affects modern autobiography is a general lack of relationship between personal and social being.[19]

On the other hand, the autobiographical mode is viewed by some as the most promising area of development of twentieth-century literature. By virtue of its plasticity and its diversity (those very features that trouble scholars eager to adumbrate its generic characteristics), autobiographical discourse may provide a means of transcending static literary forms. Jane Gary Harris asserts that autobiography "may well represent the ultimate mode of literary perception for this century."[20]

Acknowledging the critical flux in which autobiography is presently situated, there are nevertheless some parameters connected with the autobiographical mode that allow us to explicate Limonov's text more fully. *It's Me, Eddie* purports to be autobiographical; thus Limonov engages certain expectations and challenges us to apply them to his work. He offers us what Philippe Lejeune calls *le pacte autobiographique*, encouraging us to read the book as "a retrospective account in prose that a real person makes of his own existence when it stresses the individual life, in particular, the story of his personality."[21] Elizabeth Bruss suggests a systematic definition of autobiography that is most relevant to Limonov's text. Bruss' "rules" include three major assumptions: (1) the autobiographer is the subject of the text; (2) what is described in the autobiography is "true" and subject to verification; (3) the autobiographer believes in the truth of what he or she writes.[22]

In considering the *autos* of autobiography, it is certainly not the case that the selves of the author and the autobiographical narrator are usually identical. Yet the relationship between Limonov and his narrative persona Edichka is an unusually convoluted one. Not only time, space and the vagaries of memory separate the two; in *It's Me, Eddie*, the assumption that the author is the subject of his own autobiography is dubious. Moreover, Limonov creates what Pascal calls an "arbitrary standpoint" from which to narrate the story of his autobiographical hero's new life in New York. Edichka is not a great man, a public figure whose accomplishments are well known, but an obscure Russian émigré poet whose wife has recently abandoned him. What Pascal takes for weakness (*Design and Truth*, p. 10) becomes central to this satiric reworking of the autobiographical mode: Edichka is eminently worthy of artistic recognition and material rewards, but Soviet, émigré and American societies unjustly deprive him of his birthright.

The truthfulness of the work as autobiography is extremely problematic. In a letter to A. Kron, Limonov insists on the factual basis of his writing: "*If memory doesn't deceive me*, all the situations are not imagined. I have only simplified many things and thrown out a lot" (emphasis added) ("Pro babochku," 89). Indeed, the title of *It's Me, Eddie* supports our approaching the work as autobiography or as pseudo-autobiography.[23] Relying on the comfortable truism underlying our notion of autobiography – that autobiography is nonfiction – many readers and critics have approached Limonov's book as confession. Pochivalov, writing in *Literaturnaia gazeta*, asserts "from the foreword it is clear that the work is autobiographical, that the events in it are genuine" ("Chelovek na dne," 14). Matich calls the substance of Limonov's text "the unexpurgated and unedited events of his personal life and the people he has known" and claims that "his literary truth demands the uncensored representation of authentic experience."[24] Aleksandr Donde offers a more cynical assessment of Limonov's veracity: "Limonov would seem to insist that he is writing the truth. Naive enthusiasm, if not semiconscious cunning" ("Eduard, Edik i Edichka," 12). Whatever prurient interest one may have in the truthfulness of Limonov's accounts, they are ultimately not verifiable. More importantly, Limonov's truth is an aesthetic one. The events and characters he describes (or invents) to illustrate his truth are valid to the degree that they accomplish this end. All autobiography is selective, but Limonov moves beyond the assumption that the autobiographer is writing the truth as he knows it (already a significant qualification) to create a more meaningful, symbolic truth.

In *It's Me, Eddie*, Limonov casts some doubt on the sincerity and completeness of his confession, establishing another layer of uncertainty. Admitting that a conversation with a friend was accompanied by heavy drinking, Edichka insists on the rationality of his autobiographical method:

But, although a stuffed-shirt statesman may be afraid to admit he has formulated one or another state decision in the interval between two glasses of vodka or whiskey or while sitting on the toilet, I have always been delighted by the apparent incongruity, the inopportuneness, of manifestations of human talent and genius. And I do not intend to hide it. To hide it would be to distort, or facilitate the distortion of, human nature. (*Eto ia – Edichka*, p. 74)

Elsewhere he tells Roseanne about an incident from his past life when he made a pass at his best friend's wife and thus lost his friend forever. He then proceeds to confide to the reader the "real" story, whereby we learn that this was the first time he met the woman, she was receptive to his advances, her husband did not care at all, and at any rate she was accompanied at the time by her lover (*ibid.*, p. 186). That this second version may be as fictionalized as the first is not the point; Limonov suggests that truth is a relative concept and adaptable to the needs of the moment.

The tricks of memory affect all autobiographical writing to some degree, but Limonov emphasizes the unreliability of his own powers of recollection. This sometimes concerns very fine points of description, as in the following account of his dress on one particular occasion: "I was wearing a nice tight denim jacket, and jeans tucked in – no, rolled way high, to reveal my very beautiful high-heeled boots of tricolor leather" (*ibid.*, p. 76). Here Limonov makes us privy to the process of compromise between recollection and invention that must always underlie the autobiographical act. Whether Edichka's jeans were tucked in or rolled up remains in doubt – the difference is utterly inconsequential from the point of view of the narrative – but Limonov suggests that if they were not rolled up, they certainly should have been in retrospect. At times Edichka seems impatient with the demand of accuracy that the autobiographical mode would seem to impose on him. To preface his account of going to see his ex-wife in the chapter "The New Elena," he writes: "After a time she called, though I no longer remember, maybe I called; nor do I remember whether our meetings were in the chronological sequence in which I've enumerated them or in some other order. I called, I think, and it turned out she was sick" (*ibid.*, p. 262). What is significant for Edichka is not the precise ordering of events, but the emotional and psychological impact they had on him. With this brief disclaimer, he reveals that the larger aesthetic truth of his story is his primary concern.

The documentary qualities of *It's Me, Eddie* nevertheless strengthen the illusion of truthfulness. Recognizable place names in and around New York, actual people and specific times are provided by Limonov. Many of his bohemian friends and acquaintances play minor roles in his autobiographical narrative, and he often provides thumbnail sketches of their strange and unhappy lives in emigration. Edichka recalls being helped in his distress by "a former dissident and former groom at the Moscow race track, the very first recipient of the Welfare Prize... stout, slovenly, wheezing Aleshka Shneerzon" (*ibid.*, p. 9). A fellow denizen of the Hotel Winslow is the poet Zhenia Knikich, who is by training a philologist and presently spends his time cooking kidneys and sausages in his tiny room and trying to get on welfare. Lenia Chaplin scrounges food from garbage cans, saving all of his welfare money to travel in the future.

Aside from Edichka's circle of eccentric comrades in misfortune, he also mentions such well-known figures as Solzhenitsyn, Brodskii and Ernst Neizvestnyi. Limonov's disparagement of Solzhenitsyn in particular has aroused the wrath of the émigré community. Even Kron, who staunchly defended the publication of *It's Me, Eddie* in *Kovcheg*, objected to his "slander" of leading dissidents: "We have no saints and you can criticize whomever you like, but not however you like" ("Pro babochku," 90). Slanderous or not, his inclusion of such figures contributes significantly to the veracity of his account. We know that Solzhenitsyn and Sakharov existed in the time frame of Limonov's text; therefore, the lesser-known characters whom he describes are rendered less fictional, more probable.

Edichka sometimes pinpoints the location of buildings and provides precise directions as we follow him on his perambulations around New York. These references to the cityscape strengthen the reader's impression of being privy to actual events. Concluding the chapter about Carol, the leftist secretary, Edichka assures us that he still occasionally sees her and that they may be found "at lunchtime... on Fifty-third Street between Madison Avenue and Fifth, sitting by the waterfall" (*Eto ia – Edichka*, p. 108). Topographic details like these situate Limonov's narrative in real time and space. There are, however, several instances in which Limonov appears to overuse this technique. Recounting an uneventful walk in the chapter "My Friend New York," he writes:

> I go out of the park toward the Catholic student center and walk down Thompson Street, where, after passing a little Mexican restaurant, I briefly study the diverse and unusual chessmen, which never cease to astonish me, in the window of a chess shop. Occasionally I walk more

to the left, down LaGuardia, where I drop into a clothing store...
After leaving the Pole's [store], I cross Houston – a boring street,
provincial as a street out of Gogol''s *Mirgorod*, but with two-way traffic
– and go down to SoHo. (*Ibid.*, p. 242)

Saturating the text with realia, he mocks the autobiographical convention of documentary accuracy even as he employs it. Limonov would seem to have pretensions to writing a Russian émigré *Ulysses*; we can exactly retrace Edichka's steps as he wends his way through life in exile.

Some of the characters whom Limonov includes in *It's Me, Eddie* retain their own names, while some are given pseudonyms that are nevertheless easily decipherable. The author's fear of libel charges apparently does not motivate his practice in this respect; Solzhenitsyn and Brodskii, for example, are openly named and defamed. Ernst Neizvestnyi, on the other hand, is transparently rechristened "the sculptor Erast Provozvestnyi," and his name is coupled with that of the poet Genrikh Sapgir (who is referred to by his actual name) (*ibid.*, p. 183). Limonov also changes the name of the newspaper *Novoe russkoe slovo* to *Russkoe delo* in his autobiographical treatment. The bases for these and similar minor obfuscations would seem to be whimsy and an urge to dislocate the reader's expectation of verisimilitude. We are left unable to distinguish clearly the line between factual reminiscence and fiction, which is certainly Limonov's intention.

References to famous people in *It's Me, Eddie* at times give the book the quality of memoir and occasionally smack of name-dropping. Yet public figures and important events are viewed "from below-stairs," as Richard Coe puts it.[25] History is recounted from Edichka's particularized point of view, that of a little-known émigré poet on welfare. Probably the best example of this technique is his description of listening to Solzhenitsyn's speech on television while making love to his wife. This remembered scene provides a whole conglomerate of indicators of the time and place Limonov is writing about (the Cold War mentality, the West's brief honeymoon with Solzhenitsyn, the height of third wave emigration); it simultaneously accomplishes a deflation of the dissident demigod whom Limonov scorns. Even when Edichka's name-dropping functions only to inflate his own importance, there is an element of irony involved. In connection with the Glickermans, who befriended him and Elena upon their arrival in New York, he digresses a bit: "As for Tat'iana, the poet Maiakovskii was once in love with her, and if you recall, I have mentioned somewhere that in Moscow I was friends with Maiakovskii's mistress Lily Brik. It's odd how fate persistently links little Eddie with the sexual legends of another great poet" (*Eto ia – Edichka*, p. 241). Edichka is in fact repeating himself, but he suggests in this ironic aside that self-advertisement and self-aggrandizement are normative features of memoirs.

It's Me, Eddie is full of personal details of Edichka's emotional and physical life. In her discussion of women's autobiography, Estelle Jelinek notes that "intense feelings of hate, love, and fear, the disclosure of explicit sexual encounters, or the detailing of painful psychological experiences are matters on which autobiographers are generally silent."[26] In fact, such is the primary content of Limonov's text, and this saturation of the reader's sensibility is calculated to create discomfort. Limonov is intent on breaking taboos, particularly those imposed by Russian literary tradition. His praxis implies that the most intimate aspects of an individual's life are an integral part of the "truth" and deserve – indeed demand – treatment in autobiography.

Limonov's choice of the autobiographical mode for his satirical exposé is aesthetically consistent with his poetic stance. The poet's touch is evident in his evocation of scenes, his characterization and especially in his self-observation. The prose style of *It's Me, Eddie* is actually not far removed from that of Limonov's lyrical poetry; as Patricia Carden notes, "the prose poems lead directly to his diary-like prose works..."[27] Using the raw material of his own experience, Limonov imposes meaning and pattern upon it to achieve his artistic ends.

Among the motivations that underlie the writing of autobiography, at least three appear to apply to Limonov's text. In the first place, *It's Me, Eddie* is an assertion of the significance of the author's personality, of his existence in the face of chaos and extinction. Anxiety about the validity of the self may be the primary impetus for much of modern autobiography (Olney, "Autobiography and the Cultural Moment," p. 23), but Limonov's concerns are not chiefly metaphysical. Exile – specifically, the exile of the third wave Russian poet – threatens actual oblivion. It is noteworthy that critics who stress this aspect of the book are themselves émigrés. Even Viktor Perel'man, who is far from well disposed toward Limonov, writes that one option for the desperately unhappy émigré is "like the hero of the... 'novel', choking in terror and despair, to cry 'I haven't disintegrated yet, I'm still alive, look – it's Me!'"[28] The loneliness and isolation of the émigré approximate death, and *It's Me, Eddie* is an attempt to fend off non-being.

Writing one's autobiography may actualize the self. It is "one of the strategies human beings have developed to make life matter."[29] Megalomania is a central feature of Edichka's persona; he is an unabashed exhibitionist and egoist. This urge toward self-advertisement extends to his autobiographical statement. Edichka is eager to create scandal if it will call attention to himself. In admitting this, indeed trumpeting it, Edichka defies the perception that a real writer does not create with the intention of producing a bestseller. In a statement made at an émigré writers' conference in Vienna in 1987, the opinions expressed by Limonov (Edichka?) on this point were certainly calculated to be controversial:

Can I make a bold proposal? Let's talk business; we are all professionals, not beginners, and this is not a writers' workshop. All this droning on about language doesn't interest me at all. Let's talk about money, about the publishing possibilities, let's ask if we are of any interest to the foreign reader. Let's talk about critics, about what we do, and not have another boring academic conference. (Glad, *Literature in Exile*, p. 79)

If autobiography can serve to actualize the self, a scandalous and provocative autobiography can bring the self fame and fortune; both motivations were probably operative in Limonov's case.

Aside from asserting the value of the ego, the act of writing autobiography can be cathartic and therapeutic. Distancing and objectivizing the autobiographical "I" is a means of coping with loss and emotional pain that would seem to suit Limonov's needs. Retrospectively imposing design on one's life (or part of one's life) allows one to take control over it. Thus we see Edichka initially at his lowest point of debasement and humiliation; as he grows and develops and as he recounts this growth, he assumes increasing power over his own fate.[30] From his present standpoint, Edichka can apply the wisdom he has attained to the past experiences he relates. His progression toward a greater knowledge of the self and a firmer hold on life are ratified by the autobiographical act.

Finally, the distancing of the narrated self from the narrating self that occurs in autobiographical writing facilitates irony and satire. Recalling and creating Edichka, Limonov comments satirically on the image of the Russian poet, calling into question the national tradition of semi-deification. Digressive excursions into his distant past allow him to target the bohemia of underground literature in the Soviet Union and more recent reminiscences focus on the hermetic world of émigré literature. In addition, Edichka satirizes American culture as he recounts his attempts to adapt to exile. What keeps the book from being merely irritating in its criticism of Russian, émigré and American mores is Limonov's ironic stance *vis-à-vis* his autobiographical persona. Although some critics find neither irony nor parody in this work,[31] recognition of the fine irony that underlies *It's Me, Eddie* is essential to an appreciation of the text as autobiography. In this respect, a direct line can be traced from Nabokov to Limonov, and Bruss' analysis of *Lolita* as autobiography is eminently relevant to Limonov's work:

For Nabokov, autobiography is viable only when one recognizes that it creates truth as much as expresses it; thus his burlesque of autobiography in *Lolita* exposes the delusions of sincerity and the narcissistic indulgence of the confessional tradition. Not only does his own autobiography flaunt its artificiality, but achieves an almost Olympian impersonality as well, suggesting that no autobiographer ought to depict himself without first becoming aware of how much fiction is implicit in the idea of a "self." (*Autobiographical Acts*, p. 18)[32]

Indeed, *It's Me, Eddie* is suffused with what Donde defines as "a delicate combination of deep seriousness and parody" ("Eduard, Edik i Edichka," 13). Irony directed toward the praxis of autobiography itself complements and emphasizes irony directed toward other aspects of Edichka's life.

Having argued that Limonov makes use of the autobiographical mode to accomplish his critical and satirical ends in *It's Me, Eddie*, I would go further and suggest that the book is best seen as a "childhood" that examines the third wave émigré experience. For a definition of the childhood as a distinct subgenre of autobiography, I propose Coe's formulation:

... an extended piece of writing, a conscious, deliberately executed literary artifact, usually in prose (and thus intimately related to the novel) but not excluding occasional experiments in verse, in which the most substantial portion of the material is directly autobiographical, and whose structure reflects step by step the development of the writer's self; beginning often, but not invariably, with the first light of consciousness, and concluding, quite specifically, with the attainment of a precise degree of maturity. (*When the Grass Was Taller*, pp. 8–9)

Emigration entails isolation, the loss of prestige, the absence of contact with the Russian language and the necessity of coming to terms with a new culture and its unfamiliar values. Sundered (willingly or unwillingly) from the Soviet milieu, the émigré is cast adrift and must somehow adapt to his new homeland. The world Edichka confronts is chaotic, formless and incomprehensible. It is, as Nataliia Gross remarks, utterly *chuzhoi*.[33] We witness Edichka's attempts to make this world *svoi*, to impose order on chaos. *It's Me, Eddie* is essentially the history of this second childhood and as such achieves the status of a document typifying the third wave phenomenon. Edichka's tale metaphorically recapitulates the experience of his generation;[34] his extremism is validated by the fact that he writes as an insider, a witness and survivor.

We are admitted to Edichka's world after his "death" has occurred and we observe his attempts to return to life. As Donde remarks, "... to adandon one's own cosmos means no more and no less than to die, and the subsequent task turns out to be no more and no less than to be reborn" ("Eduard, Edik i Edichka," 17). Working as a laborer in a hotel restaurant surrounded by other immigrants, which Limonov describes in the chapter "I Am a Busboy," turns out to be a sort of limbo. The mechanical nature of the movements he makes, the repetitiveness of the work, resemble death itself, and Edichka must escape in order to begin his quest for life in earnest. As he leaves the restaurant for the last time, he recalls "when I shagassed out of there the last day, I laughed like a silly baby" (*Eto ia – Edichka*, p. 48). It is at this point that he gives free rein to his libido and initiates the process of growth and self-actualization that is at the heart of *It's Me, Eddie*.

The "childhood" that Edichka lives through as a new émigré is fraught with disappointments. By the time we are introduced to him, Edichka's faith in the "American dream" has been shattered and he is bitterly contemplating its ruins. One of his émigré acquaintances expresses their mutual disillusionment eloquently when he notes the impossibility of describing to Soviet friends back home what the West is like: "'You'll never explain it to him – that for all your car and your Montreal you can be up to your ears in shit here. It's impossible to explain,' Naum said. 'Fucking emigration!'" (*ibid.*, p. 21). Edichka's disenchantment with his former dreams of the West has also meant a loss of what Coe calls the "magic" of the past (*When the Grass Was Taller*, pp. 104–38). The spirit of this magic pervades his early poem "We Are the National Hero" and is, for Edichka, inextricably bound to his love for Elena.

Limonov's pseudo-autobiography in many ways parodies the genre of the childhood. Traditionally, the authors of childhoods recount gradually increasing awareness of the external world and other people (Pascal, *Design and Truth*, p. 85). Limonov's narrative persona turns sharply inward, reflecting narcissistically on himself while looking for the key to his rebirth. Indeed, awareness and acceptance of the community and integration into it – *sine qua non* of the classical childhood – are left in considerable doubt in *It's Me, Eddie*. Limonov would seem to be reacting in particular to the myth of happy childhood that is closely linked to the pastoral tradition in Russian literature.[35] His autobiography refutes this myth in form and in substance, suggesting that the émigré experience represents the antipode of Tolstoi's or Aksakov's or even Nabokov's Russian idylls.

The child's point of view is peculiarly appropriate to Limonov's evocation of émigré life. The technique of *ostranenie* that it entails allows him to present things from a fresh viewpoint, that of the *ingénue*. Focusing on American culture, Edichka writes with a double vision that is quite unique. He is both insider (a *habitué* of the streets of New York who knows the ins and outs of urban life) and an outsider (a recent arrival with only a rudimentary command of English and no marketable skills). His satirical exposé of American life from this standpoint raises *It's Me, Eddie* out of the realm of émigré literature and gives it a resonance that defies liminalization.

In autobiographical practice, the childhood is closely linked with the confessional mode and Limonov exploits this tradition. Although the element of titillation is present in much of modern autobiography (after Rousseau), the urge toward reconciliation is by and large still operative. As Stephen Spender writes:

> Even the most shamelessly revealed inner life pleads its cause before the moral system of an outer, objective life. One of the things that the most abysmal confessions prove is the incapacity of even the most outcast creature to be alone. Indeed, the essence of the confession is that the one who feels outcast pleads with humanity to relate his isolation to its wholeness. He pleads to be forgiven, condoned, even condemned, so long as he is brought back into the wholeness of people and of things.[36]

Edichka is very much the outcast, but there is no plea for forgiveness here. He insists on his wickedness as a component part of his personality and taunts the reader with the tawdriness of his revelations. It would seem, in fact, that Limonov has purposefully created a narrative persona who unites all those qualities perceived as reprehensible by his implied reader. Edichka glories in his command of the welfare system (and his abuse of it) and revels in the companionship of derelicts and criminals. He flaunts his homosexuality and relates his heavy use of alcohol and drugs as a matter of course. Not only is he not sorry about all of this, he is proud of opening up new avenues of experience and sensation previously closed to the Russian émigré (or at least to the discreet one). Spender notes that confessions of unspeakable thoughts and actions comment, if only indirectly, on the milieu in which the autobiographer lives (Spender, "Confessions and Autobiography," p. 122). Limonov foregrounds this aspect of confession and shifts the responsibility for his behavior onto external conditions. The political and social phenomenon of the third wave bears much of the blame for Edichka's unhappiness. American society is guilty of not recognizing his talent and his potential. Russian dissidents, American pseudo-intellectuals, other émigrés, middle-class businessmen and others are subjects of Edichka's ironic criticism, but he himself is blameless. He has been victimized repeatedly, first by the Soviet system and then by the American establishment. Thus the axiom that the confessional autobiographer is seeking to conclude "a peace treaty and a new alliance with himself and with the world" (Gusdorf, "Conditions and Limits," p. 39) is thoroughly subverted by Limonov. At most Edichka submits to a tenuous and fragile truce with the world, for he cannot truly forgive the world for distorting his childhood dreams.

Part of Edichka's coming to terms with his present is grasping the meaning of his past. Memories of his pre-New York life – growing up and maturing as a poet in the Soviet Union, his departure and the months immediately following his emigration – are rendered as hazy and mystical in *It's Me, Eddie*. His childhood in Kharkov is "dear and fabulously [*basnoslovno*] distant" (*Eto ia – Edichka*, p. 248). Recalling his wanderings around his native city, he finds a parallel to his present aimlessness: "I walk that way now. Again I have nothing... in Russia my life is already legend, and now I walk free, empty and terrible in the Great City..." (*ibid*., p. 231). These glimpses of his pre-emigration life indeed take on the quality of myth or dream; they suggest a preconsciousness that can only be remembered in snatches or imaginatively recreated from an adult perspective. That the versions of some events from his "past life" which Limonov provides in *It's Me, Eddie* differ substantially from versions adumbrated in his other ostensibly autobiographical works makes the issue of "truth" even more slippery. Probably the most notable example is Edichka's account of his first sexual experience. In *It's Me, Eddie*, he recalls being seduced by a prostitute in Yalta, whereas in *Memoirs of a Russian Punk*, he consummates his childish romance with Svetka at the conclusion of the book. One must assume that these are cases of fictionalized or recreated memory, each appropriate to the larger aesthetic truth of the work as a whole.

Edichka's recollections of his "Great Love" in *It's Me, Eddie* are especially vague; whatever its material privations, he remembers his marriage to Elena as Edenic. He consistently elevates her in his memory to "Fair Helen of Troy, the best woman in Moscow, and if in Moscow, in all of Russia. A Nataliia Goncharova" (*ibid.*, p. 260). (The latter epithet is particularly interesting in light of Elena's role in his metaphoric death.) Their peripatetic existence in exile is described in the sketchiest terms: "a year of tears and failures, of wanderings through Austria, Italy and America, through luxurious capitals where we lived on potatoes and onions and got one shower a week" (*ibid.*, p. 130). Finally, Edichka's visceral reaction to the tortuous memories of his "happy days" with Elena is childlike in its intense physicality: "No, I do not remember my happy days, I don't remember a fucking thing, but when I do, I feel like vomiting, as if I'd gorged myself or something or had a stomach upset" (*ibid.*, p. 128).

Edichka's descriptions of the setting of his "childhood" in New York are highly selective. Frequently he includes minutiae that serve to illuminate his inner, psychological landscape more than the backdrop of his actions. Passages such as the following have led to charges of triviality:

Well, every morning I walked through the kitchen, took a little table on casters, covered the top with a white tablecloth and the two lower shelves with red napkins. On the napkins I placed some special long, deep little bowls for butter, sometimes a few forks and knives or a stack of cups and saucers, in case the two waiters I served should lack dishes. On top, on the white tablecloth, I usually placed four imitation-silver pitchers, having first filled them with ice cubes and water, and a big bowl of butter pats, which I took from the refrigerator and sprinkled with fresh fine ice. (*Ibid.*, pp. 30–31)

Nevertheless, the exhaustive detail of this description is expressive of Edichka's state of mind at the time. Stunned and bewildered by his "tragedy" (both his loss of Elena and his exile), he moves mechanically, without reflection in order to minimize his pain and to recoup his strength. His catalogue of the busboy's equipage bespeaks his effort to focus outward rather than inward. It also, of course, serves as an exposé of the obtuseness and cruelty of America; the specifics of his menial task emphasize the inappropriateness of such work for a talented Russian poet.

Smells play an important role in Edichka's recollections. The olfactory sense is, psychology tells us, extremely powerful in conjuring up images and impressions, and writers of childhoods often include smells in their descriptions. Edichka informs us that he is very sensitive to smells and can distinguish between "society people and bohemians" and "philistines and bourgeois families" on the basis of the scent of their apartments (*ibid.*, p. 54). His intuitive class consciousness is a satirical comment on the Soviet hierarchical mindset; it also calls to mind idyllic evocations of childhood based on smell by authors like Tolstoi, Aksakov and Goncharov. Certainly parody motivates Edichka's description of the storeroom in the hotel where he worked as a busboy: "I loved the storeroom, loved its smell of clean linen and spices. Sometimes I ran in there in the middle of work, to change a towel or quickly finish chewing a piece of meat left on the plate of some surfeited customer, and then ran on" (*ibid.*, p. 38). The juxtaposition of the image of cleanliness and quiet with the rather nasty description of gulping down leftovers underscores the extent to which Edichka's "childhood" departs from the pastoral myth.

Limonov's inclusion of the curiosa of American life, ranging from various designer brands of clothing to handcuffs and vibrators, was probably interesting from the standpoint of the émigré or Soviet reader. He was, however, less interested in satisfying the curiosity of his non-American audience than in satirizing a society that elevates material values to the detriment of spiritual and intellectual values. His intentions are diametrically opposed to those of a portraitist of childhood like Nabokov. In *Speak, Memory*, Nabokov uses curiosa to create a vision and feeling of time past, specifically prerevolutionary Russia; Limonov focuses on the objects that surround him to illustrate the emptiness and degradation of the society they represent. Intended to accomplish the task of critical realism, his descriptions are for the most part straightforward and unadorned. Metaphor, simile and other elements of poetic language are rare in *It's Me, Eddie*, a feature that links Limonov's autobiographical prose with his poetry.[37]

Historical accuracy aside, it is significant that Limonov chooses New York City as a backdrop to the action of the book. The city provides a closed space for Edichka's search. He calls New York "my great house" (*Eto ia – Edichka*, p. 232), and indeed its streets, apartments and empty lots function in much the same way as the family home or estate of earlier childhood autobiographers. Moreover, the city is endowed with an animistic character of its own. It reveals its secrets to Edichka, who is not afraid of it and seeks adventure in its labyrinthine depths. In fact, New York protects and comforts Edichka, fulfilling a parental role: "Beyond the park fence, New York picks me up in its arms. I sink into its warmth and summer – summer coming to an end, gentleman – and my New York carries me past the doors of its shops, past the subway stations, past the buses and the liquor store windows" (*ibid.*, pp. 248–49).[38] Yet New York is also the city of nightmares and death. Before he comes to terms with the city, before he can refer to it as "my New York," it is "a Babylon, God help me, a Babylon" (*ibid.*, p. 85). The apocalyptic nature of the city is suppressed as Edichka recovers his inner strength, so that his relationship with his surroundings mirrors his relationship with his inner self.

Nature is almost absent as a formative influence in Edichka's autobiography. Andrew Wachtel demonstrates that nature plays a seminal role in the childhoods of most Russian autobiographers. For Tolstoi, Aksakov and others, the rural estate is associated with a golden age of innocence; furthermore, it is opposed to the "unnatural" city (*Battle for Childhood*, p. 117). Edichka's émigré childhood is spent almost exclusively in the "city of the yellow devil," indeed at its very core. Limonov debunks the arcadian myth connected with Russian childhood to express effectively the disillusionment of the émigré.

There are two important exceptions to this rule in *It's Me, Eddie* and both serve the function of contrast. When Edichka accompanies his friend John to the Tolstoi Farm outside of New York, he finds himself holding his hosts' little girl. Recalling his impressions, he calls Katen'ka a "little plant" and notes that "at her age the little girl was closer to nature, to leaves and grass, than to people." Her touch gives him "a sense of animal comfort such as I had not felt since I slept with my arms around Elena" (*Eto ia – Edichka*, p. 227). It is interesting that Edichka associates Katen'ka with Elena (and there is no sexual innuendo here at all).[39] The fleeting idyllic moment of warmth he experiences with her is connected with his cultural past (the Tolstoi Farm) and his vanished innocence (the rural setting). Both of these, represented in Edichka's mind by Elena, are irredeemably lost to him. In a second, similar passage Edichka describes a photograph of Elena as a child: "... this little girl, with her braid, in her little *white* stockings, standing in her *garden*, and behind her, like scenery in a *pastoral* opera, *birches*, shrubs, a segment of a wooden house..." (emphasis added) (*ibid.*, p. 274). The Edenic past of this photograph is so distant, so inaccessible to Edichka that one is struck more forcefully by the corruption of his present.

Most of the characters Edichka presents in his autobiography are eccentric misfits. In the accounts he provides of his fellow émigrés, madness (as defined by Edichka) is a common feature. Lenia Chaplin has been mad from birth and eats discarded food on the street; Sasha Zelenskii borrows huge sums of money and imagines himself a photographer; Sasha Zhigulin has wild ambitions but eschews work; Alesha Slavkov is an alcoholic poet who lives with a clown and a musician in an apartment where hot water flows constantly in the kitchen. They are all part of the surrealistic nightmare that is life in exile for Edichka. Their madness and in some cases their physical deformities reflect the destructive quality of emigration; this life disfigures the body and the soul. Limonov stresses the typicality of his characters: "By now there are a great many of us here. And I must confess, we have among us quite a few madmen. This is normal" (*ibid.*, p. 26). In regard to the large number of eccentrics who people Limonov's book, Kron asserts that indeed it is natural that a large proportion of émigrés are "socially maladjusted"; those who cannot adapt and find a niche for themselves in their own society are the first to leave. This fact explains, Kron suggests, the sometimes "hysterical tone" of third wave writing ("Pro babochku," 91). However closely Limonov's characterizations of his fellow émigrés may match their prototypes, they should be seen primarily as a poetic rendering of the truth. As a satirist, Limonov is not concerned with how many of these people were mad before coming to the West, nor is he interested, as Kron wryly notes, in the large number of sane and capable people to be found in the émigré community (*ibid.*); his target is the deleterious effects of emigration.

Edichka informs us in introducing Sonia that "I have always been attracted to malformed specimens" (*Eto ia – Edichka*, p. 110). However, this attraction does not extend to his fellow émigrés. He recounts avoiding their gatherings in and around his hotel and attending leftist political meetings in hopes of broadening his spectrum of acquaintances. On the one hand, his rejection of the company of other émigrés underscores his stance of extreme individuality. His isolation is at least partially self-imposed; his feeling that he has lost or abdicated his Russianness is not particularly bitter. Edichka muses: "Lately I've developed an inescapable feeling that I'm not Russian, was not fully Russian even in Russia, national traits are very approximate..." (*ibid.*, p. 138). Returning to his friends from a walk along the beach he recalls: "I returned to my own people – to choose an arbitrary term, of course, an arbitrary term" (*ibid.*, p. 224). His fellow émigrés personify the confusion and despair that Edichka is attempting to transcend. He dismisses them as "the lowest of the low, pathetic, absurd" (*ibid.*, p. 162) and despises them for their willingness to accept the social injustice of America.

On the other hand, they embody the past, now inaccessible to Edichka. They are an omnipresent reminder of his loss and of the potential for remaining an outsider permanently.[40] The ambiguity of his attitude toward his fellow émigrés is expressed concisely in his recollection of moving the belongings of Russians in New York:

> Carrying the dull green spines, the collected works of the Chekhovs, Leskovs, and other eulogizers and denizens of sleepy Russian noondays, I think vicious thoughts about the whole of my loathsome native Russian literature, which has been largely responsible for my life. Dull green bastards, Chekhov languishing in boredom, his eternal students, people who don't know how to get themselves going, who vegetate through this life, they lurk in these pages like diaphanous sunflower husks. Even the print, small and crowded, is repulsive to me. And I am repulsive to myself. It's much pleasanter to move the bright American books, not all of which, moreover, are intelligible to me, thank God. (*Eto ia – Edichka*, p. 218)

The past obtrudes into the present and obscures Edichka's focus on the future. Significantly, the logic of his vitriolic rejection of the past is markedly childlike. He blames Russian cultural traditions, represented by nineteenth-century classics, for his unhappiness. His reaction to their physical presence (the books) is visceral; he projects onto them his frustration and his fear of failure. Finally, his preference for the "bright" American books (representatives of his adopted culture) is superficial, since they are largely incomprehensible. Adding a twist of childish spite, Edichka perversely celebrates this fact.

Given Edichka's extreme emotional discomfort in relation to his fellow émigrés, our interpretation of his identification with the downtrodden and dispossessed of New York should be cautious. He professes to consider menial laborers, the poor, the homeless and criminal elements as "comrades in misfortune" (*ibid.*, p. 30). The attraction, however, is less altruistic solidarity than a desperate need to belong, to have contact with life. Introducing himself to Johnny, he explains himself to the reader: "I wanted a new world, I was sick of living an indeterminate life, being neither Russian nor anything else..." (*ibid.*, p. 160). Edichka's attitude toward his chosen soulmates is, moreover, tinged with superciliousness. Noting that one of the women in his English class has the name of a Voltaire heroine, Edichka condescendingly remarks "It is hardly likely that Zobeida herself knew this, but she was one of the best pupils in our class" (*ibid.*, p. 148). Leonid Geller charges that Edichka's vaunted identification with the poor is entirely motivated by his envy toward the rich and powerful and that his pose is hypocritical ("Prigotovitel'nye zametki," 86). Altruism and envy in fact both play a part in Edichka's identification with New York's down and out. Finding himself poor, homeless and dispossessed, he seeks human contact among those who have also suffered misfortune. However, he is still conscious of himself as a Russian poet and extraordinary man (in the Dostoevskian sense). His identification with the downtrodden is thus a childish flirtation, an experiment by way of establishing his rightful place.

Edichka's iconoclasm and his often shocking behavior are also manifestations of rebelliousness characteristic of childhood and adolescence. As an older, wiser narrator, he recognizes that his thoughts and actions were sometimes illogical. Recalling his younger self, he concedes "I did not want to be reasonable, did not want to consider assorted explanatory causes..." (*Eto ia – Edichka*, p. 27). Certainly his "badness" stems, in part, from envy and spite, and in this respect he is indebted to Olesha for his artistic prototype in Ivan Kavalerov.[41] Furthermore, he consistently shifts the blame for his actions onto others. Cast into the role of a child, he exhibits childlike reflexes. His unwillingness to accept responsibility for his own unhappiness also constitutes a (perhaps unintentional) satiric commentary on the Soviet mindset: "He begins to look for those responsible for his emigration; for him, a person brought up in the Soviet way, it is unimaginable that only he himself can be responsible for his own actions..."[42] In the tradition of Rousseau, Edichka is not really bad; his shocking behavior is the product of living in a corrupt and insensitive society. The autobiographical mode, congenial to revelations of nonconformism and revolt, facilitates Limonov's critique of America's treatment of Russian émigrés.

His identity as a poet reinforces Edichka's stance as an iconoclast. Made keenly aware of the difference in prestige enjoyed by Russian and Western poets, Limonov exploits this distinction to express the alienation of the émigré artist. In Russia, a poet is a prophet, a martyr, a spiritual leader; here, he notes succinctly, "a poet is shit" (*Eto ia – Edichka*, p. 25). His rage and defiance are explosive and resemble a child's reaction to frustration and insecurity:

> You have herds of rich men here, you have bars on every corner, and literature is reduced to the level of a professorial game. Shit if I'd go to your fucking Arlington or Bennington or whatever it is, to teach your zhlobby children Russian literature. I did not refuse to be bought in the USSR merely in order to sell myself cheap here. And please note – membership in the Soviet Writers' Union is a much better honor than a professorship, even at a university of yours. (*Ibid.*, p. 135)

Elsewhere Edichka demonstrates more restrained powers of self-analysis and remarks that he was spoiled by the glamorous life of an underground poet in Kharkov and Moscow. In order to solve this crisis of identity, to be "reborn" into his new life, Edichka must transcend the past and the Russian tradition of deification of the poet. Although Edichka is a poet in the literal sense, it is fair to interpret his calling, as L. Kornilova does, in a broader, metaphorical sense.[43] By definition, the poet is an outsider who finds it difficult to accommodate any of society's strictures and must always rebel. Edichka's poet persona is to some extent, then, conventional; at the very least, convention accords happily with Limonov's artistic demands.

There is much that is childish in the poetic stance Edichka assumes. He expresses his dissatisfaction with not receiving the recognition due him in simplistic terms: "I do my work – where's my money? Both states bullshit about the justice of their systems, but where's my money?" (*Eto ia – Edichka*, p. 11). His preference for work that is purely creative and his idealistic vision of a society in which people will not have to work for a living are attractive but naive. Kornilova suggests that his hatred for work arises from his conviction that work distracts people from attaining their dreams; it represents regimentation, soullessness and hypocrisy, all of which impede the poet's spontaneity and purity of purpose ("Poslednii romantik," 93). Edichka's poetic megalomania, while quite serious, serves an important satiric function. Because it is couched in such extreme terms, it renders farcical the traditional Russian equation of the poet and the tsar. Recounting reading his poetry to his friend Kirill and Raymond, Edichka writes "in this business I am superior to everyone; here, only in poetry am I who I am" (*Eto ia – Edichka*, p. 68). His admiration of another poet is expressed in a contrary manner; he calls him "contemporary Russia's cruelest poet, Igor' Kholin, a scoundrel and a villain, but magnificent" (*ibid.*, p. 162). Edichka focuses on the rights and privileges that accrue to the position of the Russian poet/tsar rather than on the moral responsibilities it entails. Seemingly without irony, he exposes the cultural tradition by which he defines himself as illusory. This deflation is a means of transcending the past for Edichka, of coming to terms with the reality of his new life.

The autobiographer's discovery of his sexuality is a common feature of the genre of the childhood. Having surveyed hundreds of childhoods, Coe finds that "the evidence is that the early discovery of sexuality is not merely obsessive, but seems to *demand* some kind of confession or expiation" (*When the Grass Was Taller*, p. 180). Edichka's curiosity and erotic experimentation are marked by an infantile quality. The women who frequent the hotel restaurant where he works in the chapter "I Am a Busboy" arouse a variety of strong reactions on his part: "...I stared at them with caution, disbelief, and forgive me... with delight. Alas. I stared at them in a peculiar way – I scorned them, hated them, simultaneously realizing that their pastimes would never be open to me" (*Eto ia – Edichka*, p. 37). In describing his first homosexual encounter with Chris, he recalls playing the role of a child: "I especially like to hug as children do, flinging my arms way round the neck, hugging the neck, not the shoulders" (*ibid.*, p. 83). The erotic fantasies in which he engages are also infantile. Although made in regard to a passage from another work, Carden's comments about

Limonov's fantasies are most apropos: "The fantasy contains much that is characteristic of Limonov: the world of childhood interpreted as a world of natural and free eroticism" ("Edward Limonov's Coming Out,' p. 225). Edichka dreams alternately of making love to, kidnapping and killing his former wife. A scene he imagines in relation to mannequins is particularly surrealistic and is recounted in distinctly childish terms:

Now, when I feel like fucking all the time but don't arrange it for myself, the mannequins also frighten me. With pleasure and fright I think how I could tear aside their skirts, scarves, and other frippery to get at that place, and suddenly it would turn out they had a real live peepka. *But forgive me these mystical sexual daydreams. It's because I'm not fucking much.* (*Eto ia – Edichka*, p. 234)

Although the point of view shifts to that of an adult within this passage (indicated by my italics), the dominant voice is that of the fearful, angry child. The association of the mannequins with Elena is obvious – she has found work as a model – so that Edichka's hostility may be motivated by the pain of his "tragedy."

Edichka's obsession with sex, childish as it is, is a way of affirming his existence. Within the time frame of his autobiography, he lives intensely through the body because his other connections with life (intellectual, emotional and spiritual) have been sundered. His decision to become a practicing homosexual is based on the emptiness of his life: "I was forced to grasp at anything, I had nothing, we were alien to this world" (*ibid.*, p. 53). What Donde calls Edichka's "hysterical and panic-stricken activity" ("Eduard, Edik i Edichka," 17), his sexual excess, is a symptom rather than a disease. Doubting his own self-value, fearing annihilation, he seeks human contact, warmth and protection. He tells his friend Kirill "I'm weary, no one has worried about me for a long time, I want attention, I want to be loved and fussed over" (*Eto ia – Edichka*, p. 50). Having found comfort with Chris, he analyzes his brief happiness: "Despite my everlasting honor and ironic mockery I was a hunted creature, cornered and exhausted, and this was precisely what I needed – another man's hand stroking my head, caressing me" (*ibid.*, p. 85). Matich's point that in his sexual adventures Edichka is "looking for a parent or someone to belong to" ("The Moral Immoralist," 532) is well taken.

Alienation and fear of extinction also underlie Edichka's sexual ambivalence, or what appears to be his bisexuality. His loss of Elena and his cultural bearings has cast him adrift. The sex-role reversals in which he engages reflect the "doubleness" of life in exile. Edichka wears lace shirts and sandals with heels and has, he tells us, worn his wife's underwear; in his homosexual liaisons, he assumes a "female" role. Of his encounter with Chris he recalls "the simple fact that he was considerably bigger and more virile somehow determined our roles" (*Eto ia – Edichka*, p. 83). In a curious collocation of feminine and childish images, Edichka describes being shown off by Raymond to a visiting friend: "At a request from Raymond, who was boasting about my figure, I was obliged to twirl before the Frenchman, displaying myself. I felt as if I were fifteen and my parents were displaying me to their friends. Not fifteen, younger. Ten, eight" (*ibid.*, p. 69). On one level, Edichka's attempts to be both masculine and feminine are indicative of the anxiety he feels in his search for human contact.[44] On another level, they reflect Edichka's struggle to double himself, to be both Russian and non-Russian/émigré (or in his own perception, cosmopolitan).

Undeniably, Limonov's accounts of Edichka's sexual escapades have high shock value and this has led to charges that *It's Me, Eddie* is merely pornography. Donde, who appreciates Limonov's use of the erotic, nevertheless concedes that elements of "dissipation, exhibitionism and the simple desire for literary fame" ("Eduard, Edik i Edichka," 17) enter into the text. Quite aside from his breaking the taboos of Russian literary tradition, Limonov's pseudo-autobiography may be seen as a parodic commentary on contemporary Western literature. A self-proclaimed outsider, Limonov takes the conventions of Western (especially American) confessional prose to the extreme.[45] To some degree, *It's Me, Eddie* represents a logical step in the liberalization process that is currently underway in Russian literary practice (Vail' and Genis, *Sovremennaia russkaia proza*, p. 107). However, Limonov's irony in regard to himself and the world around him often results in self-parody. An analogy can be found in the émigré director Tsukerman's film *Liquid Sky*, where everything that is possible according to looser Western strictures is included. While the film may indeed be shocking to Russian viewers, for audiences more inured to prurience and violence it is a parodic hash of erotic, science fiction and detective film conventions.

I have suggested that Elena is associated in Edichka's perception with an Edenic childhood now vanished. Given that emigration has plunged him into a sort of second childhood, it is not surprising that his present attitude toward her is tinged with infantilism. In his harsh critique of *It's Me, Eddie*, Konstantin Kustanovich insists that Edichka's love for Elena is not that of an adult, but rather that of a child.[46] Kustanovich intends this point as damning criticism, but his insight into Edichka's persona is central to our understanding of the book as childhood. It is most significant that Edichka both adores and detests his former wife. Although he initially resists the displacement of her image, Edichka is compelled to relegate her gradually to the past. The emotional security with which she is associated (in a very maternal way) must be renounced by Edichka if he is to move forward. By the end of the book, Edichka indeed seems to have transcended his ambivalent feelings of love and hate toward Elena and to be able to regard her with sympathy. Sewing a dress for her, buying her things, bringing her food, he takes on the role of a parent and she evokes pity in him:

But suddenly I stumbled upon this note [while going through her diary]: "... and Eddie, I am guilty before you. My poor, poor baby! And God will punish me; when I was a child I read a story that had the words, 'You are responsible in life for all whom you have tamed ...'" I read this and felt so sorry for my girl that I could have cried. When had she written this, evidently in Milan? Poor creature, you feel bad because you don't know that love exists. My unhappy girl who made me unhappy, how can I blame you! The loathsome loveless world is to blame, not you. (*Eto ia – Edichka*, pp. 272–73)

In describing his "tragedy," Edichka does not distinguish between the loss of Elena and the loss of his homeland. All of his identity problems as an émigré are inextricably bound to her abandoning him. He perceives himself as belonging to one of the previous waves of emigration, but his longing for Russia is qualified: "I am a man of another generation, and although I myself often sobbed into my own pillow, I wouldn't have given a shit about the emigration if it hadn't been for Elena" (*ibid.*, p. 17). As he comes to terms with Elena's departure, therefore, we also discern an acceptance of his status as émigré. The truce he establishes with America is an uneasy one and may only be temporary, but he has gained strength and wisdom along the way.

One of the most troubling aspects of *It's Me, Eddie* for many (especially émigré) readers and critics is Edichka's perceived leftist political leanings. Whatever Limonov's own politics may be, radicalism is artistically consistent with the autobiographical persona he creates. His rebelliousness is not focused but diffuse, a symptom of his disillusionment and confusion. Dancing drunkenly to Russian music, he expresses his anguish in terms of revolt: "'A machine gun, oy, give me a machine gun, my dears!' I scream hysterically, to Kirill's delight" (*ibid.*, p. 141). Edichka's fantasies of revolution, like his sexual fantasies, are rather childish. The philosophical basis of his radicalism is simplistic and myopic; he writes "I deduced my love for world revolution naturally from my own personal tragedy – a tragedy in which both countries were involved, both the USSR and America, and in which civilization was to blame" (*ibid.*, p. 99). That Edichka's convictions are still very much in the process of formation is suggested in the last pages of the book. Lamenting his relatives killed in World War II, he ironically notes that they died "For the interests of the people. For Russia. Shit" (*ibid.*, p. 280). Although he discredits the concept of nationality, a page later he fantasizes that he may join the Palestinians or Colonel Khaddafi's forces "to lay down Eddie-baby's life for a people, for a nation" (*ibid.*, p. 281). Certainly Edichka's statements are inconsistent, but his reasoning is distorted by despair and anger.

The solutions and alternatives that Edichka offers to replace existing political structures are naive. He concedes that his ideal of communes and sects is vague, but seems perfectly serious in insisting on abolishing ethnic differences:

> All nationalities must be totally mixed, must renounce ethnic prejudices, "blood" and that sort of nonsense, in the name of world unity, even in the name of stopping nationalistic wars – even for that alone it would be worth being mixed. Mixed biologically, acknowledging the danger of ethnic groupings. Jews and Arabs, Armenians and Turks – enough of all that. It must stop, at long last. (*Ibid.*, p. 93)

Furthermore, complete equality and justice in regard to property will be established, and people will no longer be slaves to work. Kustanovich belittles Edichka's utopianism ("Golyi korol'," 34) but misses the point; he approaches these ideas as straightforward expressions of Limonov's political convictions rather than as Edichka's childish dreams. Similarly, Nina Voronel' takes Edichka's threats seriously and poses the possibility of armed bands of Limonovite terrorists appearing ("Pod sen'iu," 189). In fact, Edichka's political solutions are as impossibly idealistic as the old Jew Gedali's "internationale of good people" in Babel''s *Red Cavalry*. They are raw, unmediated responses to the frustrations and disappointments of émigré life.

Edichka's indicting well-known dissidents – most notably Solzhenitsyn and Sakharov – for his predicament can also be fruitfully interpreted in this light. He charges that they were motivated by pride and the urge to self-advertisement and that they deceived the Russian intelligentsia in tempting them to emigrate. As Matich notes, Edichka's attempt to lay the blame for his personal "tragedy" at the dissident movement's door is the reaction of "a naive child or a simpleton provincial" ("The Moral Immoralist," 531). Accepting responsibility for his own actions, since they have turned out so badly, is painful for Edichka, so he must find another focus of blame. In any event, his accusations tell us much more about Edichka's character than about either Solzhenitsyn or Sakharov.

Political radicalism also offers Edichka a sense of solidarity, of belonging to a group. His longing for "a brotherhood of stern men, revolutionaries and terrorists" or "a religious sect preaching love" (*Eto ia – Edichka*, p. 232) is an expression of what George Gibian (echoing Gor'kii) calls Limonov's need for a "warm coat."[47] Opposition to the *status quo* constitutes a basis of unity with others, and it is important for Edichka that these others (potentially, since they remain abstract) are an elite minority (Gross, "Shramy rossiiskogo Odisseia," 202). His leftist convictions provide him with a weapon to fend off the specter of utter loneliness and simultaneously gratify his need to be perceived as exceptional.

Moreover, extremism and political nonconformism are almost *de rigueur* for a poet. Edichka enjoys arousing his visitors' horror with the posters of Mao Tse-tung, Patricia Hearst and Workers Party candidates that hang on the walls of his room. Refusing to recognize substantive distinctions between the Soviet and Western systems underscores his iconoclasm. He has been an outsider and suffered in both societies, so that the differences for him are negligible: "Ten years of that life in Russia, and now the whole thing over again" (*Eto ia – Edichka*, pp. 24–25). What is significant for our apprehension of Edichka's persona is the contrast he establishes between the institution, the official world, and the free individual. Kornilova interprets his equating Soviet and Western politics in this sense and suggests that his stance is essentially that of the romantic social outcast ("Poslednii romantik," 93). Edichka himself emphasizes the similarity between the world view of the poet and that of the child: "All children are extremists. I have remained an extremist, have not become a grown-up" (*Eto ia – Edichka*, p. 248).

A frequent feature of the autobiography of childhood is an account of the author's education. In *It's Me, Eddie*, Limonov subverts this convention, as his narrative persona gains knowledge and experience of American life on the rough streets and in the squalid deserted lots of New York. However, Edichka also undergoes an education in the more traditional sense. He refers repeatedly to his efforts to master English and describes his language classes. His account of the dialogues he was compelled to read underscores the vast distance between the trivial, secure world of the textbook and the real, desperate life of the immigrant struggling to adapt to unfamiliar surroundings:

[Zobeida] and I were often assigned to read a dialogue, usually between a husband and wife who constantly spilled things on themselves and on each other and then advised each other what cleaner to go to. These married couples in the book were complete idiots. Everything fell from their hands, they could not convey a morsel to their mouths; God knows how they managed to stay alive; their coffee spilled, the cups broke, greasy sandwiches fell butter-side-down on their new clothes. Things were grim. (*Ibid.*, p. 148)

Edichka's source of reading practice is magazines retrieved from trash bins. These too, with their chic advertisements and glossy illustrations, are wildly irrelevant to Edichka's life and serve to highlight the disparity between the American dream and the reality of the third wave emigration.

The author's realization of the inevitability of death is often included in autobiographical accounts of childhood. As Carden has noted, one of Limonov's primary artistic concerns is mortality ("Edward Limonov's Coming Out," p. 223). Certainly fear of oblivion is a leitmotif of *It's Me, Eddie* (as well as much of Limonov's other prose and especially his poetry). But he takes this fear one step further, as Edichka confronts and even courts death. His loss and dislocation were so debilitating that at least temporarily he lost the urge to self-preservation: "I feared no one and nothing at all in this world because I was prepared to die at any moment. I believe I was seeking death – unconsciously, but I was" (*Eto ia – Edichka*, p. 80). He refers to his "craving for death" as a factor in his attraction to Chris (*ibid.*, p. 82). Edichka does not merely struggle with the idea of death; he actively experiments with it. Once again, Limonov parodies a convention of the childhood in order to demonstrate the despair and hopelessness generated by emigration.

I have suggested in discussing Limonov's use of the autobiographical mode that *It's Me, Eddie* challenges our expectation that the author and his narrative "I" are one and the same. The relationship is made more complex by Limonov's intentionally obscuring the distinction between himself and his literary persona. The self-that-was presented to us has been shaped and altered from the raw material of *bios* by both memory and imagination. This is to some extent the practice of every autobiographer, but Limonov is exceptionally keenly aware of the double referent of his first-person "I." He implicitly acknowledges the split that exists between Edichka's point of view and his own. Recalling his purchase of a pair of handcuffs to facilitate Elena's kidnapping, he sums up the episode as "A pitiful story, very pitiful" (*ibid.*, p. 36). Describing his attire, he objectively judges his own taste: "In the end I dressed very strangely..." (*ibid.*, p. 54). Although he exploits the privileged position of the insider *vis-à-vis* his own thoughts and actions, Limonov/Edichka regards himself as if from the side, from the standpoint of an observer. This type of *ostranenie* gives Limonov's irony in regard to his narrator free play. He imagines how he appears to the secretaries watching him on his balcony: "What they see is that every other day, on a hot plate there on the balcony, a man cooks a huge steaming pot of something barbaric" (*ibid.*, p. 7). The handcuff debacle is rendered in tones of black humor: "... this gruesome scene was fit for Hollywood: Limonov weeping with grief *over a pair of handcuffs for his beloved* and filing off the safety button with a kitchen knife" (*ibid.*, p. 36). Describing his failed erotic encounter with Raymond, he muses "We must have looked like Japanese wrestlers" (*ibid.*, p. 66). Limonov even utilizes the distance between his narrated and narrating selves as a source of ironic humor. Having described himself rather grandiloquently as a "free personality in the free world," he proceeds to mock his own rhetoric a few sentences later: "The free personality got sick of sitting on the scaffold. It jumped down" (*ibid.*, p. 81). He scoffs at his posturing as he recounts it.

Limonov's frequent use of third-person narration renders the relationship between the author and Edichka still more problematic. Indeed, shifts from the *Ich-Erzählung* of the traditional autobiographical mode to the third person are seen by some critics as evidence of the destruction of genre boundaries. Writing of André Gorz's autobiography, Pascal notes that the author "speaks of himself as an object, in the third person, almost disdainfully" and that with this development "the frontiers of autobiography are reached" (*Design and Truth*,

p. 160). Pascal's objection to the third person in autobiography is that it misrepresents the nature of the relationship between the author and the narrator. It can never be as objective as third-person narration would suggest, so that there will inevitably be "contradiction between form and view-point" (*ibid.*, p. 165).

Pascal's critical stance is, however, a conservative one and practice has long outstripped theory in this regard. Limonov's use of the third person formalizes what is true to some extent of all autobiography: the self represented is not the same as the self writing. In his article "The Veto of Imagination," Louis Renza suggests that "writing's law of gravity" estranges the autobiographer from his recreated self and makes using the third person an obvious solution.[48] Limonov manipulates the distancing effect of the third person in presenting his narrator's ruminations and moods. Edichka's response to Raymond's assurance that he can eat avocado and shrimp salad because he is only a boy emphasizes his alienation both from the action described and the present act of recall: "The boy thought to himself that yes, no doubt he was a boy, but if you made a hole in his head, took out the part of the brain that controlled the memory, washed and cleaned it properly, that would be luxury. *Then* you'd have a boy" (*Eto ia – Edichka*, p. 59). Because Edichka is struggling with the reconciliation of the past (his pre-emigration life in Russia) and the present (his intolerably anonymous existence as an exile), the third person is the perfect narrative vehicle. It eloquently expresses, as Lejeune puts it, "the tension between impossible unity and intolerable division and the fundamental schism which turns the speaker into a fugitive."[49]

Limonov complicates the situation by oscillating between the first and third (and occasionally second) persons. These shifts often occur within a single sentence. He recalls attending Elena's modeling show: "Simultaneously Eddie-baby apologized for not bringing Elena flowers, I had been in such a rush to see her that I hadn't had time..." (*Eto ia – Edichka*, p. 266). The reader is sometimes drawn into the narration scheme as well, as in the following passage that ends with an insistent query: "And what's more they take away the last thing he clings to – love. Eddie has fantastic strength, how else would I hold on, with my constitution, how else?" (*ibid.*, p. 104). Narrative modes replace one another in rapid succession: "Normality is boring to little Eddie; I shied away from it in Russia, and you won't lure me into a life of sleep and work here" (*ibid.*, p. 19). Limonov's usage reflects the extreme instability of the narrative persona who is incomplete in either presentation singularly and therefore uses multiple presentations to achieve unity.[50]

Limonov's referring to himself by several different names underscores the split within his narrative persona. He most frequently calls himself "Edichka," a diminutive form of Eduard. He is alternately Eduard and Limonov, and these variations indicate the degree of intimacy and privilege accorded to other characters and to the reader. The speech etiquette associated with different forms of a proper name is particularly pronounced in Russian. Limonov manipulates these conventions, recognizing that "while this procedure [using the proper name] dispels all ambiguity, it accentuates the figured nature of the enunciation" (Lejeune, "Autobiography in the Third Person," 34). It is noteworthy that Limonov never uses his patronymic either alone or in combination with the first name; this omission suggests his estrangement from his Russian past at the time of the events described. That Edichka objects strongly to another possible diminutive of his name – Edik – is also interesting. Since the forms of appellation represent different aspects of his personality, Edik appears to be a part of himself that he suppresses and rejects.

Extended passages of direct speech, including monologue and dialogue, are unusual in autobiography. William Howarth notes that direct speech is a feature of what he calls "the dramatic autobiographer's literary technique."[51] Action is more important that description in such autobiographies, among which *It's Me, Eddie* can be counted. Moreover, direct speech may be an effective (and retrospectively privileged) means of characterization. Edichka reproduces, for example, a long exchange he had with his girlfriend Sonia on a bus. The dialogue form allows Edichka to put forth his progressive views on race relations forcefully and to present Sonia's opinions as evidence of her racism. Aware that such passages strain credibility, Limonov mockingly justifies and rationalizes his use of direct speech. The issue is complicated by Edichka's admissions that his English was weak at the time of the events described; in the case of dialogues ostensibly carried out in English, he often disregards the requirements of verisimilitude. In doing so, he insists on his right to create approximate renditions of verbal encounters. The gist and the spirit of these exchanges is preserved and thus no violence is done to the artistic truth of his account.

Limonov also toys with the autobiographical (and fictional) convention of internal dialogue. Voices that represent other aspects of Edichka's personality become independent and engage in debate with him. Limonov uses this device parodically, creating disembodied voices that criticize and provoke Edichka. The voice that speaks in his ear reiterates, but exaggerates and mocks what he himself advocates elsewhere, revealing his inability to live up to his abstract ideals:

"Don't you dare scorn her!" someone said in my ear. "You ought to love everyone who's in trouble, everyone who's unhappy and has complexes, everyone..." But what could I do – I looked at her and saw a lip exactly like my neighbor Tolik's, a boy I used to go to school with. Poor kid, he was hunchbacked and stunted, his father was an alcoholic. "Quit it, you swine!" said the voice. "You should be ashamed – you're the filthy one, she's kind and good!" (*Eto ia – Edichka*, pp. 118–19)

As he waits for his potential lover Johnny, a chorus of seven such voices discusses the reasons for his pursuing this dubious relationship (*ibid.*, pp. 166–67). They vie in exposing Edichka's baseness and hypocrisy, taking this narrative convention to its absurd extreme.

Limonov's implied reader is as unstable as his narrative persona. It is difficult to pinpoint whom Edichka has in mind when he addresses "you," and indeed this seems to change from paragraph to paragraph. He sometimes seems to address the Western world or America; this is clearly the case in his use of the Dostoevskian "gentlemen" (*gospoda*) in postulating a receptor. Edichka's spiteful introduction in the first few pages of the book in particular is aimed exclusively at an American audience. He writes "I live at your expense, you pay taxes and I don't do a fucking thing," and furthermore "I want to receive your money to the end of my days" (*ibid.*, p. 8). He anticipates his abstract American interlocutor's reaction and responds to it with undisguised malice: "You don't like me? You don't want to pay? It's precious little – $278 a month. You don't want to pay. Then why the fuck did you invite me, entice me here from Russia, along with a horde of Jews? Present your complaints to your own propaganda, it's too effective. That's what's emptying your pockets, not I" (*ibid.*, p. 9). Shukman suggests that Limonov focuses his text progressively more and more toward the émigré reader or the Soviet reader ("Taboos, Splits and Signifiers," 7). Although this may be true in roughly quantitative terms, there are still instances of addresses to the American reader late in the book. In the eighth chapter, "Luz, Aleshka, Johnny, and Others," Edichka writes "Forgive me, but though they may say that Eddie-baby knows little of America, there is less love here, gentlemen, far less…" (*Eto ia – Edichka*, p. 151). Berating Roseanne for her stinginess in the following chapter, he acidly notes that her behavior demonstrates "stinginess in my view, gentlemen, only in my view. To you, perhaps, it's the rule" (*ibid.*, p. 189).

The referent of Edichka's "you" is usually less clearly identifiable; his assumption of a common frame of reference in evoking his pre-emigration past and in describing his present exile suggests an intended reader who shares these experiences. In the following passage, for example, he poses his rhetorical questions to a receptor who implicitly sympathizes with the alienation of the émigré *intelligent* :

Fucking smart Americans, they advise men like Aleshka and me to change professions. Where am I to hide all my thoughts, feelings, ten years of living, books of poetry? And me myself, where am I to hide refined little Eddie? Lock him up in the shell of a busboy. Bullshit. I tried it. I can no longer be an ordinary man. I am spoiled forever. Only the grave will reform me. (*Ibid.*, p. 154)

The echo of the Russian proverb, "the grave will cure a hunchback, and the club a stubborn man," in the last line of this passage is also aimed at a reader who shares Limonov's cultural baggage. In alluding to this proverb, Limonov implicitly identifies himself as a hunchback, one who deviates from the norm.

The reactions Edichka solicits or anticipates from his intended reader also vary within the text. He alternately seeks the empathy of his reader ("I'm poor unlucky Eddie, put yourself in my place" [*ibid.*, p. 190]) and scorns him ("Poor, poor you! When Eddie fell apart he was nevertheless happy; though sick, he has within him *Love*. Envy him, gentlemen!" [*ibid.*, p. 268]). An interesting technique Limonov uses in addressing his intended reader directly is to debate with him, to try to convince him of his point of view: "Such were my futile dreams as I gazed on someone else's child. Why futile, you say? Of course they were futile" (*ibid.*, p. 228). His interlocutor's potential rejoinders are sometimes reproduced verbatim: "'Fool,' you will say, 'you spoiled the woman. Now you have only yourself to blame!' No, I didn't spoil the woman..." (*ibid.*, p. 257). Lejeune notes that this device has been a standard procedure in polemical literature since Plato ("Autobiography in the Third Person," 44–45). Edichka convincingly refutes the discourse of his fictive interlocutor since he controls it absolutely.

The indeterminacy of Limonov's intended reader and Edichka's intended addressee reflects the rootlessness and alienation peculiar to the exile experience. Edichka's insecurity about whom he is speaking to within the text of *It's Me, Eddie* is emblematic of the dilemma of the émigré writer. Just as Edichka addresses by turns his Western readership, the émigré community and the Soviet reader, Russian writers living in the diaspora must continually ask themselves for whom they are writing. The question has, of course, been largely obviated with the dissolution of the Soviet Union, but was still a central one for third wave writers of the late seventies and early eighties.

Unlike the traditional autobiography of childhood, *It's Me, Eddie* is not chronolinear. The original Russian text consists of thirteen chapters and an epilogue.[52] As Shukman notes, these are self-contained narrative units and could, for the most part, easily exist as independent stories ("Taboos, Splits and Signifiers," 5). The narrated time of the book is from March to October of 1976; Edichka specifies the time and place exactly, mocking his own documentary pretensions: "It was spring, 1976, twentieth century, the great city of New York at lunch hour" (*Eto ia – Edichka*, pp. 63–64). The remembered time of Edichka's pseudo-autobiography is, however, much greater. Lengthy digressions and anecdotes from his pre-emigration past and the months preceding the period treated here broaden the span of narrated time substantially. Moreover, Edichka's digressions often overlap and become mutually referential. A bottle of champagne, for example, arouses his landlady's suspicion that he is squandering his welfare payments in the first chapter of the book; this same bottle reappears a hundred pages later in Edichka's account of his liaison with Sonia and he overdetermines the connection: "I took a bottle of champagne I had laid in ahead of time, a $10 Soviet champagne, the very bottle Mrs. Rogoff screamed about" (*ibid.*, p. 113). He sometimes alludes to stories to be told in more detail later. Introducing the reader to Sonia, he writes "the term [woman] is hardly correct in respect to her, as you will see..." (*ibid.*, p. 110). Furthermore, he reminds us of stories already told, calling upon us to exert our memories to place the characters and incidents mentioned. Limonov employs what Edward Brown calls "tricks of juxtaposition and interference"[53] with memory to link his narrative and to create the sense of dislocation that informs Edichka's life.

Frequent tense shifts emphasize the instability of the narrative point of view. Rendering long accounts of past events in the present tense lends them immediacy and poignancy. Edichka's examination of Elena's apartment in the chapter "Where She Made Love" is recounted almost entirely in the present tense, heightening the anguish he experiences. At one point, Edichka briefly considers his use of tense and concludes "I say 'was,' but I might as well say 'am.' This period is not over, I am in it, in this period, even at the present time" (*Eto ia – Edichka*, p. 194).

Satire and the autobiographical mode   143

Overlapping of past and present (and sometimes future) tenses supports the open-endedness of the text. Edichka's existence in exile – his psychological, if not his physical existence – is still perilous, and he denies the reader the comfort of resolution.

We enter Edichka's life *in medias res*. He has already emigrated and begun a new life in the West, but has not yet established himself. Little historical or cultural background of the phenomenon of the third wave is provided and Edichka has no inclination to be objective or informative. Ahistoricity is not a traditional feature of the Russian autobiographical tradition and indeed we expect more or less firm historical parameters from the genre. James Olney voices this expectation when he writes "as students of autobiography we should fix autobiographical events in the moment of writing and in the history of the writer and his time" ("Autobiography and the Cultural Moment," p. 19). Contrary to this convention, *It's Me, Eddie* is an intensely personal document that relies on an informed reader to provide historical background. In fact, Edichka's focusing exclusively on his psyche and ignoring context constitutes a rejection of autobiographical canon; Limonov requires that the book be read on its own terms.

It is possible to trace a linear progression toward greater maturity, harmony and assimilation in the text. Especially in the chapter "My Friend New York," Edichka seems to have found a niche: "Washington Square is pointed out in guidebooks to New York as a place of note, and sometimes real Americans pass through, country men and country ladies, glancing over their shoulders. *To us natives* they look very funny; observing them, the guitarists, students, idlers, and joint-smokers laugh, and so do I" (emphasis added) (*Eto ia – Edichka*, p. 238). However, Limonov intentionally frustrates such a reading, for the epilogue forcefully reiterates Edichka's bitterness and alienation.[54] Like all autobiography, *It's Me, Eddie* necessarily remains incomplete, but its circularity is remarkable. The open-endedness of the text is not only that imposed by the requirements of verisimilitude (i.e. the autobiographer is still alive). Limonov's autobiography, like Michel Leiris' work, "far from concluding or being closed, remains open-ended, turns back on itself, and in its circularity, becomes endless" (Olney, "Autobiography and the Cultural Moment," p. 26). Linear progress toward peaceful accord crowned by its achievement would negate the satirical and critical force of Limonov's pseudo-autobiography. The epilogue in particular subverts our expectation of closure.

The fragmented, irregular structure of the narrative reflects the state of Edichka's consciousness. Bruss suggests that the arrangement of an autobiography can be taken as a sample of the author's epistemology and a demonstration of his capacities (*Autobiographical Acts*, p. 13). In the case of *It's Me, Eddie*, the apparent disorder and formlessness of the text do indeed underscore the chaos of the narrator's life. Plot as such is deemphasized, and Limonov concentrates instead on Edichka's psychological growth. This aspect of *bios* may not be traceable in a straightforward way across time; it rather extends downward into the consciousness. Time is experienced "like the thickness of a palimpsest"[55] upon whose restoration the autobiographer is engaged.

It is interesting that fragmentation is a typical feature of the autobiographical texts of women writers. Jelinek's explanation for the frequency of disjuncture in women's autobiography is pertinent to Limonov's work. She writes: "The narratives of [women's] lives are often not chronological and progressive but disconnected, fragmentary, or organized into self-sustained units rather than connecting chapters. The multidimensionality of women's socially conditioned roles seems to have established a pattern of diffusion and diversity when they write their autobiographies as well…" (*Women's Autobiography*, p. 17). Edichka's roles too are "multidimensional"; the fracturing of his personality into Russian poet, émigré writer, welfare recipient and busboy is expressed by the structure of his autobiographical account. Just as critical criteria need to be reexamined to approach women's autobiography, Limonov's text requires the critic to disregard genre conventions of orderliness and harmony. Most significant, in this case, is the experience motivating the structure.

Limonov employs a wide variety of stylistic levels, including obscenities and barbarisms, in his pseudo-autobiography. His mixing of registers is regarded as weakness or simple sloppiness by some critics. Kustanovich, for example, is outraged by his joining words or phrases from distinct stylistic levels "not only within the boundaries of a single page or a single paragraph, but even a single sentence" ("Golyi korol'," 32). He also sharply criticizes what he perceives as non-Russian syntax and grammatical mistakes. The stylistic hash that Limonov has concocted in *It's Me, Eddie* is, however, a wonderfully appropriate medium to express the narrator's estrangement and insecurity. One of the losses he has endured as an émigré is that of language; in the present of the text he is detached from both Russian and American cultures and his linguistic usage reflects his rootlessness.

Flowery or elaborate imagery is notably rare in Limonov's stylistic blend. Limonov aims at a realistic rendering of Edichka's world through language; metaphorical elements are not a significant part of the experience he recounts in *It's Me, Eddie*. On the infrequent occasions when Edichka is moved to employ an expressive metaphor or simile, he includes mocking disclaimers. Edichka's description of Luz is accompanied by an apology for his attempt at eloquence: "She very much liked to smile at me, arching like – forgive me this very vulgar and trite simile, but she arched like the stem of a rose" (*Eto ia – Edichka*, p. 146). He surrenders unwillingly to the temptation to write lyrically in his description of Candida's children: "I shall allow myself a flourish: they were like coffee beans, like spices, her children were" (*ibid.*, p. 146). In a third passage, he chides himself for his triteness even as he writes: "I feel like saying the banal, and I will: 'girls with the eyes of little young lambs'" (*ibid.*, p. 218). Instances of beauty that inspire Edichka to express himself in elaborate images are uncommon in the gritty, bleak world of third wave emigration. In occasionally giving voice to his lyrical impulses, Limonov ironically underscores the rule to which they are the exception.

Several critics, including Matich and Il'ia Levin, consider Edichka's speech an apt rendering of the language of new

Russian immigrants.⁵⁶ The intrusion of a large number of barbarisms – especially anglicisms – in Limonov's text is amply motivated by verisimilitude. These have been enumerated and analyzed elsewhere.⁵⁷ Limonov's use of calques is frequently justified by semantics; there are no good Russian equivalents of *velfer*, *boi-frend/gerl-frend* and *basboi*. His employment of these terms reflects the strangeness of his environment for him and for his Russian readers. That Limonov often uses anglicisms or macaronic combinations when adequate Russian equivalents do exist complicates the issue; he chooses *parti*, *sobvei* and *rummeit* over *vecher* or *vecherinka*, *metro* and *tovarishch po komnate*. Such usage is not limited to the speech of third wave émigrés; in Limonov's case, it may have its origins in the Moscow hippie movement of the seventies. In any case, it implies a rejection of the Russian tradition of retaining the purity of the literary language.

Limonov's anglicisms have the effect of distancing the work from the Russian reader. Shukman suggests that they induce both visual and phonic shock, since they appear impossible and absurd to the Russian eye and ear ("Taboos, Splits and Signifiers," 10). However, Limonov's attitude toward English is far from completely positive. Felix Dreizin concludes from his analysis of Limonov's style that he abhors the English language and the American culture it represents. His syntax is made mechanical, according to Dreizin, to reflect the rigidity of the American character: "From the author's point of view, the repulsive content deserves an adequately ugly linguistic form" ("Russian Style," 62). Indeed there is some evidence for this in Edichka's paean to Spanish (of which he knows about two dozen words): "I would much rather study Spanish, on the whole. It is richer and more congenial to me, just as all Spanish-speaking people are more congenial to me than buttoned-up clerks in neckties, or disciplined, skinny secretaries" (*Eto ia – Edichka*, p. 151). He concludes his threats to the silent "gentlemen" (bourgeois businessmen in vulgar plaid pants) with the advice "pray God to keep me from mastering correct English as long as possible" (*ibid.*, p. 9).

Although he finds English uncongenial, Edichka associates

knowledge of it with the power to which he aspires. As in many works of childhood autobiography, calling things by their proper name constitutes a kind of possession of them. As the child's horizons broaden, his or her vocabulary and control of the environment increase. Thus Edichka's struggle with English recapitulates the archetypal child's gradual mastery of language, a sometimes alienating and confusing, but necessary step in his development (Coe, *When the Grass Was Taller*, pp. 253–66). The ironic twist in Edichka's case is that as a poet, he has an extraordinary command of his native language; that no one values his prior knowledge is an indictment of the conditions of emigration.

In order to describe more evocatively the experience of his first years of emigration, his second childhood, Limonov sometimes resorts to infantile language. He consistently uses the terms *popka* and *pipka* to refer to his and others' anatomy and he employs the childish expression "make pee-pee" (*delat' pi-pi*) for urination. With few exceptions, autobiographers of childhood have traditionally been compelled to convey the experience of the child in the language of adults (*ibid.*, pp. 83–84). Edichka's reversions to infantile language emphasize the uncomfortable closeness of the narrated self and the narrating self, the self-that-was and the self-that-is. His grip on "adulthood," here the security of belonging within a culture, is tenuous and continually threatens to loosen, throwing him back into chaos.

Limonov's use of Soviet propaganda clichés and journalese is troubling to some émigré readers. Geller ("Prigotovitel'nye zametki," 87) hears the cadences of Soviet radio in passages like the following:

It all started with Messrs. Sakharov, Solzhenitsyn, and company, who turned us against the Soviet world without ever having laid eyes on the Western world. They were prompted not only by specific purposes – the intelligentsia were demanding a part in governing the country, demanding their share – but also by pride, the desire to advertise themselves. As always in Russia, moderation was not observed. They may have been honestly deceived, Sakharov and Solzhenitsyn, but they deceived us too. Whatever the case, they were "dominant influences." (*Eto ia – Edichka*, p. 153)[58]

That Limonov applies this language to well-known anti-Soviet dissidents is, of course, particularly outrageous. However, as Donde has wisely observed, it is perfectly natural for Edichka to employ clichés that he has heard since childhood; indeed their illogicality is perfectly suited to his spontaneous, angry outbursts ("Eduard, Edik i Edichka," 13).

The presence of obscenities (*mat*) in *It's Me, Eddie* has been the focus of a great deal of controversy within the émigré community and more recently, in the former Soviet Union. Readers' and critics' reactions to his liberally sprinkling his text with taboo words have been quite extreme. On the one hand, his language has been reviled as vulgar and indecent. Geller charges him, moreover, with using *mat* in a heavy-handed, unimaginative way: "The great, powerful Russian *mat* has earned worldwide renown. But Edichka for some reason expresses himself extremely poorly – not in terms of quantity, but in terms of quality" ("Prigotovitel'nye zametki," 85). Kron suggests somewhat ingenuously that permitting the intrusion of *mat* into the literary language to the extent that Limonov does may impoverish oral speech; what will be left that is exclusive to this stylistic level, if *mat* becomes acceptable in print? ("Pro babochku," 90). Others see Limonov's text as a linguistic *tour de force*. Dreizin applauds his breaking of linguistic taboos, asserting that he employs *mat* like a virtuoso. His obscenities, to the extent that they are peculiarly Russian, are "an oasis of the author's national identity" ("Russian Style," 65).

Quite apart from issues of Limonov's skill in reproducing spoken *mat* and the appropriateness of non-normative elements in literature, Edichka's language is most effective as a means of expressing his childhood/émigré experience. Obscenities are essential to Limonov's art in that they permit Edichka to describe not only what his world looks like, but what it *feels* like. In this respect too, *It's Me, Eddie* parodies the conventions of childhood autobiography. Traditionally, language conveys the magic and wonder associated with the author's budding consciousness. Limonov subverts this convention by employing obscenities to express his ineffectuality, his helplessness and his frustration. Moreover, he often uses them impressionistically or inexactly (Coe, *When the Grass Was Taller*, p. 253) to reflect his irrational, angry response to the conditions of life in exile. Edichka's friend John speaks "viciously" in discussing class inequities in America: "'What's the name of that car?' I asked. 'Mercedes-Benz!' he replied. Staring at the car, he added, 'Fuckin' shit!'" (*Eto ia – Edichka*, p. 229). This is, perhaps, as forceful an indictment of capitalist inequality as any penned by Upton Sinclair. At any rate, it is linguistically and psychologically true to the milieu Limonov describes. As Shukman notes, Limonov's obscenities are "words used in an emotive function and without referential content: signifiers without signifieds" ("Taboos, Splits and Signifiers," 11). He closes his pseudo-autobiography with a purely obscene, irrational curse emblematic of all his pain, dislocation and angst: "'Fuck you, cocksucking bastards,' I say, and wipe away tears with my fist. Perhaps I'm addressing these words to the buildings around me. I don't know. 'Fuck you, cocksucking bastards! You can all go straight to hell!' I whisper" (*Eto ia – Edichka*, p. 281). The gesture of wiping his face with his fist and his whisper are powerful images of childhood grief. Thus Limonov superimposes the language of his first, Kharkov childhood on a reminiscence of his second, New York childhood.

CHAPTER 4

The family chronicle revisited: Dovlatov's Ours

> Before you is the history of our family. I hope it is sufficiently ordinary.
>
> Sergei Dovlatov: Ours

The satirical works of Sergei Dovlatov have found an enthusiastic and appreciative audience among Russians émigrés, Western readers and with *glasnost'*, his own compatriots. Dovlatov was born September 3, 1941 in Ufa, Bashkiria, where his parents had been evacuated during World War II. After his family's return to Leningrad in 1944, he spent his childhood and youth in that most Western of Soviet cities. Indeed, his work may be seen as an outgrowth of the Leningrad Prose movement of the sixties and seventies. His parents were both connected with the theater, his father as a director, his mother as an actress. Dovlatov himself has more than once commented on his unusual ethnic heritage; he was Jewish on his father's side and Armenian on his mother's side.

Reaching maturity during Khrushchev's Thaw, Dovlatov was a member of the disaffected and alienated post-War and post-Stalin generation. Like his literary peers Aksenov, Bitov and Voinovich, he rejected (implicitly if not explicitly) the tenets of socialist realism and sought inspiration in the gritty, sometimes seamy aspects of Soviet urban contemporaneity. The literary influences most clearly operative in his prose are Ernest Hemingway, Erich-Maria Remarque and J. D. Salinger, whom he read in translations that appeared during the Thaw period. Obvious traces of these Western influences aroused the wrath of cautious Soviet editors in the sixties; they paradoxically made his prose more accessible to his American audience following his emigration.[1]

Although he enrolled in Leningrad University to study Finnish in 1959, Dovlatov abandoned his philological studies after two years. In one of his last works, "The Subsidiary,"[2] he recounts the events leading up to his being dismissed from the university. These are connected far less with academic weakness than with a tempestuous first love affair. It seems safe to assume that this *povest'*, like Dovlatov's other works, is largely autobiographical, though the degree of fictionality is difficult to determine. In any case, both in "The Subsidiary" and in reality Dovlatov was drafted soon after leaving the university.

Dovlatov subsequently served as a guard of strict-security prison camps in the Komi Autonomous Republic from 1962 to 1965. The novel which resulted from this experience is *The Zone*, written in 1966 but published in the West in 1982 and in the Soviet Union in 1991. This was a highly controversial work, for Dovlatov's narrative perspective is diametrically opposed to that of other "camp writers." As Il'ia Serman has perceptively noted, "He saw and got to know the camp simultaneously from outside and from within, which no writer had yet accomplished. Hence his aphorism 'It's the same world on both sides of the forbidden zone' and consequently the same people" ("Teatr Sergeia Dovlatova," 143). Dovlatov's treatment of the camp theme focuses on the psychology of the prisoners and those who guard them. His thesis that little distinguishes the inmates from their guards is reiterated in *The Invisible Book*: "The police and the thieves have an extraordinary resemblance to each other. Special regime prisoners and camp supervisors are absurdly similar in all sorts of things: speech, style of thinking, folklore, aesthetic canons, and moral judgements. This is the result of the mutual influence on each other."[3] This stance, quite predictably, led a considerable portion of the dissident and émigré communities to regard Dovlatov with suspicion. Quite absurd rumors, e.g. that he had stood guard over Solzhenitsyn (who was imprisoned in the late forties and early fifties), circulated widely.

Returning to Leningrad after his military service, Dovlatov

completed his studies in the Faculty of Journalism and became a professional journalist. Journalism was, by all accounts, primarily a means of making a living for Dovlatov, both when he lived in the Soviet Union and after his emigration to the United States. While he worked for various newspapers in Leningrad, he simultaneously wrote stories and *povesti*, submitting them to journals and magazines for consideration. Aside from a few miniatures in *Krokodil* and brief, rather mediocre pieces in *Iunost'* and *Neva*, Dovlatov's literary prose remained unpublished in his homeland until *glasnost'*. According to Aleksei Zverev, the thought that only stories about the working class, such as that printed by *Iunost'*, could appear in the Soviet Union left Dovlatov disgusted, and he turned to *samizdat* channels.[4]

Although he was a latecomer, Dovlatov was nevertheless a member of the Leningrad literary group "City Folk" (*Gorozhane*), which also included Vladimir Maramzin, Igor' Efimov and Boris Vakhtin. These writers, consciously setting themselves in opposition to the Village Prose movement, cultivated a bohemian lifestyle in the sixties and seventies. Like many of his contemporaries in the Leningrad intelligentsia, Dovlatov experienced Americaphilism, enthusiastically adopting the external forms of American culture. America was, Dovlatov said in a 1984 interview "everything we didn't have. It was the land of cowboys, jeans, jazz, Coca-Cola, the sexual revolution, Hemingway."[5] Dovlatov's ultra-liberal literary affiliations, his unorthodox lifestyle and his lack of steady employment made him susceptible to charges of "social parasitism." It was to circumvent these charges that he became the literary secretary of Vera Panova, a well-established Soviet writer and, coincidentally, the mother of Boris Vakhtin.

In 1974, Dovlatov moved to Tallinn, Estonia in search of a more liberal atmosphere and better prospects for publication. While living in Tallinn, he wrote for the newspaper *Sovetskaia Estoniia*. His experiences in this capacity are recounted (and fictionalized) in *The Compromise*, published 1981 in the West and 1991 in the Soviet Union.[6] His attempts to break into literature, however, were unsuccessful. A book which had been accepted by the Estonian publishing house Eesti Raamat in 1975 was dropped as a result of an anti-dissident campaign, and Dovlatov returned to Leningrad the following year.

As early as the late sixties, Dovlatov's works were circulating in *samizdat*, and within a few years several pieces found their way to the West and appeared in *tamizdat*. His stories began to be published in leading émigré journals such as *Kontinent*, *Vremia i my* and *Ekho*. *The Invisible Book* came out in the West in 1977. Despite his trafficking in *samizdat* and *tamizdat*, Dovlatov was not a political dissident in the ordinary sense. His resorting to unofficial, underground channels was more a result of personal frustration with the conservative Soviet literary apparatus than a display of political principles.

In 1978, submitting to police harrassment and steady pressure to leave the country, Dovlatov emigrated to the West, following his wife and daughter. His decision was surely prompted by his arrest and brief imprisonment for parasitism and the dissemination of illegal literature (including his own works). He alludes to this experience in *Craft* by way of explaining his fondness for America: "After the Kaliaevskii Special Detention Center, I liked absolutely everything. And still do."[7] In *Ours*, he provides a telegraphic summary of the events leading up to his emigration: "The accusation of social parasitism and promoting dens of vice. The signed oath not to leave town while under investigation. Investigator Michalev. Some unexplained beatings at a police station. A series of broadcasts on the West German radio. Arrest and trial on Tolmachev Street. Nine days in Kaliaevskii Prison. Unexpected release. Summons to the Office of Emigration."[8] Thus Dovlatov became a member of the third wave of emigration, albeit a reluctant one.

After settling in New York in 1978, Dovlatov began to publish prolifically in émigré journals and newspapers such as *Posev*, *Al'manakh Panorama* and *Novoe russkoe slovo*. Blessed with a sonorous bass voice, he also found work at Radio Liberty broadcasting Russian-language programs. This latter role is also given to the autobiographical narrator of "The Subsidiary," who is charged (as was Dovlatov) with covering an émigré conference in Los Angeles for Radio Liberty. In 1980, he co-founded the weekly newspaper *Novyi amerikanets* with a small group of émigré friends. For the two years of the paper's existence, he served as editor-in-chief and contributed a regular column. These articles have been collected and published under the title *The March of the Lonely*; they provide a unique view into the splintered, often contentious world of Russian émigré life in America. In addition, Dovlatov recounts the story of the conception, genesis and ultimate disintegration of the newspaper in *The Invisible Newspaper*.[9] Its demise was largely due, according to Dovlatov, to the jealous protectionism of *Novoe russkoe slovo*, the New York émigré paper which enjoyed a virtual monopoly for several decades. Dovlatov's iconoclastic position within the émigré community was reinforced by the impact of his literary works, which began appearing with considerable frequency in the early eighties. These were judged by many émigré critics to be excessively "light" and lacking in ideological substance, conclusions with which Dovlatov himself mockingly concurred: "I understand that my judgments are rather trivial. Not for nothing did Vail' and Genis pronounce me 'the troubadour of intensified banality.' I'm not offended. Indeed there is now an extreme shortage of commonplace truths."[10]

Nevertheless, Dovlatov enjoyed far greater success as a satirical writer in the United States than in his homeland. In a little over a decade, he published eleven books, many of which were translated and subsequently issued by major presses. Several stories and excerpts from larger works were printed in *The New Yorker*; this was, with the possible exception of Iosif Brodskii's case, an unprecedented coup for a third wave Russian émigré writer. His prose elicited the praise of American writers such as Kurt Vonnegut and Joseph Heller and in 1986, he received the Pen Club prize for the best story of the year.

In evaluating his success in America, it is important to appreciate his attitude toward his adopted homeland. As Serman notes, Dovlatov was more interested in understanding America than in judging it ("Teatr Sergeia Dovlatova," 155). Certainly his ability and willingness to adapt to circumstances served him well in this regard. Moreover, America provided rich resources for his satirical sensibility. Dovlatov's significant innovation was to see America as it is, in all its puzzling complexity, its beauty and its ugliness. America has quite frequently found reflection in Russian literature, most prominently in the period of the Thaw.[11] But it is with Dovlatov that we are afforded a privileged view simultaneously from within (as an immigrant and permanent resident) and from without (as a recent arrival who does not speak English and only marginally grasps cultural nuances).[12] He elaborates upon his attitude toward America in *The March of the Lonely*:

My interrelationships with America are divided into three stages. At the beginning everything was wonderful. Freedom, abundance, benevolence. All the groceries you could want. All the publishing houses you could want. More than enough newspapers and magazines. Then everything was terrible. Got tired of chicken gizzards. Got tired of jeans. Publishing houses print all kinds of nonsense. And they don't pay the authors. And then there is crime. And inflation. And then those endless bills, invoices, accounts, payments... And then everything became normal. Life is full of bitterness and joy. There is both the funny and the sad, the good and the bad in it. And the saleswomen are of various kinds (which is completely natural). And there are criminals, as there are everywhere. And for one, let's say, Brodskii, there are at least forty graphomaniacs. Which is also completely natural... And the main crises, naturally, happen inside a person, and not outside. And as before fools are lucky. And as before you can't buy happiness for money. The surrounding world is normal. Isn't that what we were striving for?[13]

It is, in all likelihood, Dovlatov's openness to America, his acceptance of its quirks and conundrums, that made his works accessible and meaningful to Western audiences and assured his success in American publishing.

With *glasnost'*, Dovlatov returned to his homeland in print (though he himself never revisited Russia). That his emigration was retrospectively justified and even lauded by Russian literary critics is symptomatic of the prevailing attitude toward "returnees" under *glasnost'*. Zverev speculates that he was particularly sensitive to the atmosphere of the seventies that bred "absurdity, incoherence, confusion, hopelessness, weariness" ("Zapiski," 69). Andrei Ar'ev cites ideological pressure as the cause of his departure from the Soviet Union and praises his stance of moral resistance.[14] Iunna Morits considers his emigration logical and necessary, arguing that "no contemporary writer can live where he is not published. And even if he lives there, all the same he cannot."[15] Virtually all of Dovlatov's works have been published in the former Soviet Union, including excerpts of a work tentatively called *The Refrigerator*, upon which the author was working at the time of his death.[16]

He has belatedly been claimed as a genuine Russian writer and identified specifically as a member of the Leningrad Prose movement. Some critics, such as Zverev and Viacheslav Kuritsyn, maintain that Dovlatov's focus is exclusively Russian and that America is quite beside the point. Stressing the nostalgic elements of his work, they interpret his treatment of the third wave as tragic, downplaying or ignoring its comic and satirical aspects.[17] While these claims are comprehensible in light of the historical circumstances and the specific point of view of these critics, Dovlatov actually transcends nationalist labels and delimiting definitions. His appeal to Western audiences may be quite different from his appeal to Russian readers, but it is none the less valid. Following Dovlatov's sudden death in August 1990, an obituary mourning the loss of a writer only recently rediscovered and appreciated appeared in *Literaturnaia gazeta*.[18]

Dovlatov's stated intention in writing *Ours* was to record a history of his extended family. In the closing chapter, he concludes "Before you is the history of our family. I hope it is sufficiently ordinary" (*Nashi*, p. 220). The English translation of the book is subtitled "A Russian Family Album" and the work is structured as a series of portraits of several generations of Dovlatov's relatives. The chronology of the text extends from the author's own prehistory to his future (in the person of his infant son). This "stratification" of time is a typical feature of the genre of the family chronicle. It is both a structural principle and, according to an investigator of the American family chronicle, a "method of discovering whatever meaning lies folded away in its characters' lives."[19] As is true of most examples of this genre, three generations of the chronicler's family constitute the object of his attention in the text. The opening chapter of *Ours*, "Grampa Isaak," is the most remote in time; commencing with the story of the narrator's grandparents constitutes a genre marker, a "signal that before us is a family chronicle."[20] In a parallel fashion, the closing chapter, a brief paragraph about the narrator's young son born after his emigration, looks forward to the future and leaves the chronicle open-ended.[21]

Despite this structure within which the narrator moves his lens from one family member to another in succession, his primary focus remains himself. His presence, his reactions, his interpretations and his experiences provide unity in the text. His voice is the glue that holds this rather eclectic family album together. Nevertheless, he must sometimes rely on others' eyewitness reports and documentary evidence. Although he does not explain how he came to know their contents, he describes the letters exchanged by his father and his Uncle Leopol'd, who left the Soviet Union when he was young (presumably in the late twenties or early thirties). He recounts the anecdotes about famous writers – quite possibly apocryphal – told to him and to others by his aunt, a literary editor:

> She had a very good memory. Many of the stories she told have stayed with me to this day. Such as this one: She happened to meet Mikhail Zoshchenko on the street. The difficult time of official disfavor had already begun for him. Zoshchenko turned his head and quickly walked past her. My aunt caught up with him and asked, "Why didn't you say hello to me?" Zoshchenko grinned and said, "Forgive me. I'm trying to make it easy for my friends not to talk to me." My aunt edited Iurii German, Kornilov, Seifullina, even Aleksei Tolstoi. She had something to tell about each of them. (*Nashi*, p. 162)

The narrator uses passive verbs to recount the discovery of the secret of his cousin Boria's paternity: "When my aunt fell ill and died, a portrait of a gray-eyed, handsome man was found in her papers..." (*ibid.*, p. 103).[22] It is not clear whether he himself was present for this event, but it is ultimately not important. This is family lore to which the narrator has become privileged by his heritage and the reader grants it as much credibility as Dovlatov's own eyewitness accounts.

The genre of the family chronicle, although quite widely used in Russian literature, has received scant scholarly attention. S. Mashinskii, in his discussion of Aksakov's *Family Chronicle* (1856), notes that giving the work this title was a tacit refusal to allow readers and critics an exact genre definition.[23] In the 1840s, portraiture predominated in Russian literature; gradually, over the next decade, the idea that human processes of growth, discovery and interaction could be fruitfully portrayed in the novel began to take hold. The span of the novelist's attention was broadened to include the entire birth–death cycle of his heroes and heroines. Childhood experience in the formation of character became an object of fictional attention.[24] Tolstoi's *Childhood* (1852) and Aksakov's *Family Chronicle* and *Childhood Years* (1858) are early examples of the Russian family chronicle. Later in the nineteenth century Leskov adopted the genre in his *Old Times in the Village of Plodomasov* (1869) and *A Decrepit Clan* (1874). Saltykov-Shchedrin's *Golovlev Family* (1880) and *Old Days in Poshekhonie* (1887–89) also take the form of family chronicles. There were indeed many works of this type published in the nineteenth century; according to Andrew Wachtel, at least five bore the subtitle "A Family Chronicle" (*Battle for Childhood*, p. 63).

The popularity of the genre in this period reflected increased interest in historical themes and memoir literature in general. In combining these elements, the family chronicle often treated minor, personal aspects of history. Family chroniclers dealt with lives and events peripheral to the major, sweeping changes occurring in the same time frame. Dovlatov's *Ours* observes this tradition as well, as the narrator provides only the sketchiest historical framework. The events of World War II are allotted only a sentence: "In the next few years, a great deal happened: war, victory, yet another flare-up of terror."[25] The post-Thaw years are recounted with similar lack of detail:

The country was ruled by a bunch of nondescript, faceless leaders. A depressing, colorless uniformity held sway in the arts. On the other hand, father would point out, people were not being shot, or even imprisoned. Well, they were sent to prison, yes, but not so often. At any rate, if they were, it was for some concrete action, or at least for some imprudent public remark. That is, for a reason. Not the way things used to be. (*Nashi*, p. 180)

Dovlatov, like his literary predecessors Aksakov, Saltykov-Shchedrin and others,[26] can limit his treatment of major historical events to brief synopses and concentrate on his personal history because the reader is already conversant with the spatiotemporal background of his text. World War II and the atmosphere of the "time of stagnation" are well enough known to Soviet and Western readers not to need elaboration; brief asides are sufficient to evoke rich complexes of associations.

Another reason for the popularity of the family chronicle in the mid-1800s that has relevance to our understanding of Dovlatov's text is the appearance of the literary "little man." With the Natural School and the rise of Russian Realism, the simple man became an interesting and novel object of exploration. Moreover, the choice of a "little man" protagonist could suggest implicit criticism of the *status quo*. As Mashinskii observes, "the contradiction between the individual and the ruling system was for progressive circles of Russian society the most striking expression of the tragic disorder of contemporary reality."[27] Dovlatov's narrator and his extended family are, he stresses, ordinary people in the Soviet context. Although far removed in terms of time and, more importantly, political framework, they too embody alienation and disaffection.

Between its peak in the nineteenth century and its revival with Dovlatov's work, the family chronicle underwent a period of decline and neglect. Interest in the genre waned in the late 1800s, but was briefly revived in the revolutionary period. Works such as Bunin's "Sukhodol" (1911) and I. S. Rukavishnikov's *Four Centuries* (1914) signaled a minor rebirth of the form, but the prevailing theme of these and similar works was quite different than that of earlier examples. The disintegration and breaking up of gentry families and the inescapability of class heritage became leitmotifs of the early twentieth-century family chronicle.[28] Following this brief revival, the family chronicle lost its distinctive features and merged with more established genres such as the novel, the *povest'*, the short story and the autobiography.

Fictionality has been a traditional feature of the family chronicle since the nineteenth century. Tolstoi's *Childhood* can best be called an "imaginative reconstruction of the past,"[29] and Aksakov continued this blending of fact and fiction in his works. In Dovlatov's text too, the broad sequence of events he recounts corresponds more or less to that of his own family's history. The veracity of the details of his account, however, is by no means a foregone conclusion. As is the case with Leskov's *Old Times in the Village of Plodomasov*, the family chronicle form may be utilized to give the illusion of factual, documentary accuracy (Mashinskii, *S. T. Aksakov*, p. 210). Thus truth and invention merge imperceptibly, and it is difficult if not impossible to ascertain their boundaries. *Ours* occupies middle ground between history and pseudo-autobiography; its apparent authenticity encourages the reader to accept it as documentary, but its status as fiction leaves the issue unresolved and ambiguous.

In fact, the family chronicle has traditionally occupied a position on the fringes of *belles-lettres* in Russian literary culture. The genre is extraordinarily plastic and flexible, allowing tremendous freedom to the individual author in the application of its conventions. As E. P. Viduetskaia notes, "the boundaries of this literary form are mobile, they fluctuate from memoiristic sketches to the novel" ("*Poshekhonskaia starina*," p. 217). Its very marginality accords with Dovlatov's informal, journalistic style.

Before examining Dovlatov's satirical adaptation of this genre, we should consider the function of the family chronicle in the Russian tradition. In the nineteenth century, the family chronicle was a vehicle of testament and preservation of Russian culture. Ostensibly historical narratives provided pictures of a bygone era in encyclopedic detail for present and future generations. Certainly Slavophilism played a significant role in this view of the genre; according to Andrew Durkin, Slavophilism sought "to elaborate an indigenous past to validate its claims of being the truly Russian intellectual movement" (*Sergei Aksakov*, p. 90). Thus the family chronicle purported to present a representative but particularly crucial slice of time within a historical continuum. The events recorded acquired additional significance through their links to past and future events.[30]

This temporal perspective may give the family chronicle protreptic, prescriptive resonance. Aksakov, in concluding his *Family Chronicle*, stresses this aspect of his work when he addresses his characters:

> You are not great heroes, not famous personalities; in silence and in obscurity you spent your earthly existence and long ago, very long ago left it. But you were people, and your outer and inner life is as full of poetry, as curious and *instructive* for us, as we and our life in turn will be curious and *instructive* for our descendants. (emphasis added)[31]

The reader presumably has the opportunity to learn from the behavior (positive and negative) of earlier generations and to benefit morally. Underlying the didactic aspect of the genre is considerable generalizing potential. The characters portrayed in nineteenth-century and early twentieth-century family chronicles and the stages of life through which they pass have archetypal significance. They represent classes of Russian society and more broadly, the evolution and fate of Russian culture (Gracheva, "'Semeinye khroniki'," 65; Mashinskii, "O memuarno-avtobiograficheskom zhanre," 136). The specific, eccentric qualities of the family members portrayed are thus subordinated in this view of the genre to their general, representative elements.

Conversely, the family chronicle served in the past as a means of delving into the writer's self, his or her individual nature. As in autobiography or pseudo-autobiography (gaining in popularity in the middle of the nineteenth century as well), tracing one's ancestry was a way to understand the forces that shaped one's personality and character. Generational continuity affects the individual, so that the act of writing a family chronicle may be an exercise in self-discovery (or self-invention). Soviet critics tend to downplay or eschew this psychological aspect of the genre. Mashinskii, for example, praises Herzen's *My Past and Thoughts* for demonstrating the evolution of the personality as a result of complex interactions with historical phenomena (*S. T. Aksakov*, p. 367).

In *Ours*, Dovlatov subverts and parodies these canonical aspects of the family chronicle genre even as he adopts them. He relies on the reader's knowledge of nineteenth-century models in reshaping their form and content to his own ends. Tolstoi's *Childhood*, Aksakov's *Family Chronicle* and *Childhood Years*, and Saltykov-Shchedrin's *Golovlev Family* are probably the best-known examples of the genre. As we have seen, Dovlatov's chronicle shares with them an autobiographical quality, a structure of a series of character portraits and a chronology spanning the author's own prehistory to his present. Certainly it is not Dovlatov's purpose to mock or ridicule these models themselves. Instead, he adopts the external features of the genre in order to underscore and emphasize the significant ways in which his version departs from the "norm." The operative technique Dovlatov employs in *Ours*, then, is parody in the sense of repetition with critical distance. That is, the reader's expectations are engaged by the use of the recognizable genre conventions of the family chronicle. These expectations are then thwarted when it becomes apparent that the similarities between *Ours* and its nineteenth-century models are quite superficial. Much more important for appreciating the satirical effect of Dovlatov's work are the divergences, the ways in which *Ours* pointedly resists conforming to genre canon.

The targets of Dovlatov's satire are in fact peculiarly twentieth-century phenomena linked to the specific milieu of Soviet culture. His choice of the family chronicle genre is felicitous in this respect, since the models on which he relies tend to depict an idyllic, pastoral world vanished with the passing of the Russian gentry in the late nineteenth century. The past and present of Dovlatov's text are, on the other hand, the bleak and oppressive years of Stalin's and Brezhnev's respective reigns. The ample potential for contrast in terms of the political, material and spiritual parameters of these radically different Russian societies is richly exploited by Dovlatov. The vast distance between the norms established by the models he poses and the parallel features of his own chronicle emphasizes the foibles and the perversities of Soviet reality.

The family chronicle revisited

Ours is neither explicitly nor implicitly didactic. Dovlatov's family chronicle is satirically critical, but no prescriptions or antidotes are offered for the negative phenomena he exposes. As Kuritsyn notes in a review of his prose, "Dovlatov is very far from any kind of moralizing, he does not intend at all to teach anyone how to live" ("Vesti iz filiala," 41). In relating the story of his grandfather Stepan, for example, Dovlatov paints a portrait of a stern, irascible, often domineering man without condemnation. He emphasizes the quirky, humorous aspects of his behavior in his account and manages to render him sympathetic. Similarly, his references to his own and his family's future are ironic and skeptical, but never ominous. Having told the story of his mad uncle Roman, he ponders rhetorically "Whither, O Lord?" (*Nashi*, p. 153). In closing his chronicle, he looks to the future with self-deprecation and pragmatism: "It's not likely I'll become an American rock singer. Or a movie star. Or a drug dealer. It's doubtful I'll ever get rich enough to shield [my daughter] from material worries" (*ibid.*, p. 219). Dovlatov's brief account of his son's birth in New York suggests his cautious optimism in regard to the future, but this is not overt or prescriptive.

Underlying Dovlatov's satire in *Ours* is, instead of a protreptic motive, a desire to understand. In this respect, his family chronicle resembles Babel′'s cycle of childhood stories. It is with the same kind of ironic introspection that Babel′ delves into his memories of his eccentric, unlucky family to understand himself. Dovlatov searches the lives of his ancestors to find the sources of his behavior, his appearance and his character.[32] He explains some of his own eccentricities as an inheritance from his grandfather Isaak:

I often think of my grandfather, though I never knew him. For instance, if one of my friends says in surprise, "How can you drink rum out of a teacup?" I immediately think of Grandpa. Or my wife may say to me, "Tonight we're going to the Dombrovskiis for supper. We should get you something to eat beforehand." Again he comes to mind. He also came to mind when I was in a prison cell... I have a few photographs of Grandpa. When my grandchildren leaf through the family album, it won't be hard for them to mistake us for one another. (*Nashi*, p. 146)

The reference to his arrest and imprisonment links Dovlatov's fate with that of his grandfather and adds a solemn note to an otherwise quite frivolous catalogue of shared qualities. An element of catharsis, though unobtrusive, is nevertheless discernible in Dovlatov's effort to chronicle his past.

By and large, the satiric tonality of *Ours* is Horatian, reflecting Dovlatov's conviction that the role of the satirist is criticism and exposure precluding caustic ridicule and vituperation. In *A Foreign Woman*, the narrator explicitly justifies his passing over certain events in silence as resisting the urge to calumniate: "... we always want to show what's funny, humiliating, stupid and pathetic, to curse and swear. That's a sin."[33] There are exceptions to this rule of restraint in *Ours*, notably in Dovlatov's treatment of particularly egregious examples of injustice and brutality perpetrated by the Soviet state. In respect to individual human failings and weaknesses, however, his attitude is consistently one of bemused mockery. To quote the narrator of *A Foreign Woman* once again, "There are things more important than justice ... specifically, mercy" (*ibid.*, p. 80). Dovlatov's satire has been called "Chaplinesque" and has been compared to that of Milan Kundera for its "gentle black humor."[34] Nevertheless, the crucial distinction between satire and humor is maintained in his prose generally and in *Ours* specifically; Dovlatov underscores the difference metaphorically in "The Subsidiary": "My mother says that once I used to wake up with a smile on my face. This was, one must suppose, in about 1943. Imagine – all around war, bombers, the evacuation, and I lie and smile... Now everything is different. For about twenty years now I have been waking up with a disgusting grimace on my neglected physiognomy."[35] Dovlatov's narrator in *Ours*, like the narrators of his other works, observes and comments wryly on the world around him without drawing definitive, negative conclusions. His sympathies lie with the eccentric, flawed, often ridiculous characters whom he recreates (or creates) and the reader's sympathies are elicited as well.

Ours, for all its quirkiness, does have the potential of

typification and generalization common to earlier examples of the family chronicle genre. Dovlatov presents his clan as an average Russian intelligentsia family of the twentieth century. His aim, however, is quite unlike that of nineteenth-century chroniclers, who attempted to idealize or preserve the past. He recounts his family's being scarred by the Stalinist purges, poisoned by anti-Semitism and compelled to make moral compromises. Zverev, in noting the commonality of experience that underlies *Ours*, writes "... we read in his stories about ourselves, because, for better or worse, we belong to that time and there is no hiding from it, even if we want to" ("Zapiski," 67).

Recounting his uncle Aron's peripatetic life and wild swings of political conviction, Dovlatov points out "The biography of my aunt's husband, Aron, fully reflects the history of our government" (*Nashi*, p. 48). Growing up in tsarist Russia, he became a radical student, a Red Army soldier (presumably during the Revolution), then fought on both sides in the Civil War. Following the Civil War, he studied in a workers' university program, became a NEPman, helped dispossess kulaks and carry out the purges and finally, fell victim to the purges himself. His life is as inconsistent and contrary as that of Russia in the early twentieth century and thus comes to represent, in miniature, the fate of the Soviet people. Dovlatov's own ambivalence toward his heritage is expressed in the conclusion of his portrait of his uncle: "As I said, my uncle's biography reflects the whole recent history of our country, of our *beloved and awful* land" (emphasis added) (*ibid.*, p. 170).

Dovlatov's experiences of growing disillusionment with the Soviet system, vacillation and finally, emigration are tragically common in his generation. His becoming *persona non grata* as a result of his *samizdat* and *tamizdat* activities, his being fired and harrassed, his painful decision to leave all take on a generalized quality in the telling. Moreover, Dovlatov pointedly rejects delimiting spatial and temporal parameters in concluding his chronicle. He insists that his son's history "will be the history of another, American family"[36] and this is not necessarily a tragedy or a loss. In creating an antipode to the traditional

Russian family chronicle, Dovlatov revises the specifically nationalist elements of his models and broadens their scope. Paradoxically, the typicality of *Ours* lies in its chronicling the experiences of alienation and departure (metaphorical or actual) from Russia and the establishment of a new life in exile (internal or external).

Structurally, *Ours* resembles a cycle of stories, linking it to such notable literary predecessors as the *Decameron* and *A Thousand and One Nights* (Ar'ev, "Teatralizovannyi realizm," 20).[37] A more immediate precedent for this structure in a satirical work can be found in some of Saltykov-Shchedrin's works. Dovlatov, like Saltykov-Shchedrin, clearly found the blurry distinctions between the cycle and the chronicle congenial to his publicistic bent:

> The chronicle in its genre structure is generally very close to the cycle, inasmuch as it can be a series of sketches, connected only by a single narrator. Like the cycle, the chronicle does not require a consistent plot and the conclusion of events. The presence of a main protagonist, around whom the action is concentrated in a novel of the usual type, is not necessary. (Viduetskaia, "*Poshekhonskaia starina*," p. 218)[38]

The chapters of *Ours*, like those of most cycles, are discrete literary entities and can stand independently. In fact, a number of them were originally published separately as sketches or short stories. Each portrait treats the life and fate of one individual centrally (though others are connected peripherally). *Ours* has little plot as such and is, like any family chronicle, left open-ended in the sense that the narrator's life is unfinished.

None of this is to suggest that *Ours* lacks unity. Taken as a whole, the work has the structural coherence of a *povest'*.[39] The narrative voice of the work is very consistent, and the component portraits are further unifed by recurrent stylistic features. Characters who reappear serve to link rather disparate events. Perhaps most importantly, *Ours* is characterized by "a central vision,"[40] in this case nostalgia significantly tinged with irony. The stories that comprise *Ours* are not so much consecutive developments as variations on a theme, additional illustrations of the narrator's perception of his (and his country's) past. As the building blocks of the cycle-chronicle, these stories introduce additional information about events and characters already described and provide commentary on one another.

The structure of the whole depends, of course, on the arrangement of the component stories. Dovlatov's family portraits are arranged in roughly chronological order, but in addition to the principle of chronolinearity, considerations of comparison and contrast are operative in *Ours*. The parallel stories of the narrator's grandfathers that open the work, for example, illustrate the two distinct sides of his past and the diverse sources of his character. Grandfather Isaak, his paternal grandfather, was a Jew from the Far East who bankrupted the family's business, served in the tsar's Guards, settled down as a manager for a housing office, and ended by being arrested and executed on trumped-up charges of being a Belgian spy. Despite his great size and strength, Grandfather Isaak was peaceable; Dovlatov calls his life, so senselessly cut short, "daft and amusing" (*Nashi*, p. 146). Grandfather Stepan,[41] the patriarch of his mother's side of the family, represents the narrator's Caucasian heritage. Taciturn and tyrannical, he spent his life as a salesman and co-owner of a clothing store in Tbilisi and walked off into a ravine when he tired of old age and decrepitude. That Dovlatov begins his family chronicle with parallel portraits of his grandfathers is in accordance with genre convention. What is unusual is that neither of these figures is epic in a traditional sense and neither would appear to be a serious contender for the role of "embodying the creative force of the family" (Gracheva, "'Semeinye khroniki'," 66). Dovlatov thus parodies the device as he makes use of it, emphasizing the unorthodoxy of his own contribution to the genre.

Following the portraits of his grandfathers, Dovlatov provides sketches of two of his uncles, Roman and Leopol'd. These parallel stories are illustrative of alternative ways of coping with life's travails. Specifically, his uncles' stories suggest two possible modes of reacting to the disaffection and alienation endemic to the generation that came to maturity under Stalin. Roman, the narrator's maternal uncle, becomes neurotic and paranoid, suspecting everyone around him of complicity in an ill-defined plot. Dovlatov's paternal uncle Leopol'd, on the other hand, withdraws physically from a society he finds uncongenial and hostile; he emigrates and assimilates, becoming a successful businessman in Belgium. Although Roman ostensibly becomes well again after his stay in a psychiatric hospital and Leopol'd presumably finds happiness selling lumber and building materials, Dovlatov presents both his uncles' fates in a sad, ironic light. Neither of the alternatives they represent is very attractive.

The chapter called "Glasha," in which Dovlatov provides a portrait of the family dog, constitutes a lighthearted satiric diminution of genre canon. Domestic animals have certainly been included in family chronicles before, but rarely have they taken on a literary status equal to that of other family members. Glasha, like her owners, has a fully developed personality and accompanies them in exile. Furthermore, Dovlatov adroitly juxtaposes this sketch to one called "The Colonel Says I Love You." The former has purely personal interest and illustrates the difficult emotional experiences connected with emigration. The latter recounts the intrusion of the state into the delicate decision-making process, as an anonymous KGB colonel pressures Dovlatov to leave the Soviet Union and join his family in the West.

Finally, the presence of the fragment entitled "Kolia," with which *Ours* closes, is justified by the cyclical structure of the work. This extremely brief sketch is an exception to the rule that the component chapters of *Ours* are independent stories. However, it emphasizes the open-endedness of the text and the forward-looking perspective of the narrator, as it focuses on the future, embodied in the person of the narrator's American-born infant son.

Dovlatov is at pains to provide linkage between the strands of his chronicle. Often the chronology of successive stories is interwoven and overlapping, complicating the broader, basically chronolinear structure of the text. At the beginning of the chapter "Uncle Leopol'd," the narrator writes "His fate excited my imagination for many long years, though that's all over now" (*Nashi*, p. 153). He simultaneously introduces an element of suspense and a note of anticlimax, underscoring his own distance (temporal, spatial and emotional) from the events to be related. Uncle Leopol'd's emigration and subsequent contacts with his family are recounted in the first chapter, but references to these events recur elsewhere in the text, serving as echoes of his grandfather's absurdly unjust fate. Similarly, asides concerning the narrator's own emigration are scattered throughout the text, reminding the reader of the centrality of the motifs of loss and separation.

The stories that comprise *Ours* frequently end with a leap in chronology into the narrator's present. "Mother" closes with an account of the narrator's leaving the Soviet Union accompanied by his mother and his dog; he then skips intervening events in America, concluding cryptically "Now we live in New York, and we'll never part. Just as we never parted before, even when I went away for a long time" (*ibid.*, p. 176). "Father" also ends on a minor note that brings the narration up to the present time: "After we had been in the United States for a year, my father came. He settled in New Jersey. He plays bingo. Everything's normal. There is no applause to wait for, from anywhere" (*ibid.*, p. 182). Viduetskaia notes that one of the functions of the family chronicle is to contrast the past with the present ("*Poshekhonskaia starina*," p. 212) and these endings are particularly effective in this sense. By concluding his accounts of his relatives' eccentric and unsettled lives in the Soviet Union with such abrupt shifts into an alien milieu, Dovlatov emphasizes the themes of disjuncture and loss that inform *Ours*. Perhaps the most poignant use of this device is the end of the chapter "My First Cousin," that recounts the adventures of the narrator's recidivist cousin Boris. Having refused to emigrate with the narrator's family, Boris sends a package of souvenirs to his relatives and the narrator interprets these and past gifts from his cousin as metaphors for emotional links irrevocably severed: "I thought to myself, What were the most precious things I ever got in my life? And I realized: four pieces of lump sugar, Japanese cigarettes called Hi-Lites, and now this corkscrew. I covered my face with my hands. I understood that I was alone" (*Nashi*, p. 198).[42] Despite the pathos evoked in these passages, this device contributes to the generally satiric tone of the text as a whole. Beneath the narrator's ambiguity about the present and the mild sense of nostalgia for a more familiar way of life lies a serious indictment of the conditions that made life unbearable in his homeland.

As is true of any family chronicle, the memoiristic quality of *Ours* enhances the verisimilitude of the text. Dovlatov endows all of his texts, and especially his "family album," with many autobiographical elements, and it is tempting to read the work as straightforward history. Yet there are a number of considerations that militate against such a reading and remind us of its primarily belletristic character. E. Tudorovskaia points out the distinction in a review of *Craft*; her words could easily apply to *Ours* as well:

> The author himself speaks in the role of the main hero; moreover, in the first part the names and events of real life are in general given. This should convince the reader of the truth of what is depicted ... unreal, unlikely Soviet reality, the witnesses and victims of which were the author and his writer friends. But what they are like, these witnesses, and what the course of events was like – this is already literature. The truth here is artistic, and not memoiristic, and that should be kept in mind.[43]

One effect of Dovlatov's utilizing autobiographical details is the creation of a sense of sincerity and shared intimacy. More importantly in terms of the satirical motivation of the text, this technique demonstrates the author's conviction that the reality he describes is farcical and absurd in and of itself; invention and hyperbole are superfluous. This is not to say that invention and hyperbole are absent from the text. Rather Dovlatov seeks to minimize our apprehension of these by employing the trappings of autobiography.

Moreover, the narrator of *Ours* undercuts his own veracity, playfully reminding us that we believe in the literal historical truth of his text at our peril. He includes highly improbable, mythical accounts of some events, such as the "incident from life" told by a prison guard. One of his prisoners, he maintains, used a pine tree and rigging belt to catapult himself to freedom. Having told this tall tale, he concludes with a detail that he says is "pure literature: When they grabbed him, he bit the commanding officer on the nose" (*Nashi*, p. 193). This last element is, of course, no more unlikely than the rest of the story, so that the distinctions between truth and legend are completely obscured. Dovlatov's accounts of his grandfather Isaak's feats of strength (heard secondhand) are similarly improbable, but they are so closely intertwined with realistic details of his life that it is virtually impossible to be sure where truth ends and where myth begins. The narrator himself points out the illusory nature of his "truth," implicitly insisting on his right to create family legend as much as to record and preserve it.

The events of large-scale, public history alternate rapidly with those of the narrator's own private history in *Ours*. This is, as we have noted, a canonical feature of the family chronicle genre, but there are particular, satirical motivations for Dovlatov's application of this device. In recounting the evolution of his father's political outlook, for example, he closely intertwines the public with the personal:

The years went by. I was growing up. The Great Leader was debunked. Grandpa's name was rehabilitated, as they say. My father again took heart. It seemed to him that the third and final act of the life drama was beginning, and now Good would finally triumph. One might even say it already had. He married for the second time. A nice young woman technician had fallen in love with him. She may have taken him for a brilliant eccentric. That kind of thing sometimes happens. In short, things were getting better. The play had regained its lost momentum. The long-breached rules of classical drama were being restored. And then what happened? Nothing much. The country was ruled by a bunch of nondescript, faceless leaders. (*Ibid.*, p. 180)

His father, though particularized, represents his generation's ambivalence, for his world view is colored by the historical events that transpire in his lifetime. This technique of mingling the public and private sides of life also affects the reader's perception of the scale and significance of the former. Events that have traditionally been treated by Soviet (and Western) historians and propagandists as grandiose, heroic and epic are diminished. World War II, the siege of Leningrad and the renewal of Stalinist terror after the war are covered in two sentences in Dovlatov's chronicle; they are mentioned chiefly as background to the more immediately relevant events of deaths and divorce. The life of a family, Dovlatov reminds us, is played out against the backdrop of national disasters and crises, but has its own internal rhythm as well.

Another stylistic peculiarity of Dovlatov's text is the frequent intrusion of anecdotal digressions. These include accounts of Uncle Roman's failing his entrance exams to the university, an inexplicable, brutal attack on Aunt Galina, his father's receiving a mysterious package from his brother Leopol'd, the arrival and departure of an importunate "nonrelative" from the provinces, and many others. Often these digressions begin with catchy leads, a carryover from Dovlatov's journalistic praxis: "One of my grandfather's duels with God ended in a draw" (*ibid.*, p. 147); "His second duel with God ended tragically" (*ibid.*, p. 148); "Before his eighteenth birthday, he had brought off his first genuine scam. It happened like this..." (*ibid.*, p. 147). It is worth noting that most of these anecdotes do little to advance the plot of the stories or chapters in which they are included. Indeed, some of them closely resemble the apocryphal miniatures that comprise Dovlatov's collection *Solo on the Underwood*. The dialogue that he recounts between Aunt Mara and Ol'ga Forsh, for example, is of this sort:

One time Ol'ga Forsh was at a resort for writers and was looking through the "complaint book." She found the following entry: "We keep finding all kinds of forest insects in the kasha. Not long ago at supper I came upon a large horned beetle." "What do you think?" Forsh asked my aunt. "Was it a grievance or a note of appreciation?" (*Ibid.*, p. 162)

What these anecdotal digressions do accomplish is characterization, enrichment of the portraits Dovlatov is painting in his album. In addition, they enhance the impression that absurdity and incongruity are normative features of Soviet life.

Dovlatov's character portraits are on one hand larger than

life. His ancestors in particular tend to be endowed with epic qualities of physical strength and honor.[44] His grandfather Isaak is almost seven feet tall and capable of dragging artillery cannons and turning over trucks single-handedly. He speculates that his grandfather Stepan was morose because of his dissatisfaction with "the changing of the seasons... the indestructible order of life and death... the law of gravity... the contradiction of sea and dry land" (*Nashi*, p. 148). His cousin gains notoriety for urinating on an unpopular teacher and later distinguishes himself by committing twelve robberies. Folk motifs are discernible in these characterizations, especially in that of Grandfather Isaak. Like a mythical *bogatyr'*, he eats hugely and accomplishes feats of superhuman strength. Furthermore, he has three sons, whose lives and fates are recounted by Dovlatov in fairy-tale fashion. These legends provide contrast, so that the distance between the heroic past and the more mundane present becomes palpable. Finally, his narrative ends with the birth of a son (yet another fairy-tale element). An important difference, however, is that Kolia is an American, utterly unlike a Russian *bogatyr'*. In using this folk convention to close his text, Dovlatov thus paradoxically emphasizes the extent to which his family chronicle departs from its models.

Aside from such epic figures as his grandfathers and some representatives of his own generation, Dovlatov includes rather ordinary characters in his account. A survey of his other prose works indicates that in fact his heroes are generally low or *déclassé* types, socially unsuccessful or alienated.[45] An important distinction to be made, however, is that while they are frequently eccentric, even mad, they are not grotesque. Uncle Roman, whose mind gives way to paranoid delusions, enjoys the narrator's considerable sympathy and is not caricatured.

What can be said about both Dovlatov's epic characters and his "little people" is that they are neither heroes nor dissidents in a conventional sense. For the most part, his relatives find ways to coexist with the Soviet regime with a minimum of moral capitulation. His father, for example, rationalizes widespread arrests under Stalin by noting that "In each of [these people], if you really thought about it, there was something negative, something that allowed you to come to terms with the loss" (*Nashi*, p. 178). He objects to the Thaw, expressing nostalgia for the grandiose stature of Stalin. When confronted with the confession of an acquaintance who had informed on people, he is initially outraged, demanding "Just who appointed you judge, Arkadii?... Who are you, Jesus Christ?" However, when his interlocutor explains that he informed only on bad people, "the ones who never buy dinner for their friends... people who drink alone...," he concedes that such behavior was reasonable (*ibid.*, p. 181). It is significant that Dovlatov treats the ethical hedging and moral ambivalence of these characters, his relatives, directly. He is interested not in judging his characters, but in exposing the distorted values of the milieu which formed them. As Zverev notes in a review of *The Suitcase*, Dovlatov writes about "normal people who are only partially to blame that an abnormal life turned them into neurasthenics, cynics or alcoholics."[46] The narrator's aunt, who conveniently forgets about the scabrous behavior of the famous writers she knew, simply prefers to remember "humorous instances"; Dovlatov concludes "I don't fault her for this. Our memory is selective, like a ballot box" (*Nashi*, p. 163).

The cumulative effect of Dovlatov's characterization techniques, which combine the epic and the low, is mock-heroic. Although his grandfather has superhuman strength, he is arrested and summarily executed. Boris, who is distinguished by his boldness and cunning, ultimately surrenders to the authorities without resisting. Epic prowess — both physical and moral — is easily overcome by force. Furthermore, honor and courage, traditional epic-heroic attributes, are rendered ambiguous in *Ours*. What constitutes honor in the grandfathers' generation has become seriously compromised in the narrator's and Boris' generation. In the sixties and seventies, pilfering, tacitly refusing to work, writing politically unorthodox stories and so on are in their own way heroic acts. The diminution of the proportions of heroism is less a comment on the characters depicted than on the society that forms them; successive decades of Soviet rule have reduced the epic nearly to bathos.

Dovlatov's descriptions contribute significantly to the satiric effect of his text. Often the details he includes in descriptive passages are absurd and illogical. Without commentary, the narrator recalls that a visitor from Belgium "brought Grandpa a tuxedo and a huge inflatable giraffe. The giraffe, it turned out, was really a hat rack" (*ibid.*, p. 145). The implicit irony is twofold: not only are these items utterly superfluous, but they provide grounds for his grandfather's being accused of spying for Belgium. After Stalin's death, the narrator's father sends a similarly incongruous assortment of gifts to his brother Leopol'd: "He sent him a whole flotilla of wooden spoons and bowls, a cupronickel replica of Leo Tolstoi's samovar, several figurines in semiprecious Ural stone, and a jubilee edition of Shevchenko the size of a headstone" (*ibid.*, p. 157). The hyperbole of Dovlatov's catalogue – "a whole flotilla," "the size of a headstone" – is striking, and underscores the absurdity of the brothers' long-distance exchange of gifts. There is a bizarre element of competition between these men who have not seen each other for several decades but who insist on maintaining their respective illusions of happiness and prosperity.

Dovlatov reports dialogue between characters in a similarly telegraphic manner. What appear to be *non sequiturs* are not accompanied by explanation or commentary. When Leopol'd tells the narrator "'It's good you look like your mother... You resemble her a great deal,'" he replies "'Yes, we're often mistaken for each other'" (*ibid.*, p. 160), and the conversation continues smoothly. The narrator recalls someone at a party saying "'Let's go get something to eat at Eliseev's! It's three blocks there, and about the same distance back'" (*ibid.*, p. 206). The reality depicted by Dovlatov emerges as strange and illogical, reflecting the familiar absurdity of contemporary Soviet culture. As Zverev has noted in appraising the farcical aspects of Dovlatov's prose:

> We know well where this bent for such extremism arose that forces one to urinate out of a window on the director of the school (formerly a prison camp guard) or to create a scandal in a restaurant because the waiter refuses to sing "Suliko." We know that in these acts there is a great deal that is wild, but nothing inexplicable. For it is impossible

always to adapt to the conventional farce which has been playing now for many years without intermissions. Any extreme situation is more human. ("Zapiski," 68)

Dovlatov articulates the surreal nature of the *status quo* in his account of how his wife was given permission to stay with his daughter in the hospital. An old acquaintance whom he meets by chance places a call and orders the hospital authorities to admit her, prompting the narrator to conclude "the only weapon against the Soviet administration turned out to be the absurd" (*Nashi*, p. 216).

Dovlatov's humor tends toward the scatological. Monia, the visitor from Belgium, is characterized by his ill-bred behavior in the toilet. The narrator's mother judges his friends on the basis of whether or not they wash their hands after going to the bathroom. Boris initially gains notoriety by urinating on the director of his school and Glasha the dog likes to relieve herself "behind a certain building, at the base of a four-meter-tall portrait of Brezhnev."[47] This emphasis on low detail suggests the decline of the level of culture in general. The physical, base aspects of human nature are more central, more prominent than the spiritual or ideological in Dovlatov's universe. The effectiveness of these scatological descriptive elements depends at least in part on knowledge of Dovlatov's parodic models. Excessively physical details were previously taboo; even Bunin's "Sukhodol," the most naturalistic of these models, treats such matters as rape and miscarriage with comparative restraint. Quite aside from parodic motives, there is a marked similarity between some of Dovlatov's black humor and the flavor of Soviet-era anecdotes. Having been invited to visit a KGB museum, the narrator muses "'I wonder what they have in that museum of theirs,'" to which his interlocutor replies "'God knows... maybe Bukharin's fingernails'" (*Nashi*, p. 202).

Incongruity is a favorite satiric device of Dovlatov that similarly purports to reflect reality. Words that mask or distort the truth are exposed as false when the narrator "translates" their real meaning. Sometimes Dovlatov's intention seems to be exposure of political euphemisms. For example, his grandfather was "given ten years 'without correspondence privileges.'" What this really meant was that he was shot" (*ibid.*, p. 146). More often, his target is the human tendency to prevaricate, to prettify unpalatable or unflattering truths. When his uncle is hospitalized, "Galina Pavlovna said it was a 'neural clinic,' but it was actually a psychiatric hospital" (*ibid.*, p. 152). He provides explanatory notes to accompany his father's letters to his brother Leopol'd:

> My father's letters sounded a bit sunnier: "I am a writer and theater director. I live in a small, cozy apartment." (He referred here to his tiny room, partitioned off with plywood.) "My wife has just been driving through the Baltic republics." (Actually, my father's second wife did sometimes take a union bus to Riga to buy stockings.) "And, as for inflation, I have no idea what it is." (*Ibid.*, p. 156)

Beneath this gentle mockery of his father's pretensions, of course, is satiric commentary on the housing crisis and the shortages of consumer goods. It is characteristic of Dovlatov's praxis that these elements – the broadly human and the specifically Soviet – are inextricably interwoven.

Understatement is used by Dovlatov ironically, i.e. for emphatic effect. Recalling his grandfather Isaak, the narrator states blandly "Grandpa did not like disorder. For that reason, he held a negative view of the Revolution" (*ibid.*, p. 144). The deportation of the family of his cousin's father is "not very pleasant" (*ibid.*, p. 183). The reader, it is assumed, is capable of grasping the import of these events without much narrative commentary.

The style of Dovlatov's prose is, for the most part, markedly colloquial. More than one critic has noted its terse, laconic quality and its closeness to *razgovornaia rech'*.[48] To some extent, the language of *Ours* constitutes a subversion of the smooth, eloquent prose of its parodic models. Whereas Aksakov and Tolstoi attempted to recreate the flow of time in convoluted, verbally rich prose, Dovlatov conveys a sense of disjuncture and isolation stylistically. Dialogue tends to be especially clipped in Dovlatov's chronicle. The narrator and his Uncle Aron communicate mostly by exchanging insults: "'A provocateur, a syphilitic, and a German spy,' I said of Lenin. 'Blasphemer and blockhead!' my uncle said to me" (*Nashi*, p. 167). He establishes a relationship with Reinhardt, the owner of the hotel where the narrator stays in Vienna, on a level of spiritual sympathy that makes words superfluous:

"Do you know Latin?" "Neither do I. And my children won't know it, either, which is a pity. I suspect that Latin and Rod Stewart don't go together." "Who is Rod Stewart?" "A madman with a guitar. Would you like a glass of vodka?" "I would." "I'll bring some sandwiches." "Not essential." "You're right." (*Ibid.*, p. 158)

Certainly the influence of Hemingway and the stylistic tendencies of the Leningrad School of Dovlatov's generation are discernible in such passages of dialogue.

Occasional use of foreign words unfamiliar to Russian as well as Western readers gives *Ours* a somewhat exotic quality. The narrator provides glosses on these, as with his grandfather's use of the expletive *Ka-a-kem*! "(which translates – please excuse this – as 'I crap on you!')" (*ibid.*, p. 147). He defines his Uncle Roman as a *kinto*, offering a variety of translations and settling on "hell-raiser" as a reasonable equivalent (*ibid.*, p. 149). Elements of prison camp slang intrude now and then, but these instances are rarer than in Dovlatov's other works and tend to reflect the degree to which these terms have infiltrated urban colloquial speech. Anglicisms serve to render the narrator's present reality; *bingo*, for example, has no Russian equivalent and thus eloquently conveys the strangeness of life in emigration.[49]

Considering the colloquial level of Dovlatov's prose and the strata of society about which he writes, it is perhaps surprising that *mat*, or obscene language, is used only sparingly. Dovlatov chooses to employ *mat* in small, measured doses in specific contexts. In so doing, suggest the critics Vail' and Genis, he convincingly reproduces the speech patterns of the urban intelligentsia (*Sovremennaia russkaia proza*, p. 106). As a general rule, *mat* appears in other characters' direct speech. The school director's outburst when he is urinated upon by Boris is distinctly vulgar and characterizes him effectively: "'I'll make you eat shit... You son of a bacilli-laden bitch!'" (*Nashi*, p. 185). *Mat* in direct speech expresses the paradoxical extremes of human nature, as in the parting cry of a unnamed prisoner: "'Nadka, if you fuck around, I'll kill you. I'll hunt you down and cripple you like a monkey – this I guarantee. And remember, you bitch, Vovik loves you!'" (*ibid.*, p. 196). Whether in direct speech or, more rarely, in the narrator's own voice, vulgar language is forceful and striking in *Ours* precisely because it is infrequently used.

One occasionally senses an echo of political or propaganda clichés in Dovlatov's prose. Although it is perfectly natural that these should be part of the narrator's stylistic repertoire (they were part of the culture in which he grew up), he generally employs them ironically. In describing his cousin's early successes, he recounts: "He... was a terror to petit-bourgeois thinking and all vestiges of capitalism in the consciousness of the people" (*ibid.*, p. 186). However, we already know that Boris has a penchant for anti-social behavior and a flair for unorthodoxy and the narrator's praise rings hollow. Alternatively, political clichés are mouthed by other characters, but this usage too tends to be incongruous. It is Boris (now a prisoner) who complains of "no military discipline at all" (*ibid.*, p. 196) when a guard is slow about delivering the vodka he has ordered; another prisoner proposes a toast "'To our mighty Motherland! To Comrade Stalin personally! To our victory over fascist Germany! Let's hear it for the surface missiles – ba-boom!...'" (*ibid.*). Whenever clichés enter into Dovlatov's text, they are "others' speech" psychologically. That is, they are felt as foreign within the speech of other characters as well as within the narrator's own discourse.

The form of the family chronicle, then, is the vehicle of Dovlatov's parody, but not his primary target. A more central satiric theme of *Ours* is Soviet totalitarianism over the span of about six decades. The scope of the text is chronologically coincident with the establishment and entrenchment of Soviet power. Beginning with his grandfathers' generation, Dovlatov proceeds from the prerevolutionary period to the Brezhnev years. Moreover, he uses the conventions of the genre to demonstrate that for ordinary people, life is roughly the same in all the diverse stages of Soviet rule. That is, he refutes the distinctions historians would establish between "liberal" and "repressive" periods, suggesting instead that life remained essentially unchanged. His father's evaluation of the Thaw stands unchallenged by the narrator: "Nevertheless, it had been better under Stalin. Under Stalin, they would publish books, and then shoot the authors. Now they didn't shoot writers and they didn't publish books. Jewish theaters weren't being closed down; there just weren't any" (*ibid.*, p. 180). Zverev recalls that Dovlatov dismissed the notion of the *zastoi* period as "pure fiction"; he believed, Zverev writes, that the slight changes that occurred in the political arena meant no substantive changes in the quality of life for ordinary Soviet citizens ("Zapiski," 67).

The most direct focus of Dovlatov's satire is his own contemporary reality, i.e. Soviet culture of the seventies. In particular, the literary and artistic avant-garde comes in for considerable demystification and mockery. Its members, for the most part, are part and parcel of the system and as vulnerable to ethical compromise as any other segment of the population. Describing a bizarre sugar carving which his father obtained to send to his brother abroad, the narrator comments: "Such objects were very much in vogue in the Khrushchev years. The intelligentsia would decorate their apartments with antiques, which were difficult to obtain. They were sold only in special stores closed to everyone but members of the high-ranking elite."[50] Dovlatov leaves it up to the reader to draw the logical conclusions, that the intelligentsia is materialistic and pretentious and that the myth of its spiritual superiority is an exaggeration.

Dovlatov tends not to address broader moral questions directly. Unlike his dissident peers Solzhenitsyn, Maksimov and Vladimov (to name a few), he does not judge the Soviet state explicitly, but rather treats its representatives and its victims as individuals. This relatively benign attitude toward the Soviet Union and this apparent hesitancy to condemn have left Dovlatov vulnerable to charges of triviality in the often extreme world of Russian émigré literature. Serman, by way of examining these charges, notes the similarity of Dovlatov's focus on "trifles" and "frivolousness" to Gogol''s satiric method.[51]

Another theme of Dovlatov's satire in *Ours* is nationality in the Soviet sense of this term. Hyper-awareness of ethnicity is treated as a peculiarly Soviet trait, and he plays on widespread stereotypes in order to expose them as fallacious. Noting that there was something almost unnatural in his great-grandfather Moses' being both a Jew and a peasant, he summarizes his grandfather Isaak's moving back to the city: "he got things back to normal" (*Nashi*, p. 143). The narrator's cousin Boris ponders their likeness to one another, which defies his reasoning: "'How strange! Both of us with Armenian mothers, and I'm half Russian, you're half Jewish. But we both like vodka with beer'" (*ibid.*, p. 198). To this kind of thinking the narrator opposes common sense and his own ostensible naiveté. Recalling his uncle Roman's anti-Semitism, he notes disingenuously that many Armenians did not like Jews, but counters "it would have been more logical for them to dislike Russians, Georgians, or Turks... Apparently, people at the bottom of the social ladder don't much care for others like them" (*ibid.*, p. 151). He mildly conveys his doubt about his mother's conviction that "A Georgian cannot possibly be a decent man," commenting that this was a "rather original way" of arriving at contempt for Stalin (*ibid.*, p. 170).

An even more striking aspect of Dovlatov's treatment of ethnicity is his dismissal of national (in particular Russian) sensibility as a unifying force. The narrator finds more spiritual community with his Viennese host, Reinhardt, than with his own uncle, despite their blood ties. He mocks the appeal he made to his wife to put off emigrating: "I talked about the motherland, about God, about the benefits of enduring intense social pressure, about the linguistic and cultural range available to us. I even spoke of birch trees – something for which I will never forgive myself" (*ibid.*, p. 212). It is characteristic of Dovlatov that he attributes this argument to himself even as he exposes its emptiness; he does not attack these sentiments or those who express them directly, but demonstrates the impotence of this line of reasoning in the face of reality. In *Craft*,

Dovlatov develops this theme further, exploring how Russians can not only be strangers to one another, but can do active harm to their own community. Finding the same mutual empathy with his American agent that he found with Reinhardt, the narrator muses in *Craft*: "Such a thing can really happen! An American, speaking a foreign language, and in addition a bit 'pink,' a leftist, is closer and more comprehensible to me than my longtime acquaintances. It's a mysterious thing, this human contact" (*Remeslo*, p. 166). Dovlatov's rejection of traditionally held conceptions about ethnicity and his tentative discoveries reflect an important function of the family chronicle in its modern variant, what Kenneth Mason terms "the quest for an identity suited to the moral, spiritual, and social exigencies of modern living" ("The Family Chronicle," p. 11).

Institutionalized anti-Semitism is a special target of Dovlatov's satire in *Ours*. The historical reality of anti-Semitism in Russia and the Soviet Union is mentioned only in passing, but is treated as a normative feature of life. His grandfather Isaak quite reasonably assumed that the disturbances associated with the Revolution were the beginnings of a pogrom, and an ordinary insult hurled at him by a truck driver was "kike face" (*Nashi*, p. 145). Being Jewish in the society Dovlatov describes is presumed to be a handicap. Therefore, it is most significant that Grandfather Isaak is not at all a stereotypical Jew, but rather a Benia Krik figure; his heroic-epic characteristics have already been noted. Dovlatov's ambivalence in this regard may well be connected with his own mixed parentage, but he is primarily interested in dispelling preconceptions about ethnicity.

Alcoholism is a pervasive aspect of the lives of Dovlatov's extended family and by implication, of Russian and Soviet culture. The narrator's male ancestors and relatives of his own generation without exception drink excessively and destructively. His grandfather Isaak drinks up his wealth, his grandfather Stepan begins imbibing Napareuli wine as a child, Uncle Roman is a drunkard (among other things), his father drank "perhaps... no more than others did, but it was somehow more noticeable" (*ibid.*, p. 179), and his cousin Boris goes on wild alcoholic binges. Moreover, the drinking habits attributed to non-relatives suggest that this is nothing out of the ordinary. His neighbor, a certain Genadii Sakhno, "was an alcoholic journalist and, like many lushes, a man of blinding nobility of character" (*ibid.*, p. 176). The chief physician attending his sick daughter "was a generally slovenly person who had usually had too much to drink" (*ibid.*, p. 216). Aphoristic asides about the central role of alcohol in Russian culture are uttered by the narrator and other characters. The narrator explains his suddenly calming down during an angry confrontation thus: "No matter how furious a Russian may be, offer him a drink and his mood immediately improves" (*ibid.*, p. 200). His grandfather Isaak drank vodka out of cream-soda glasses, the narrator himself drinks rum from a teacup; Americans, in the narrator's opinion, drink from ridiculously small glasses.

Alcohol is a kind of levelling agent in *Ours*. Both scoundrels and decent people drink. A scene at the prison where Boris is incarcerated is emblematic: "Everyone took a swallow [of vodka] – the zeks, their relatives, the guards, the soldiers, the guard on duty himself" (*ibid.*, p. 196). The narrator is the direct heir of this tradition and does not shrink from exposing his weakness. Relating his failures as a soldier, a journalist and a writer in the Soviet Union, he notes: "I ... drank occasionally"; "I started drinking more"; "I began drinking heavily" (*ibid.*, pp. 174–76). He even meets and consummates his relationship with his wife as the result of binges. His relationship with Reinhardt is based on the consumption of vodka; he wins his host's admiration by relating how he once made do with only an eyeglass case from which to drink. It is significant that Uncle Leopol'd, who has effectively opted out of the family and Russian culture, does not drink and discourages others – notably his wife and the narrator – from drinking.

All of this is not to say that *Ours* constitutes a tract against alcohol. Certainly the omnipresence of excessive drinking in the text is a commentary on Soviet culture as Dovlatov knew it. Nevertheless, what underlies the destructive alcoholism that he describes is more significant for our understanding of the text as satire. The narrator and his relatives share a desire to escape from reality, to achieve a state of numb indifference to their surroundings. Thus the metaphorical function of alcohol in *Ours* on one level resembles its role in Erofeev's *Moscow-Petushki*. Here, however, the philosophical aspect of alcoholism is relatively muted and the fantasmagoric element it introduces into Erofeev's text is absent. The leitmotif of alcohol also links *Ours* with Saltykov-Shchedrin's *Golovlev Family*. Alcoholism is a consistent and pernicious trait passed from generation to generation of the Golovlev clan. Indeed it comes to symbolize the deterioration of the family. In Dovlatov's chronicle, there is not even the semblance of propriety or moderation; hypocrisy is not a target of Dovlatov's satire. The alcoholic in *Ours* is rather a victim and the responsibility falls on Soviet society.

America, Dovlatov's adopted homeland, is a secondary focus of his satire. His treatment of America and Americans is, as I have shown, relatively benign, but it is not the case, as some critics have suggested, that these themes are beside the point. That nostalgia is perceptible in *Ours* is quite true and Dovlatov's characters are indeed almost exclusively Russian.[52] Nevertheless, Dovlatov's treatment of "exile" is significantly different from that of his predecessors in the family chronicle genre. As A. M. Gracheva notes: "Leaving the family 'nest' for the heroes of Aksakov's and Leskov's 'family chronicles' is equivalent to breaking ties with one's national roots and means that the family will certainly perish in the future and the idyll will be totally destroyed" ("'Semeinye khroniki,'" 67). In this respect, Dovlatov would seem to be closer to the tradition of chroniclers of immigration such as Charles Reznikoff, Mary Antin and Gertrude Stein. America fills him with bewilderment and intensifies his sense of isolation, but also inspires awe and respect. His attention is focused, for the most part, on Russian émigrés' inability to cope with American culture and the English language.[53] The "vast quantity of squirrels" in New York City strikes the narrator as mildly curious,[54] but his own slowness to adapt to the pace of American life – to learn to drive, to develop a taste for American music, to speak English – is a more central target of his Horatian satire.

Dovlatov, unlike Limonov, qualifies his judgments of

America with self-deprecation and restraint. His viewpoint too is simultaneously that of insider and outsider, but he utilizes this vantage point to emphasize cultural differences rather than to praise or condemn. His musings on the chief trait of Americans, for example, may be read as admiring as well as mocking:

> What is the main quality of Americans? I immediately decided it was their optimism. In the courtyard of our building there was a man who got around in a wheelchair. If you asked him, "How are things?" he answered, "Fine," without the slightest trace of self-consciousness. Or else you saw a girl on the street, pale, disheveled, heavy-legged, wearing a T-shirt that said, "I'm Ursula Andress." Again, not the least bit self-conscious. And so on.[55]

His daughter surprises him by insisting on an expensive operation for their old and chronically ill dog and he remarks that he had thought she was "a typical American girl – happy and carefree, with a dollop of pragmatism."[56] Yet he concedes that his perception of Americans may be flawed. The attitude of tolerant mockery that is evident in these passages is characteristic of Dovlatov; the absence of nostalgia for or praise of Russian culture constitutes an important break from the genre tradition he has adopted.

A pervasive element of Dovlatov's satiric prose is irony. Zverev calls irony Dovlatov's "chief distinguishing quality" and notes the particular effectiveness of this technique in critically examining Soviet life ("Zapiski," 70). Irony colors the world view of the narrators of all of Dovlatov's works and reflects the absurdity of the universe he depicts. It is also directed inward, toward the persona of the narrator himself. He does not spare himself in his caustic appraisal of Soviet education: "The competition came and went, and a long series of F's began again. These I got due not to independence of mind but to being dumb" (*Nashi*, p. 174). Moreover, his critical irony is focused on sympathetic and unsympathetic characters alike, on his friends and relatives as well as Soviet bureaucrats and hacks. Summarizing the bohemian life of his literati friends, he writes:

> They were, after all, my friends. They didn't get published either. Their reaction to this situation was generally neurotic and noisy. They

drank fortified wine and regarded one another as geniuses. Almost all my friends were geniuses, and some were even geniuses in several areas at once. Sasha Kondratov, for instance, was a genius at mathematics, linguistics, poetry, physics, and church art. On his pinky he proudly wore a homemade tin ring in the shape of a skull. (*Ibid.*, p. 175)

The last detail is remarkably apt, succintly conveying both this person's pretensions to originality and iconoclasm and the narrator's retrospective skepticism.

There is something palpably postmodernist about Dovlatov's irony[57] and this may help to explain his success in Western literature. The ironic tenor of his prose fits the prevalent tone of modern American stories of the sort, for example, that are published regularly in *The New Yorker*. Nevertheless, Dovlatov's irony is first and foremost satiric and has as its goals attack, mockery and exposure. His father's fate is related in *Ours* with an ample dose of bitterness: "... my father himself was forced to leave his job in the theater. As he should have been, in keeping with his own theories: a Jew, with a father who had been shot, with a brother living abroad, and so on" (*Nashi*, p. 178). The irony of his politically loyal father's being fired is primary, but beneath the surface of this passage lurks the secondary irony of the "normalcy" of this way of thinking.

To claim that Dovlatov's irony is satiric is perhaps to beg the vexing question of what exactly the relationship between irony and satire is. Certainly this is a thorny problem. Wayne Booth, in his exhaustive treatment of irony, concludes that it is a device used in some satire, but by no means in all; that some irony is satiric, but much is not (*Rhetoric of Irony*, p. 30). Considering the question at some length, George Test suggests "Irony then can be coessential with satire when the overall technique or structure is itself inherently ironic. It may on the other hand be merely pervasive or at least basic without being an exact overlay."[58] In the case of Dovlatov's family chronicle, irony and satire are nearly indistinguishable, so closely do they interact in the text. As we have demonstrated, even irony that appears to be "cosmic" on the surface contains an element of satire on closer examination.

There are numerous instances, however, when irony also

overlaps with tragedy in *Ours*. This type of irony, in which the reader's sympathy for the victim is elicited (Muecke, *Compass of Irony*, p. 51), is often found at the close of Dovlatov's individual character portraits, i.e. at the end of chapters. Having recounted his failure to establish a relationship with his uncle Leopol'd, the narrator concludes "A couple of times I've thought of calling him. I should send him a Christmas card" (*Nashi*, p. 161). In closing the chapter that describes his aunt Mara, a professional editor, he emphasizes the irony of the hopeful, optimistic tone of her poetry: "My aunt was mistaken. Her life was coming to its close. The errors could no longer be corrected" (*ibid.*, p. 165). Recalling his Uncle Aron's regret at never looking behind a certain brown fence, the narrator writes "Then my uncle actually did die. A pity, and that tall brown fence gives me no peace" (*ibid.*, p. 170). Although the satiric quality of these passages should not be overemphasized, it is significant. Uncle Leopol'd is a stranger to his nephew because he long ago emigrated in order to escape a stifling, repressive society; Aunt Mara's "errors" (*oshibki*) euphemistically suggest all kinds of excesses, particularly those of the Stalinist variety; the brown fence represents externally or internally imposed limits on intellectual or creative inquiry. Even when Dovlatov's irony shades to pathos, then, there is an undercurrent of critical commentary.

In general, irony supports satire in *Ours* through the principle of what Muecke calls "double exposure" (*Compass of Irony*, p. 45). Appearance and reality are effectively juxtaposed and the contrast is strikingly revealed to the reader. Coming into the room upon hearing the children laughing, the narrator's aunt says "'Whatever people say, children need their father! See how happily they play, joke, and laugh with him'" (*Nashi*, p. 151). The reality of the situation, to which the reader is privy, is that they are laughing at their father's breaking wind; the touching moment is also qualified by the fact that their father is only visiting, for he has a second family.

To appreciate fully Dovlatov's use of irony, the reader must recognize the masquerading of appearance as reality that is endemic in the society he describes. Appearance becomes, in a sense, an alternate reality irreconcilable with the truth. The clash of these perceptions produces most effective satire. Dovlatov juxtaposes two planes of reality in the following account of Uncle Roman's career: "Like all discharged lieutenant colonels, he was put in charge of security technology at his place of work, the Lightbeam factory. (Full colonels are assigned to head personnel departments.) It's possible that he knew something about security technology, or at least it shouldn't be ruled out. What all his energy went into, though, was planning mass athletic events" (*ibid.*, p. 150). That he is given a job for which he has no experience (and probably no aptitude) is, of course, illogical. What Dovlatov does is call our attention to a familiar breach of common sense. More poignant is his brief summary of his Uncle Aron's life. Having helped to dispossess the kulaks and purge the Party, he was himself purged. This scenario is perhaps too familiar to a Russian reader to evoke surprise, but Dovlatov compresses the sequence of events to make the irony of his fate more striking. Urging the narrator to speed up his demise by smothering him, Uncle Aron offers him his set of Lenin's complete works which he can then exchange "for a really good edition of *Pinocchio*" (*ibid.*, p. 169). No explanation is provided (or needed), and the absurdity of Soviet publishing practices is underscored.

Irony is inherent in Dovlatov's material, not imposed as a pattern by the satirist.[59] In exposing the clash between appearance and reality or between alternate realities, he effects a kind of catharsis. The reader frequently experiences the shock of incongruity on reading *Ours*, whenever ingrained acceptance of an absurd reality is reversed. This may, in part, explain why Dovlatov's satiric prose is so satisfying. As Max Eastman suggests, "Our lives in all departments consist so largely of the cultivation of insubstantial pretenses and amenities...that almost any perfectly candid speech about anything contains an element of release."[60] Eastman was not writing specifically about Soviet literary culture, but his remarks are particularly apropos to our understanding of Dovlatov's satiric praxis.

Dovlatov's ironic devices in *Ours* tend to be rhetorically quite simple. His favorite technique of verbal irony is hyperbole.

The family chronicle revisited

Uncle Aron's enthusiastic support of Khrushchev is described as falling in love (*Nashi*, p. 166). A neighbor who acts as a lookout and warns the narrator's family of approaching police is "a man of blinding nobility of character" (*ibid.*, p. 176). Boris' young wife, who joined him in penal exile (where he went for committing robbery), "acted like the wife of a Decembrist" (*ibid.*, p. 188). Dovlatov employs understatement less frequently, but with similar wry effectiveness. Recommended for admission to the Party by his colleagues, Boris is tormented by a moral dilemma: "Namely, how was it possible to be a communist with a criminal past? The old communists assured him that it was possible" (*ibid.*, p. 189). Any narrative commentary on the implications of this statement would be superfluous, and Dovlatov's restraint is eloquent.

The narrative techniques of *Ours*, like those of Dovlatov's other works, are superficially straightforward and simple. Although he experiments elsewhere with relatively complex narrative strategies (notably in *The Zone* and *A Foreign Woman*), he writes in *Ours* what Franz Stanzel calls an "authorial" text. That is, the author of this work frequently obtrudes by addressing the reader, commenting on the actions he recounts, reflecting on the meaning of events, and so on. The narrator, however, is consistently intradiegetic and character-bound, a participant (except in the earlier chapters) in the events he relates.[61] Even when he was not a direct participant, Dovlatov's use of the conventions of the family chronicle allow him to report events *as if* he participated in them or witnessed them because they constitute family lore. This should not obscure the tension, which is nonetheless present, between the realm of the author and the *literary* realm of his text.

In the manner of Hemingway and the Leningrad School, Dovlatov favors direct speech as a narrative mode. The narrator himself frequently engages in the dialogue reported and these exchanges serve to characterize his interlocutors and to illuminate family interrelationships. His responses (and his silences) eloquently reveal his attitude toward his Uncle Aron in the following dialogue:

"Sergei," he said very quietly, "I'm dying." I said nothing. "I'm not afraid of death." He paused for a moment and then went on. "I've made honest mistakes... I've felt anguish over the wrong steps I've taken. Here is what I have understood: The holy tenets I upheld all my life have turned out to be false. I've cracked up ideologically." He asked for water. I lifted a cup to his lips. "Sergei," he said, "I always scolded you, but it was only because I was afraid. I was afraid they would arrest you. You're very unrestrained... I criticized you, but deep down I agreed with you. You should understand me. Forty years of that" – and here Uncle used a very dirty word – "Party. Sixty years under this" – here he repeated the word – "system..." "Please calm down," I said. "...have turned me into a whore," he said, finishing the sentence. He had to make an effort to go on. "You were always right. I only argued because I was afraid for you. Forgive me." He started to cry. I felt very sorry for him. (*Nashi*, pp. 167–68)

In this and similar passages of reported speech, Dovlatov the author consistently retains control, summarizing and commenting upon his own reactions. His authorial hand is still more obvious in cases of indirect dialogue, where he both formulates and responds to questions. Against his father's objections to emigration ("Whoever heard of such a thing – leaving the stage in the last act?"), he replies with his own rhetorical questions: "What could I tell him? That we weren't onstage but in orchestra seats?" (*ibid.*, p. 182).

Positioned as it is between history and autobiography, *Ours* (like any family chronicle) encourages equation of narrator and author. The concept of an implied author is most useful in elaborating this complex relationship in *Ours*.[62] Interposing the persona of an implied author allows us to perceive separately Dovlatov the author and his satirical narrator. Nevertheless, the *ostensible* unity of these personae in *Ours* helps to establish the narrator's reliability. His intimate, confidential tone is rhetorically persuasive, an important element in any satirical text. Moreover, his emotional or physical involvement in the events he recalls softens the didactic import of his observations. As he writes in *The Compromise*: "In this story there are no angels or villains, and there couldn't be. One of the protagonists is me."[63]

The narrator of *Ours* often presents himself as a naif. This is, however, a carefully cultivated device. Having established that his parents knew of Stalin's crimes during his reign, he poses the wickedly naive question: "There's one thing I don't understand. How come my ordinary parents knew everything, while Il'ia Erenburg didn't?" (*Nashi*, p. 170). He is a "little man" in the Gogolian tradition, but this stance is qualified by echoes of a bohemian, vaguely criminal past.[64] The narrator regards himself with self-deprecation, mercilessly diminishing his heroic anti-establishment reputation. Recalling his literary activities in Austria following his emigration, he writes: "I wrote something or other for émigré journals and newspapers, mostly elaborating on my nonexistent dissident exploits" (*Nashi*, p. 214). This is equally true of his retrospective accounts and of passages situated in the present of the text. He is loath to name-drop and employs the persona of Glasha the dog to avoid inflating his own literary status: "Glasha was acquainted with Evgenii Evtushenko, Vasilii Aksenov, Anatolii Naiman, Evgenii Rein. She sat on Daniil Granin's lap and Vera Panova's, ate from the hands of Akhmatova and Kornei Chukovskii, tore the trousers of the esteemed critic Efim Etkind."[65]

Alternately, the narrator is a knowledgeable, savvy witness-observer of the phenomena of Soviet and Western life. In respect to the Soviet press, "the only truth in our newspapers is in the misprints" (*Nashi*, p. 171); his father's consternation at being denounced by a communist colleague bespeaks "a deep and stubborn lack of understanding of the way things are" (*ibid.*, p. 182); Glasha's receiving 400 grams of tenderloin for saving the family from suffocating charcoal fumes is "possibly the first time in the history of the Party that exclusive privileges were awarded to someone worthy of them" (*ibid.*, p. 203). Thus in regard to injustices and paradoxes he witnesses, Dovlatov the narrator stands apart, an objective and caustic observer.[66]

The narrator is at times also a philosophic commentator, intruding to summarize and comment on the events he recounts. For the most part, these asides pertain to specific characters, but occasionally he extends the scope of his inquiry. Recalling his grandfather's arrest and execution as a foreign spy, he writes: "For me the questions are: Just what was going on back then? In the name of what, exactly, was that daft and amusing life cut short?" (*Nashi*, p. 146). That there are no satisfactory answers to these questions is self-evident, and the narrator's indictment becomes broad.

Finally, the narrator emphasizes his selectivity, his prerogative not to tell the reader everything. This is particularly evident in the treatment of his prison experience. Three times he refers obliquely to his arrest and imprisonment. He qualifies his conviction that the prisoner and the prison guard are essentially the same: "I don't much feel like writing about it in detail. I'll say only this about it: I didn't like being in jail" (*ibid.*, p. 176). Another time he allows himself a jibe at a Soviet literary icon by way of demurring: "I don't really want to write about it. Otherwise everything would come out sounding overliterary, like Mikhail Sholokhov's *Tales from the Don*" (*ibid.*, p. 188). Like any family chronicler, Dovlatov exercises his privilege to omit unpleasant or disturbing reminiscences, but his repeated references to his prison experience indicate that it was indeed central in forming his present world view. In this case he relies on the reader's knowledge of twentieth-century camp literature. Dovlatov knows well the power of allusion; detailed description would be superfluous in light of the models of Solzhenitsyn, Shalamov, Evgeniia Ginzburg and others. In his reticence to touch upon this event directly, he focuses attention away from external political events and back to the hearts and souls of his eccentric relatives. In all their moral hesitancy, their vulnerability and their tragic displacement, they become a case study of Russian twentieth-century social history.

CHAPTER 5

Dystopia redux: *Voinovich* and Moscow 2042

> "Take Orwell, for example. Didn't he predict in detail the system that exists in Russia today?" "Of course not," I said. "Orwell wrote a parody of what already existed at the time. He described a totalitarian machine that worked perfectly and could simply never exist in a real human society."
>
> Vladimir Voinovich: *Moscow 2042*

Born in 1932 in Dushanbe, the capital city of Tadzhikistan (at that time Stalinabad), Vladimir Nikolaevich Voinovich is one of the most popular and prolific of contemporary Russian satirists. In respect to his style and his thematics, he has often been compared to Gogol'. Both in his homeland and in emigration, Voinovich has subjected the Soviet system to caustic and often very funny satirical scrutiny. Nevertheless, he has consistently resisted wearing the mantle of satirist, arguing that he merely depicts reality – absurd, often grotesque reality – "as it is."[1]

A formative event in what he has called an "ordinary" youth was the arrest and imprisonment of his father when he was still a small child.[2] When his father was released and rehabilitated after five years (which was actually quite extraordinary), his family resettled in Ukraine. Voinovich managed only seven years of formal education while he was growing up and began working at the age of eleven. Over the course of the next decade, he worked at a wide variety of jobs, including herdsman on a collective farm, construction worker, factory laborer, carpenter, teacher, aircraft mechanic and railway worker. He served four years as a private in the Red Army in the early fifties.

While still in the army, Voinovich began to write verse and published some of his poems in a military newspaper. His applications for admission to the Gor'kii Institute of World Literature in 1956 and 1957 were rejected, but he obtained a job at Moscow Radio a few years later that gave him entrée to the world of literature (albeit through the back door). It was song lyrics that first brought Voinovich success; he wrote about fifty songs in all and published the texts of many of them in 1960. His composition "Fourteen Minutes To Go" became the unofficial anthem of the Soviet cosmonauts, sung by Khrushchev himself from the tribune atop the Lenin Mausoleum at a celebratory parade for Nikolaev and Popovich upon their return from space.

Voinovich's debut in literature proper was less surrealistic but equally auspicious. In the sixties, five of his stories were published in *Novyi mir*, the most prestigious liberal literary journal in the Soviet Union. "We Live Here" appeared in 1961 and was received – at least initially – with enthusiasm and praise by critics. His next two works, "I Want to Be Honest" and "A Distance of Half a Kilometer" (1963), aroused more controversy and spurred a retrospective evaluation of the ideological soundness of his previous work. Treating shoddy building practices and the pressure exerted by the state to make ethical compromises, "I Want to Be Honest" was regarded as slanderous by orthodox critics. Another *povest'*, "Two Comrades" (1967) and a much slighter piece, "In the Sleeping Compartment" (1965) were published in this period. "The Sovereign" appeared in the journal *Nauka i religiia* in 1969. Voinovich's only other significant work to appear in the Soviet press prior to *glasnost'* is an historical novel about Vera Figner called *A Degree of Trust*, which was published in the "Ardent Revolutionaries" series in 1972. This was, it seems, Voinovich's sole attempt to write an ideologically correct piece of literature and he later dismissed its publication as part of a strategy of coercion by the state; the regime "handed me a cookie instead of whipping me."[3]

The decline of Voinovich's career in Soviet literature was almost as meteoric as the ascent. What galvanized Voinovich's resistance to the official line in literature and in politics was the Siniavskii and Daniel' case of 1966–68. He has suggested that had he not already become a writer and a public figure, he might have withdrawn and lapsed into silence as did many members of his generation who were disillusioned by the failure of Khrushchev's reforms.[4] In signing – along with Kornei Chukovskii, Il'ia Erenburg, Bella Akhmadulina, Bulat Okudzhava and fifty-seven other writers – a letter protesting their arrest and imprisonment, he initiated his fall from grace. Over the course of the next few years, Voinovich signed several other open letters to the Soviet authorities protesting treatment of dissident intellectuals. These letters were circulated in *samizdat* and smuggled to Western correspondents; through Voice of America, they reached a large audience within the Soviet Union. Although there was little official reaction for several years, a letter which Voinovich signed calling for a fair trial for Ginzburg, Galanskov and other *samizdat* figures in 1968 had serious consequences. He was reprimanded by the Writers' Union, a book that was scheduled for publication was withdrawn, his plays and film scenarios were banned, he was expunged from library catalogues. After his vociferous protest of Solzhenitsyn's expulsion from the Writers' Union in 1973, his position became untenable. Voinovich's initial reaction to official sanctions and reprimands was to look for a way to compromise, to continue his career in Soviet literature. However, the banning of his works essentially deprived him of the means of making a living; his expulsion from the Writers' Union in 1974 meant that he was in the eyes of the state no longer a writer. (On the day following his expulsion, however, he was made a member of PEN.)

The publication of Voinovich's works abroad, which began with the appearance of the first part of his *Life and Extraordinary Adventures of Private Ivan Chonkin* in the émigré journal *Grani* in 1969, exacerbated the situation. He complied with the authorities' demand that he protest the publication of his novel without his approval and his letter, with some additions, was duly published in *Literaturnaia gazeta* (Voinovich, "Voinovich o sebe," p. 144). Nevertheless, as his foothold in Soviet literature eroded in the seventies, he turned more openly toward the West and began to publish his works through the émigré press. The *povest'* "By Way of Mutual Correspondence" appeared in 1973, *The Ivankiad* in 1976; *Pretender to the Throne*, which comprises the third and fourth parts of *Ivan Chonkin*, was published in 1979.[5]

During the seventies, Voinovich and his family were under steady surveillance and were followed, questioned, sometimes threatened by the KGB. In a 1975 article called "Incident at the Metropole," Voinovich recounts being interrogated and poisoned by Soviet security agents. As a result of the systematic harrassment that went on for seven years – an attempt, Voinovich has said, to force him to emigrate – his health suffered and his relations with the authorities became increasingly acrimonious: "Later on they said that I became bitter. That's true. But if they embitter a person, and he doesn't become bitter, then you have to think that perhaps he's stopped being a human being" ("Voinovich o sebe," p. 144). In 1980 he agreed to leave the country on the condition that he be allowed to take his books and papers with him. Although his departure was set for immediately after the close of the Olympic Games, various complications prevented him from leaving until December. His stay in the West was ostensibly temporary; he was invited to the Barvarian Institute in West Germany for a year. In July of 1981, however, he was stripped of his Soviet citizenship and became a member of the third wave.

Voinovich was a very visible and vocal figure in emigration, but he resisted aligning himself with any particular camp. His voice has generally been a moderate and liberal one; his polemics with Solzhenitsyn illustrate his distaste for dogmatism and political extremism of any sort.[6] He rejects the notion that emigration adversely affects a writer's talent and insists that good literature may be produced in the diaspora: "Writers emigrate not only from one country to another, but from one book to another" (Glad, *Literature in Exile*, p. 90). Voinovich taught and lectured widely in the eighties, dividing his time between West Germany and the United States. His works, translated into many languages and disseminated through major Western publishing houses, received considerable critical attention by émigré and Western critics alike. His first major work to appear in emigration was a collection of essays and feuilletons, *The Anti-Soviet Soviet Union*.

Moscow 2042, the futuristic satire treated in the present chapter, followed two years later (excerpts had been published previously in the émigré press). As a result of the widespread interpretation of the book as an *ad hominem* satirical attack on Solzhenitsyn, Voinovich found himself ostracized by a sizeable portion of the émigré community. There were some "punitive sanctions" imposed on him – he became *persona non grata* at Voice of America and his books were shunned by an American agency that sent émigré literature to Soviet readers – on account of the scandal (Bek, "Iz russkoi literatury," 252–53). Within the Soviet Union, where Solzhenitsyn had achieved the status of a cultural icon under *glasnost'*, journals initially refused to publish *Moscow 2042*. It was finally printed in 1990 in a collection of utopian and dystopian works and as a separate volume by a Russian-German cooperative publishing house.[7]

Indeed, despite his initial skepticism,[8] *glasnost'* made possible the publication of all of Voinovich's works in his homeland. His repatriation in print began with the publication of *Ivan Chonkin* in *Iunost'* in 1988–89; at the same time, excerpts from the novel were printed in *Ogonek*. The publication of *Ivan Chonkin* was connected with a proposal by the preeminent Soviet director El'dar Riazanov to make a film based on the novel; to make this possible, the book had to become a part of *Soviet* literature. Voinovich himself spent some weeks in Moscow working on preparations for the film, but problems arose over the ownership of film rights and the project was eventually scrapped. The misunderstandings and mutual recriminations that resulted from this incident are important in that they demonstrate some of the complications of merging émigré and Soviet art and literature.[9] In 1989, when Voinovich's *povest'* "The Fur Hat" appeared, it came out almost simultaneously in the Soviet Union. In addition, several of his works have been successfully staged in Moscow. *Ivan Chonkin*, "The Fur Hat" and *Moscow*

2042 have all been adapted to the stage in some form and "The Fur Hat" has been filmed.

Voinovich himself has been dubbed a "half-returnee" by an unsympathetic critic (Murikov, "... Bez slez," 146), and the appellation is quite apt. He professes a strong attachment to his homeland and suggests that his books find their most suitable audience there. They are, he believes, read differently than in the West and are "more necessary" to Russians.[10] Before he would consider returning permanently, Voinovich insisted on the reinstatement of his citizenship and the return of his apartment. These conditions, which constituted a public apology on the part of the government, were granted in 1990 and he now maintains a residence in Moscow. Nevertheless, practical considerations have prevented Voinovich from returning completely, and he has retained his German citizenship.

Moscow 2042, which marks a distinct departure from Voinovich's earlier satirical writing, may be read in the tradition of utopian and dystopian literature. In some sense, the Moscow represented in Voinovich's futuristic portrayal draws upon the utopia, a genre that has conventionally presented a "community where sociopolitical institutions, norms and individual relationships are organized according to a more perfect principle than in the author's community."[11] The word *utopia* is a neologism coined by Thomas More that punningly incorporates the notions of non-existence (Greek *ou*) and good (Greek *eu*), so that combined with *topos* ("place"), it means both "good place" and "no place." Literary utopias, from Plato's *Republic* to More's *Utopia* to Bellamy's *Looking Backward*, share several positive ideals. These include material abundance, leisure, peace and justice. S. K. Vohra, in his study of modern utopian and dystopian fiction, convincingly traces the genesis of literary utopia to medieval chiliasm; the existence of utopia presupposes that man can influence and shape his destiny through his own powers.[12]

In considering Voinovich's work in relation to utopia, it is important to avoid common critical confusion of utopian thought, utopian practice and utopian literature. Although utopian thought has been applied in the establishment of utopian communities (notably in America in the late nineteenth century), the literary utopia as verbal artifact is more pertinent to our discussion here. The literary utopia does not necessarily lead to social reconstruction, but rather delineates a scheme of the ideal society.[13] It will also be useful to distinguish between planned and escapist utopias, since *Moscow 2042* bears a relationship to both types. The escapist utopia, or *retropia*, as Eduard Gevorkian terms it,[14] typically portrays a fantasy world where man enjoys complete gratification of every desire and unlimited pleasure. Planned utopias, by contrast, emphasize the technological or legal organization of the perfect society; they describe the institutions and mechanisms of civilization. Although the literary utopia predates science fiction by many centuries, the relationship between these genres has been altered by the rise in status of science fiction. Specifically, the technological utopia intersects with science fiction, beginning with Wells. The synthesis of the utopian novel and science fiction has proceeded unabated in the twentieth century in the West to the extent that the utopian novel – a rare phenomenon these days – is now considered a sub-type of science fiction.

More interesting in terms of Voinovich's work is the close connection between utopia and satire that has been demonstrated by Robert Elliott. Elliott posits a link between the idea of utopia (in particular escapist utopia) and the myth of the Golden Age. The transference of the ideal elements of the myth to utopian tales of the future occurred at the point when man rejected eschatology and assumed the role of creator himself. Furthermore, Elliott suggests that the ancient Saturnalia was "a sanctioned way to the Golden Age," a ritual "negative means to a positive end." Thus both modes – the satiric and the utopian – derive from release and license. With the Renaissance, satire (perhaps through a confusion of etymology) became more closely associated with the bellicose aspects of Saturn.[15]

Literary utopia indeed has a dual character. Because it describes the ideal, it implicitly (and sometimes explicitly) encourages comparison and contrast with the real. Salient features of the author's own society are inverted, so that the inconsistencies or illogicalities of that society are exposed. The difference between utopia and satire is really one of degree; in the utopia

> ... the author's intention is obvious: to show, in contrast to his ideal pattern, the aberrations of present society. The irony is all the more sharp when the distance between idea and reality is greatest. And when the distance is enormous, as in the fourth book of *Gulliver's Travels* or Cyrano de Bergerac's *The Other World*, we are clearly in the domain of social and political satire.[16]

Of course, the functions of these two modes is another way of distinguishing utopia from satire. The utopist distorts reality in order to bring about positive change, while the satirist is concerned primarily with criticism and mockery. Utopian satire – a hybrid form – utilizes the conventions of the literary utopia to focus a critical lens on the present.[17] Classical examples of utopian satire include Voltaire's *Micromegas*, Swift's *Gulliver's Travels* and Butler's *Erewhon*.

Another relative of the literary utopia is variously known as anti-utopia, reverse utopia, negative utopia, mock utopia, *aipotu* (utopia spelled backward), cacotopia, *roman-preduprezhdenie* ("novel-warning") and dystopia. Although these are often used loosely, even interchangeably, there are important distinctions among them. Gevorkian's suggestion that we understand utopia as a quintessentially good society, dystopia as an ideally bad society and anti-utopia as something in between is rather facile ("Chem vymoshchena doroga," 11). Alexandra Aldridge's formulation of anti-utopia as a genre historically and formally between utopia and dystopia brings us closer to an understanding of the relationship.[18] Gary Saul Morson's formulation is the most precise; he posits dystopia as a subgenre of anti-utopia which discredits the ideals of utopia specifically by "portraying the likely effects of their realization" (*Boundaries of Genre*, pp. 115–16). Generally, the term *anti-utopia* encompasses those works directed specifically (dramatically, satirically or parodically) against utopian thought. Dystopias typically expose the dangers inherent in utopian idealism, such as fanaticism, dogmatism and totalitarianism.

Literary dystopia seems to have emerged as a peripheral genre in the nineteenth century. It has, in the course of the twentieth century, undergone a marked shift toward the center. This change in the relative status of utopian and dystopian literature is, according to Chad Walsh, very significant. It may, he postulates, "foreshadow one of those really massive psychological shifts that sometimes occur over a whole culture."[19] While the roots of the modern dystopia may ultimately be traceable to Greek utopian satire through Swift's Lilliput, the twentieth-century variety is probably a response to relatively recent events. World War I and the Bolshevik Revolution gave a strong impetus to dystopia; World War II, the Holocaust and the nuclear arms race seem to have given the genre definitive priority in contemporary Western literature. The fact that fascism and Nazism were propounded in utopian terms fueled a dystopian reaction.[20]

More generally, the rise of dystopian fiction appears to be connected with the failure of utopia in the present century. Advances in technology have made many aspects of utopian schemes realizable, but this has paradoxically spawned disillusionment, even horror. As the means of creating the ideal society have become more accessible, the fear that they will be misused has grown apace. Chiliasm, the belief system that motivated nineteenth-century utopists, has been largely abandoned. Perhaps more to the point, utopian ideals have undergone a profound reevaluation that has left them seeming at best naive, at worst static and oppressive. Dragan Klaic summarizes Karl Popper's critique that "implemented utopia would be the model totalitarian state, that every utopian dream contains a nucleus of totalitarianism" (*ibid.*, p. 63). This intellectual rejection of utopia has been reinforced by broad acceptance of Freud's view that man is not always a rational being. Indeed, the twentieth century has provided good evidence – in contradistinction to nineteenth-century utopian thought – that man is not perfectible. For utopian idealism to be put into practice, an essential change in human nature would have to be accomplished, and this has been discredited as impossible in our age.

The critical function of utopian satire is far more pronounced in dystopia. That which is often only implicit in utopia – subversive commentary on real social or political conditions – is made explicit in dystopia. The writer of dystopia also describes a futuristic society, but his or her vantage point is different:

> Utopias, as a rule, look forward from a world in which ... basic human values are still in force – though very imperfectly, to be sure – to a future world in which they will be fully operative; anti-Utopias look back from a future world in which those values have completely vanished to a past world in which they still existed, even though imperfectly. (López-Morillas, "From 'Dreams of Reason'," 58)[21]

A prominent element of dystopia that is secondary or absent from utopia is prophecy. Whereas utopia posits the future in wishful terms, dystopia warns that the future depicted is possible, indeed inevitable, if steps are not taken to avoid its actualization.

For the criticism inherent in dystopia to be effective, there must be recognizable links between the world described and the author's own social and historical situation. Furthermore, it must be clear that the author regards the society he describes as unpleasant, if not frightening and repulsive. Authorial intention, then, is a defining characteristic of dystopia; it is up to the reader to discern the author's attitude toward his fictional world if he is to interpret it accurately.[22] This is why we understand B. F. Skinner's *Walden Two* as a utopia, but read Aldous Huxley's *Brave New World* as a dystopia in spite of the similarities in the societies described in these works. Although the metric of intentionality might be highly suspect in regard to analyzing other types of literature, it is crucial to an understanding of the dynamics of dystopian literature. Dystopia is, after all, a variety of satire, and we cannot divorce the satirist's critical intention from any meaningful interpretation of the text.

Given that the literary dystopia is a twentieth-century phenomenon and that it has assumed a prominent place in satirical writing, it is probably best defined in terms of its exemplars. Proto-dystopias may be adduced, but the most obvious model of modern dystopias is the writing of H. G. Wells. Wells' own œuvre, however, offers ambivalent evidence. Some of his works are thoroughly utopian, while others – *The Time Machine*, *When the Sleeper Wakes*, *A Story of the Days to Come* – display his apprehension that scientific progress may have undesirable social ramifications. Unambiguous examples of the modern dystopia include Evgenii Zamiatin's *We*, Huxley's *Brave New World* and George Orwell's *1984*. One can cite many other works, of course,[23] but these three dystopias effectively define the generic paradigm.

Although Zamiatin's work is certainly the best-known Russian dytopia, both the utopian and dystopian traditions are broadly represented in Russian literature as a whole. The first literary utopias produced in Russia may be traced to the eighteenth century, to the writing of Sumarokov ("The Dream of the 'Happy Society'") and Radishchev (the utopian dream in *A Journey From St. Petersburg to Moscow*). Often utopias were contained, as is the case of Radishchev's dream interlude, within a larger work. The eighteenth century also saw great interest in Western utopian literature; translations of English and French utopias became very popular in Russia. Viacheslav Shestakov suggests that the literary utopia was perceived differently in Russia from its inception: "The Russian writer and thinker often felt the disparity between the ideal and reality more keenly than his European counterpart. What seemed to the European philosopher and author ... could possibly be created very soon ... was for the Russian utopist a striking dream existing only in the very distant future."[24] Nineteenth-century utopias were written by Kiukhel′beker, Vel′tman and Odoevskii; the dreams in Chernyshevskii's *What Is To Be Done?* and Dostoevskii's *Dream of a Ridiculous Man* are also rooted in the utopian tradition. Utopian science fiction was tremendously popular in Russia from about 1890. Some of these works drew on Western models that were widely translated and serialized at the time, some updated earlier Russian utopian visions with technological innovations and some were proto-dystopias, warning of the dangers of collectivism and materialism.[25]

Russian utopian literature of the nineteenth century has a

close relationship with utopian socialism. Based on the idea that man is essentially good, rational and perfectible, utopian socialism was adopted by Russia intellectuals as a political theory upon which to reform society.[26] Works that expounded the ideas of utopian socialism, such as Nekrasov's *The Story of Poor Klim* and Herzen's writings, were subject to strict censorship. Nevertheless, the ideas of utopian socialism were made the basis of the political programs of various secret societies, including the Petrashevskii Circle. In the wake of the reforms of 1861, widespread disillusionment among intellectuals was added to the effects of government suppression to render utopian socialist thought *passé*.

Marxists use the term *utopia* disparagingly, but Russian literary critics have of late conceded that utopian socialism was one of the theoretical sources of Marxism.[27] Indeed, the Soviet Union itself was a utopian experiment and this is reflected in twentieth-century Russian literature. First published in 1908, Aleksandr Bogdanov's *Red Star* is probably the best example of Marxist literary utopia. Sergei Esenin depicts an agrarian, populist utopia in his poem "Inonia," written in 1917; Vladimir Maiakovskii shows the pure communist Ivan triumphing over the wicked capitalist West in his 1920 verse utopia "150 Million." The twenties were a productive decade for the literary utopia, but the genre virtually disappeared in the thirties; Shestakov summarizes the Stalin period: "After the rapid rise and development of utopian literature in the twenties came a sharp decline, and beginning with the thirties, utopias rather rarely appear in book shops" ("Evoliutsiia," p. 20).

The literary dystopia in Russia is connected with the repudiation of rationalism, Marxism and communism. In particular, the direction taken by the Soviet experiment motivated Russian dystopian writers. It has been pointed out that the bleakest of dystopian works have been created by disenchanted leftist writers, e.g. Zamiatin and Orwell. However, in considering the connection between Soviet sociopolitical reality and dystopian literature, it is important to note that it was not so much the failure of utopian idealism that led to the disillusionment of dystopian writers as the distortion and deformation of utopianism.

Modern Russian dystopia finds its most important literary antecedent in Dostoevskii's "Legend of the Grand Inquisitor." The Grand Inquisitor, in describing his utopian vision, is the archetypal spokesman for elitism and totalitarianism in the name of man's happiness. He prophesies absolute control over people, a situation that will be fictionally portrayed in twentieth-century dystopian works:

> And they will have no secrets from us. We shall allow or forbid them to live with their wives and mistresses, to have or not to have children – according to whether they have been obedient or disobedient – and they will submit to us gladly and cheerfully. The most painful secrets of their conscience, all, all they will bring to us, and we shall have an answer for all. And they will be glad to believe our answer, for it will save them from the great anxiety and terrible agony they endure at present in making a free decision for themselves.[28]

Dostoevskii dramatically treated the paradox of utopia in theory ending in slavery in practice earlier in *The Devils*; Shigalov is a utopist who loses sight of the end when the means become central. A bleak portrayal of the socialist future is offered by Nikolai Fedorov in his tale *An Evening in the Year 2217*, published in 1906. I have already mentioned Zamiatin's *We* (1920) as a literary dystopia that occupies a pivotal position in both Russian and Western tradition. Responding both to Dostoevskii's concern with the balance of freedom and happiness and to Wells' ideology of science, Zamiatin satirized the dehumanization associated with collectivization and mechanization. As we shall see, Voinovich's *Moscow 2042* has a close relationship with *We* and, through Zamiatin, with Dostoevskii's "Grand Inquisitor."

In the post-Stalin period, the utopian/dystopian tradition has been carried on by Mikhail Emtsev, Eremei Parnov and Arkadii and Boris Strugatskii. Their works exhibit traits of both literary dystopia and science fiction and until very recently, were published only selectively in the Soviet Union. In general, the reception of dystopia in the Soviet period has been chilly.

The following criticism of dystopia as politically reactionary is representative:

> The victorious march of communist ideology gaining control of the minds of the broad masses, the successes of socialism inevitably gave birth to a corresponding reaction on the part of ideologists of the old world. The anti-utopia is one of the forms of this reaction against socialist ideas and socialism as a social system. Vicious, slanderous fantastic novels aimed against Marxism and the socialist state become more and more widespread as the crisis and decay of world capitalism increases.[29]

According to Soviet criticism, the best examples of dystopian literature were those targeting Western, bourgeois society. A measure of how much this attitude has been challenged under *glasnost'* is the public debate surrounding the publication of Aleksandr Kabakov's bleak dystopian tale *No Return* in 1990.

Literary dystopia bears a parodic relationship to utopia in that it addresses certain conventions of the model. On one level, dystopia carries on an intertextual dialogue with the utopian genre or with a specific work of that genre. In the modern period, as I have shown, dystopia has transcended its dependent status *vis-à-vis* utopia to become at least a subgenre with its own established conventions of theme, plot, characterization and style. The most cursory reading of *Moscow 2042* suggests that Voinovich was very much aware of the topoi associated with the literary dystopia in composing the work. However, what makes this dystopia innovative is his subversion of the generic norms he acknowledges. Voinovich himself suggests that the designation of the work as an "anti-antiutopia" is appropriate.[30] In the interest of satirizing his targets more forcefully and more effectively, Voinovich parodies the literary conventions of the dystopia, creating a kind of satiric palimpsest. Near the surface we find a dystopian vision of the future Soviet state that reflects the author's antipathy toward the present Soviet system; peeling away this layer, we encounter sophisticated aesthetic play with the dystopian tradition itself. And it is on this level, I believe, that much of the humor and the paradoxical optimism of the text may be understood. Morson observes that the function of parodic recontextualization is to reverse the task set by the model (*Boundaries of Genre*, p. 111). The catalyst for Voinovich's parodic reworking of the generic conventions of the dystopia would seem to be his perverse faith that man can never design the perfectly unfree society.

Voinovich's examination of alternative versions of utopia and dystopia within the framework of *Moscow 2042* is an explicit element of parody. Early in the novel, before embarking on his journey into the future, the narrator Kartsev dismisses the possibility that communism can ever be achieved, asserting that "Utopias are utopian."[31] Although Kartsev is not identical to Voinovich and expresses himself somewhat crudely, it is clear that the pejorative connotation given the term *utopian* in this judgment stems from the author's point of view.

The contradiction between personal freedom and utopian harmony has been a recurrent theme in Voinovich's work. *A Degree of Trust* is primarily an historical treatment of Vera Figner and her involvement in the People's Will, the radical revolutionary group that assassinated Alexander II in 1881. Voinovich wanted initially to entitle his biography *A Wooden Apple*, an allusion to Figner's writing that she perceived freedom to be a "wooden apple" that she could not savor. Voinovich's Figner is more attracted to a vision of the future offered by a fellow revolutionary, Nikolai Morozov, than to freedom:

> ... life will be completely different from how it is now. Everyone will be healthy, beautiful and shapely. Everyone will do some physical labor in equal measure. They will devote their free time to the sciences and art. Then even the city will be completely transformed. All the roofs of the houses will be at one level, and they will all be flat like the decks of steamships.[32]

Morozov goes on to describe the regulation of citizens' lives in his imagined utopia, how they will walk, sit, drive and so on. The architecture of the city reflects the extreme orderliness and rigidity of his vision. It is certainly true, as Robert Porter suggests, that Voinovich is mocking the naive utopian ideas of the early revolutionaries in this passage (*Four Contemporary*

Russian Writers, pp. 117–18).[33] His juxtaposing this dialogue about utopia to one in which Morozov points out the home of an intended assassination victim to Figner strengthens the association between utopian dreaming and coercion.

In one of his early *povesti*, "Two Comrades," Voinovich also treats this issue. A passage in which the young first-person narrator muses about his relationship with his mother and grandmother raises essentially the same question posed by Dostoevskii in "The Legend of the Grand Inquisitor": "I didn't have a girl. I had only mama and grandma, who required that all the processes of my personal life should take place before their eyes for complete peace of mind. At twelve years of age I understood that the limitation of personal freedom is a terrible punishment, even if it is the result of someone's boundless love."[34] Though framed in a purely personal context and lacking the grandiose scale of Dostoevskii's dilemma, this scene suggests the importance of the conflict between security and the play of free will in Voinovich's world view. Here and elsewhere he consistently endows a sympathetic character with the urge to struggle for the right to act as a free individual.

Dreams are a generic convention of the utopia that allow the author to construct an entire alternative world. Dreams were particularly well suited to nineteenth-century utopian works in Russia in that they could "assume the role of fantasies that are not to be taken seriously (especially by the censor)" (Reeve, "Utopian Socialism," 384). Kartsev's extended dream of utopia, the first chapter of the third part of the novel called "The Enjoyment of Life," parodies this convention. Here there is plenty of everything, money is superfluous, no one has to work, it is always summer and gravity has been reduced. Kartsev is ecstatic at finding himself in this paradise and busily loads up on caviar and vodka until he sees Zilberovich, an old Moscow acquaintance and now Karnavalov's aide, kissing his (Kartsev's) wife. On the one hand, this dream is a spoof of the escapist utopian tradition. Voinovich enumerates all of the foods and beverages available for free in utopia, concluding that the variety equals "all the goods we could buy in our Stockdorf supermarket, or perhaps a little less" (*Moskva 2042*, p. 143).[35]

Having deflated the grandeur of his vision through this aside, he proceeds to experience greed and jealousy in spite of the optimal environment. Although every consumer's wish can be gratified here, Kartsev – and, Voinovich implies, people in general – are flawed by nature and cannot be cured of their passions.

Another version of utopia included in *Moscow 2042* is that offered by the terrorist seated next to Kartsev on the plane to the future. His conception of communism turns out to be a simplistic rendering of the traditional utopia. Small cities will be covered with glass domes, the climate will be comfort-controlled, there will be no illness or death and people will have plenty of leisure time to engage in philosophical discourse. Yet to Kartsev's question about whether people will be able to read whatever they want, he replies that "books with high intellectual and moral content would of course be available to everyone through public libraries" (*ibid.*, p. 89). Even in this fantasy proto-utopia, there is censorship and control of individual liberties.

The most damning indictment of utopia made by Voinovich in *Moscow 2042* is his depiction of Karnavalov's revolutionary regime. That Moscowrep in all its nightmarish, dystopian stasis is overthrown is very significant. Destroying or planting the seeds of destruction within the fictive vision of dystopia is very much part of the Russian tradition of this genre. Indeed, this is a seminal difference between Dostoevskii and Zamiatin on the one hand, and Huxley and Orwell on the other.[36] Like his predecessors both Russian and English, Voinovich structures the plot of his dystopia around an attempt at subversion. The extent to which his revolutionaries succeed, however, is unprecedented in dystopian literature. This generic topos is radically undercut when the system that Karnavalov establishes becomes cruel and repressive in its own turn. Dissenters are torn limb from limb, beheaded and hanged; *ukazes* are issued regulating clothing, hair, means of transportation, religion and other aspects of personal life. Most importantly, coercion is an integral part of this state as well. The security agent Dzerzhin tells Kartsev after the revolution: "'they need specialists like me. Any regime does. No matter what kind of revolution you make, you have to have something to protect it with after. And who's going to do that? We are. Any individual can be replaced but you can't replace all of us at the same time'" (*Moskva 2042*, p. 334).[37] Karnavalov's ascension to power and the establishment of his personal vision of utopia in place of Moscowrep is on one level a satiric attack on the conservative, nationalistic camp of the third wave of Soviet emigration. By having Karnavalov destroy Moscowrep and create a new dystopia, Voinovich introduces a darker, apocalyptic strain into his work.

Moscow 2042 is, I have suggested, both a satire on contemporary Soviet mores and a parody of literary dystopia. However, the tone of Voinovich's work is remarkably light, and we can discern positive values underlying the negative images he creates. In the first place, Voinovich's choice of genre implies interest in and concern about the future; the text may paradoxically be read as "the last refuge of utopian hope" (Klaic, *Plot of the Future*, p. 7). I would not suggest that a utopian counterimage can be read into the novel through simple inversion of its negative images. Yet the work offers – even endorses – a positive alternative to the nightmarish vision it presents.

Kartsev, for all his moral ambiguity, champions the positive virtues of individualism and freedom. Voinovich invests him with the creativity and irrationality that he posits as antidotes to communism. The free will that he exercises in refusing to edit his novel causes his expulsion from the "Communist Hotel" and results in physical deprivation and discomfort. Nevertheless, it allows him to retain his humanity and some degree of dignity. Voinovich seems to insist that the equation of the collective happiness of society with the happiness of its individual members is hopelessly flawed. In the final analysis, the Grand Inquisitor's choice of freedom or happiness still presents a dilemma, but in *Moscow 2042*, Voinovich comes down decisively on the side of freedom. In rejecting the utopias posited by communism and nationalism, he mocks the notion that human happiness can be built according to a blueprint. As an alternative to the dystopias he portrays, he would seem to endorse Nikolai Berdiaev's hope that "... cultured and intelligent people will dream of ways to avoid ideal states and to get back to a society that is less 'perfect' and more free."³⁸

In depicting the structure and institutions of Moscowrep, Voinovich draws upon preexisting models offered by the utopian and dystopian traditions. He subverts and transcends these paradigms in various ways to intensify and particularize his satire. Both utopia and dystopia involve more description than plot development, and here too plot is largely subordinated to Kartsev's account of communist society. Escorted by Iskrina and the other Communites, he contemplates unfamiliar aspects of life in 2042 and relays this information to the reader.

The time differential that Voinovich sets up in *Moscow 2042* is relatively short. The tendency of major dystopian works considered chronologically has been a foreshortening of the time lapse between the present and the envisaged future; Zamiatin imagined his United State a thousand years hence, Huxley posited his new society six hundred years in the future and Orwell placed Ingsoc in this century. *Moscow 2042* would seem to follow this pattern, as Kartsev visits Moscow only sixty years in the future. It may be that the acceleration of the pace of technological and social development in the recent past has contributed to dystopia's being brought closer to us in successive texts. Voinovich has stated that he set *Moscow 2042* sixty years in the future because that is about as far ahead as his imagination reached.³⁹ And the reason that he travels sixty years into the future instead of fifty years – because all the tickets on the earlier flight are sold – is comically banal. The very specificity of the date serves to subvert the uchronia associated with utopia. Voinovich exaggerates the historicity of his dystopia in order to relate it firmly to the present, to make it an imaginable, potential future. His satiric vision gains immediacy and urgency through his use of what Irving Howe calls "the narrative psychology of 'one more step'."⁴⁰

The dystopian state usually comes about as the result of mankind's being nearly destroyed by a global war. In the case of *Moscow 2042*, the state is formed as a result of the "Great August Revolution" (a transparent allusion to the Soviet

"Great October Revolution"). Smerchev recounts the history of Moscowrep to Kartsev immediately upon his arrival. Even as Voinovich parodies the inflated and hyperbolic language used to describe the birth of the Soviet state in official accounts, he pokes fun at the rather artificial generic convention of a historical monologue; Kartsev archly comments that "It must have been a long way from the plane to the terminal, because Smerchev also had time to explain how and why the Great August Communist Revolution took place":

> At times vulgarizing the great teaching [of communism], previous party and state leaders had attempted to build communism without taking local and general conditions into account. At one point, even the great Lenin thought that he could build communism immediately throughout the planet by carrying out a world revolution. Later the position was taken that the first stage of communism, socialism, could be built only in one country. And that was done. However, the transition from socialism to communism proved much more complex than it had seemed at the start. All the attempts to build communism in one country proved failures. After analyzing these attempts thoroughly and developing his own revolutionary theory, the future Genialissimo, even back then, drew the sole correct conclusion that the root of the problem lay in the previous leaders having been guided by vulgarized ideas. Overly hasty, they failed to take into account the scale of the country, unfavorable weather conditions, and the backwardness of a considerable portion of the multiethnic populace. Ultimately, the future Genialissimo came to a decision – simple, but a decision of genius – that there could be, indeed must be communism in one city. (*Moskva 2042*, p. 106)

Couched in the euphemistic cant characteristic of glorifications of Stalin, Smerchev's discourse is actually a rationalization of reducing the Soviet Union to a tiny, isolated fortress state. Voinovich has subjected the process of ideological compromise carried on by successive Soviet regimes to *reductio ad absurdum* in this concise history of Moscowrep. His satirical indictment charges that instead of "building" communism, Soviet strategists have steered Russia down a path of isolationism and stagnation.

Continual war is a common motif in dystopian literature. In Voinovich's scheme, a siege mentality is fostered by the communist elite of Moscowrep; the rings encircling the city are called "rings of hostility." This structure is, of course, an extension of the actual physical layout of the city of Moscow, which is encirled by ring-shaped highways. But Voinovich shifts these rings from the purely geographic sphere to the ideological realm: "The First Ring of Hostility was formed by the Soviet republics which the Communites called the filial republics, the Second Ring was composed of the fraternal socialist countries, and the Third by the capitalist enemy" (*ibid.*, p. 121). Moscow's being besieged by "filial" and "fraternal" neighbors is a wonderfully symbolic paradox. Voinovich satirizes the doublethink that allowed reconciliation of Soviet dominance and control of the entire Eastern Bloc with territorial paranoia.

However, the basis for outsiders' antagonism toward the citizens of Moscowrep is not ideological, but material. As bad as things are within the city, conditions in the outer rings (at least in the First and Second Rings) are deplorable. We never learn what life is like beyond these rings, in the capitalist countries, and the truth is ultimately irrelevant. What is important is that the citizens of Moscowrep believe that people suffer terrible deprivation there. Convinced that others live much worse than themselves, the Communites appreciate their own situation and are motivated to behave well. There is, after all, the constant threat of exile to the outer rings. Like the citizens of E. M. Forster's dystopian tale *The Machine Stops*, the Communites are taught that they will surely perish if they are forced to live outside the city. Disinformation and propaganda are powerful and pernicious influences for Voinovich, as for Forster. The Communites' perception is probably wrong, but it effectively keeps them in a state of submission.

Whereas utopias often have a pastoral, arcadian bent, dystopias are usually urban. Indeed, as Eric Rabkin suggests, a defining feature of dystopias is their anti-pastoral, technological nature.[41] Zamiatin, Huxley, Orwell and other dystopian writers have been keenly aware of the political connotations of architectural space in their imagined societies. They have created glass-enclosed, sanitized bubbles that facilitate coercive surveillance and constructed high walls to keep wildness and disorder (natural and political) at bay. Voinovich implicitly mocks the idea, common to communism and Western utopianism, that increasing control over the environment means increasing control over human nature.

For the most part, the realization of communism in *Moscow 2042* has meant regression to a primitive, pre-technological state. Moscowrep is protected by concrete slabs and barbed wire instead of a huge glass dome or electric fence. The descriptions of the city recall those in Zamiatin's story "The Cave," where the revolution has reduced culture to barbarism. On the outskirts of Moscowrep, where Kartsev is exiled for refusing to revise his novel, there is no electricity at all; the "Socialist Hotel" is pitch black after dark. Given the role of electrification in the Soviet collective psyche, it is very significant that Voinovich makes electricity a luxury item in his dystopia.

There are also satirical asides directed toward specific aspects of Soviet reality in Voinovich's text. Kartsev's description of the Leningrad Highway, for example, quite accurately reflects the present condition of the infrastructure: "The asphalt was cracked in some places, swollen in others, and, here and there, missing entirely" (*Moskva 2042*, p. 120). His account of trying to use a public phone in the First Ring is a good example of the narrator's dual insider/outsider viewpoint:

> I went outside again, figuring on calling from a booth, especially since public phones in the Moscowrep were free. One of the public phones by the hotel entrance was out of order, and another was minus a door and the receiver had been torn off. Another one around the corner had a receiver, but the glass had been smashed and I was afraid of cutting my feet. The next phone booth was about a block away. It had both a door and a receiver; the only thing lacking was a dial tone. (*Ibid.*, p. 293)

To the uninitiated Western reader, this passage may seem hyperbolic and improbable. But Voinovich's satire is calculated to have a different effect on the Russian reader, who will recognize an all-too-familiar experience with the Moscow public telephone system (which is virtually free but horribly unreliable). When asked by an interviewer in 1990 if the

Moscow he was visiting resembled that he depicts in *Moscow 2042*, Voinovich replied: "...unfortunately, things are on a downhill slide; that is, it's not that the book reflects reality, but that reality is beginning to reflect fiction."[42]

Social equality is a common motif in utopia and a rigid hierarchical order its converse in dystopia. Many utopian schemes posit a classless society as an ideal.[43] Dystopias portray the distortion of that ideal, its extreme opposite in which a ruling elite controls and conditions the rest of humanity. The acme of power in dystopian works generally rests with a dictator figure, a demigod who is "omnipotent, omniscient, omnipresent, a face and voice that is, has been, and ever more will be, a god of judgment who demands self-denying love and unquestioning faith."[44] A conventional plot device in dystopia is an encounter between the hero and this dictator figure.[45] Aside from this confrontation, the dystopian ruler is generally not seen; it is part of his mystique to be inaccessible. What is often revealed in a meeting with the subversive hero is that the dictator has good intentions, that he genuinely believes the society he heads optimizes the happiness and well-being of its citizens.

The political structure of Moscowrep is utterly authoritarian, with near deification of the state's putative leader. In *Moscow 2042*, the Genialissimo fulfills a role parallel to that of Zamiatin's Benefactor, Orwell's Big Brother and Huxley's Mustpha Mond. He holds the five highest posts in Moscowrep; he is general secretary of the Party, chairman of the Supreme Pentagon, commander-in-chief, chairman of state security and patriarch of all the Russias. Virtually everything in the city is named after him or a tome of his writing and the media report the condition of his health in detail every morning. Initially Kartsev assumes that he is a mythical being, a convenient fiction, for he is reputed to be immortal and omnipotent. Furthermore, Kartsev is bringing to bear (and calling upon the reader to bring to bear) the generic convention that requires a leader of this type.

Therefore, Kartsev is quite surprised to discover that the Genialissimo actually exists, and as we learn more about him, the extent to which Voinovich subverts the convention becomes clear. A fundamental paradox of dystopia is that the leader is superfluous. Voinovich intensifies this irony by making the Genialissimo a prisoner orbiting endlessly around the earth. Although he was instrumental in carrying out the Great August Revolution, the oligarchy deemed him too meddlesome as stasis was established, and he was jettisoned into space. The Genialissimo's image is further diminished when it turns out that he is none other than Leshka Bukashev, an ineffectual careerist known (and despised) by Kartsev during his previous life in the Soviet Union and Germany. The media's health bulletins also undercut his demigod status, reducing him to his component parts: "His pulse and blood pressure were always just a bit better than they needed to be. His lungs, liver, and kidneys functioned superbly, and the results of his urine and blood analysis were excellent" (*Moskva 2042*, p. 173).

When Kartsev meets the Genialissimo in prison, they replay Dostoevskii's encounter between Christ and the Grand Inquisitor in an utterly farcical context. The Genialissimo's profession of good intent and self-sacrifice ironically reveals his impotence: "'Whenever I wanted to make some concrete reforms, and convoked congresses and meetings and told them we couldn't go on living this way, let's finally do something, let's try a new approach, once again the reply would be stormy applause and cheers. The newspapers and television would extol me for my exceptional boldness and breadth of vision'" (*ibid.*, p. 329). In case the parallel is not clear, Voinovich includes an explicit point of contact with reality; Kartsev muses: "I didn't find anything novel about his confessions. In my time, the Soviet system had operated in roughly the same way" (*ibid.*). The expectations that we bring to the text as experienced readers of dystopias are radically and humorously undercut by Voinovich's characterization of the Genialissimo as a hapless political pawn, pickled on the "elixir of life," floating in a fishbowl-like satellite. Through an absurd rationalization of his actions, he claims that his doing great evil will result in great good; in realizing communism, he "gave mankind the chance to come down with the disease and develop an immunity which will last for many generations into the future" (*ibid.*, p. 328).

Dystopia redux

In any dystopian state, agents of surveillance play a significant role and this is true of the society Voinovich depicts in *Moscow 2042* as well. It is the duty of all citizens of Moscowrep to display vigilance and to inform on any utterances, behavior or thoughts that appear to be anticommunist. The ubiquity of spying and informing is represented for Kartsev by a poster of a soldier in the bathhouse accusing him of using an extra basin. It is important that the figure pictured looks "like a Red Army soldier from the Civil War" (*ibid.*, p. 137). That is, the pervasive atmosphere of distrust and reproach has not changed in the Soviet Union over its entire history. Moreover, Kartsev suspects that this communist society has instituted something resembling Orwell's Thought Police, for the Communites seem to be able to read his mind. The twist Voinovich gives to these dystopian topoi is that the entire surveillance system in Moscowrep is a sham. The KGB has been infiltrated by the CIA to the extent that no one knows who is who, and it really makes no difference. The specter of the Thought Police turns out to be illusory; the guardians of Moscowrep know Kartsev's thoughts because they have read *Moscow 2042*. And the most banal impediment to the effectiveness of the security system – that there is no paper on which to write denunciations – saves Kartsev from the necessity of compromising his morals.

There is, however, a more serious aspect of Voinovich's satirical exposé of Soviet security practices. The agents of Internal Security who arrest Kartsev as a suspicious character are not only inept, but also frighteningly brutal. That their methods have remained primitive is initially suggested by the objects they use. The duty officer at the station where Kartsev is brought records information in a thick notebook with a wooden pen and uses ink from a glass inkwell.[46] Within a few lines, the scene has degenerated into a graphically described beating, complete with blood, spit and cursing. Just as significant as the explicit brutality associated with the security organs in Moscowrep is the utter lack of trust and moral corruption engendered by institutionalized paranoia. Berii Il'ich Maturin, chief marshal of Moscowrep, confesses to Kartsev that "in our republic you can never tell who are your own people and who aren't" (*ibid.*, p. 235). Not trusting anyone else, Voinovich suggests, results in the loss of one's own sense of identity and integrity. As Dzerzhin says to Kartsev, "In this country nobody knows who he really is any more" (*ibid.*, p. 308). This by-product of spying and surveillance is more profoundly destructive on the level of national culture.

As Geoffrey Hosking has noted, the capacity to construct our lives around illusions has always fascinated Voinovich.[47] The chief marshal of Moscowrep assures Kartsev that "we all live on illusions" (*Moskva 2042*, p. 224). What gives this dystopia a peculiarly Soviet flavor is that absolutely *no one* believes in the illusions promoted by the state. The very core of this futuristic society is rotten because "everyone knows everything, but everyone pretends to know nothing" (*ibid.*, p. 205). Although the citizens of Moscowrep superficially subscribe to the ideology purveyed from above, the most important element of any dystopia – mind control – works very poorly here. Bukashev, while still in the present, makes an observation about Soviet society that establishes a direct link with Voinovich's futuristic vision: "'The system is idiotic and I serve it. But that doesn't oblige *me* to be an idiot. And the others aren't idiots either. Everybody understands everything, but there's nothing they can do'" (*ibid.*, p. 28).

Advanced technology frequently contributes to coercion in the literary dystopia. This convention developed in reaction to the glorification of technology by Wells, Jules Verne and others. Their works prophesied that science would enrich and ease mankind's life in the future. Concurrent with the rise of dystopia, the question of feasibility became moot; the focus of dystopian writers has become how man will utilize scientific means. The emphasis has shifted "from the absolute or relative increase of resources (that is, from problems of production and distribution) to the restriction, control or 'guidance' of unlimited desires."[48] Science itself is perceived as neutral, but the abuse of science can cause atrophy or brutalization of men's physical and moral selves. Aldridge makes the distinction that dystopian writing is not anti-scientific, but anti-scientistic (*The Scientific World View*, p. ix).

Voinovich's exploration of the relationship between technology and despotism takes an unusual direction. In the first place, he charges that the subordination of rational, scientific procedure to ideological concerns leads to inefficiency and waste. Furthermore, he draws a clear parallel between this practice in Moscowrep and the policies of the Soviet Union. Iskrina explains the rationale for dispersing cloud cover over the city to Kartsev: "... this does have a negative effect on the climate and the harvests, but we put the ideological struggle first and the harvest second." And Kartsev replies succinctly "I can see that. It was like that in my time, too" (*Moskva 2042*, p. 185).

Kartsev forewarns us that he is not interested in technology; he advises readers curious about details of his trip through time to read science fiction instead. As it turns out, technology is all but nonexistent in Moscowrep (except in the closed, secret scientific complex). Computers are virtually unknown, vehicles are mostly steam-powered and production of consumer goods is primitive. This return to a pre-technological state has not, however, meant rediscovery of utopia or arcadia. In fact, Moscowrep is characterized by limitation of personal freedom without material security (the exchange typical of dystopian literature). Voinovich reinforces the irony of this situation in his depiction of the secondary dystopia established by Karnavalov. Sim Simych Karnavalov decrees the Communites' return to a primitive lifestyle: he issues an *ukaz* abolishing science and replacing it with obligatory study of Scripture, Dal's *Etymological Dictionary* and his own works. His regime, we soon see, will be even more cruel and rigid than that of the Communites. Voinovich thus replies to fears about technology unleashed voiced by previous dystopian writers. In particular, he suggests that tyranny does not bear a direct relationship with advances in technology and that absolutism without the benefit of science is a frightening possibility. Indeed computerization is treated positively in *Moscow 2042*; Kartsev himself has composed some of his novels on a word processor.

Like any work written in the dystopian mode, *Moscow 2042* focuses considerable attention on the *modus vivendi* of the citizens of the fictional state depicted. But in this respect too Voinovich parodies the conventions he adopts. Like the citizens of any dystopian state, Communites wear standardized uniforms. Men wear shorts and women wear short skirts, and the quality of the cloth from which they are made varies according to the rank of the wearer. Voinovich thus formalizes an observable fact of life in the Soviet Union of his day. The variable quality of consumer goods reflects the hierarchical structure of the Soviet system. The disparity between reality and the ideal of the classless society is the source of Voinovich's satirical irony. That all the Communites dress in short clothing also presents a paradox, for men were actually forbidden to wear shorts in Moscow (and women wearing short skirts were frowned upon) until very recently. The prescription of short pants and skirts is due to severe shortages of cloth in Moscowrep; Iskrina initially disapproves of Kartsev's robe because "'There's plenty of extra material here, enough for two or maybe even three people'" (*ibid.*, p. 178). Moreover, the length of clothing is charged with ideological significance and Kartsev is hounded by the security organs for being a "longpantser" (*dlinnoshtannyi*). As in the Soviet world view, pragmatic considerations drive philosophical ones, but once established, the latter become utterly rigid.

The ideological architects of Moscowrep, like the elite of other dystopian works, have recognized that man is incurably religious and longs for the security of ritual. And as is common in dystopia, eschatology is elaborated within a purely secular system. What Voinovich adds to this formula is normalized hypocrisy. Faith in God is renounced, but the church is a powerful state institution that "ceaselessly struggles for the propagation of new communist religious rites among the Communites" (*ibid.*, p. 186). Representatives of the church wield enormous power and prestige because they have made a compromise with the state and preach "faith in communist ideals and the person of the Genialissimo" (*ibid.*, p. 122). Voinovich's futuristic scenario satirically reflects the position of the Russian Orthodox Church within the Soviet Union. As the fierce polemics between émigré clergy and Orthodox clergy within Russia attest, the situation of the church under Soviet rule was indeed paradoxical; Voinovich has only slightly exaggerated inconsistencies and compromises associated with the church in his satirical exposé.

Father Starskii (*otets Zvezdonii*), a "major general in the religious service," is a fanatical proponent of this communist religion. His faith in the Genialissimo is so strong that he chooses a gruesome crucifixion over renunciation when Karnavalov's monarchy is established. Yet Voinovich portrays him as sadly deluded rather than bravely loyal; he reveals his ignorance as he explains the church's doctrine: "'We worship [Christ],' said Father Starskii, flustered and stomping his foot, 'not as any son of God but as the first communist, a great predecessor of our Genialissimo, of whom Christ once rightly observed, But those who will come after me will be stronger than I!'" (*ibid.*, p. 108). Starskii's reinterpretation of Scripture echoes the Soviet falsification of history that gave Stalin political primacy and legitimacy after Lenin's death.

In the cultural sphere too, Voinovich borrows a great deal from dystopian models, but individualizes his satiric vision. Education is equivalent to indoctrination in Moscowrep, as children are taught to idolize the Genialissimo and to dedicate themselves to him above all else. They memorize facts and figures about him, read his works exclusively and go on field trips around the city to view the innumerable statues erected to him. From an early age, children are taught "to inform on one another, to report their parents' transgressions to their teachers and those of their teachers to the kindergarten principals" (*ibid.*, p. 187).

Voinovich's preface to his discussion of education in Moscowrep emphasizes its programmatic quality. He prepares the reader to approach what follows in the context of the utopian/dystopian tradition when he begins: "My account of the Communites' customs and ways would not be complete if I did not touch on the subject of their education, which occurs in the following manner" (*ibid.*). Our reading of this chapter about indoctrination practices in Moscowrep is therefore colored by our prior knowledge of this topos. The force of Voinovich's irony lies in the proximity of this scenario to Soviet (especially

Stalinist) reality; it is not particularly futuristic or fantastic. It is satirically effective precisely because this society's deification of the Genialissimo resembles Soviet glorification of Stalin (and to a lesser extent, other leaders). Regarding denunciation as a positive and useful skill seems less preposterous when we remember the cult of Pavel Morozov. These pernicious aspects of Soviet education stand out in grotesque relief through Voinovich's careful and restrained application of hyperbole.

The possibility of achieving immortality underlies many utopian schemes. Fending off death and making time stand still are ways of establishing paradise on earth for architects of utopia. Dystopians frequently utilize this convention as well, but suggest that the quality of life must diminish with its prolongation. Although Voinovich's recontextualized dystopia does not include increased longevity on a broad scale, experiments are being carried out in the scientific complex to perfect the elixir of life. The Genialissimo and Edison Ksenofontovich are the primary beneficiaries of this discovery and already Edik envisions how the elixir will be used as an instrument of coercion.

The awareness that death is inevitable renders certain people fearless, even desperate. But the elixir will make everything different. In fact, we'll be able to rescind many punishments, including prison and the death penalty. Why? We'll simply distribute the elixir strictly on the basis of behavior. If you behave – you'll get your monthly portion. And if you behave well next month, you'll get it again. But anyone who displays any disobedience will be deprived of the elixir. Some temporarily, and some permanently. (*Ibid.*, pp. 274–75)

Immortality becomes, in Voinovich's dystopian scheme, another privilege to be distributed on the condition of conformism and obedience. He adopts this motif familiar to readers of dystopias to suggest the pervasive influence of the reward system operative under Soviet rule. Voinovich emphasizes the danger of tampering with the natural order of life and death through the figure of Karnavalov. While Kartsev repeatedly insists that he can have no influence on events in Moscowrep because he must be long dead, it turns out that he has been frozen. His preservation – though bizarre, not without a basis in cryogenic theory[49] – has instructively disastrous results for society.

Euthanasia, a frequent motif in both utopia and dystopia, is touched upon in *Moscow 2042*. Here, however, the decrepit and ill are not actively euthanized, but only dispatched to the First Ring. This may well hasten their death, but that is not of primary importance; what matters for propaganda purposes is the extremely low death rate within Moscowrep. Voinovich's employment of a dystopian convention again ricochets back at his target of contemporary Soviet mores. In Moscowrep (and by implication in Soviet society), reality is not as significant as statistics, and statistics show that people do not die.

Eugenics is practiced in Moscowrep, but like immortality, it is still in the experimental stage. Edison Ksenofontovich heads the Institute for the Creation of a New Human Being, where he attempts to breed specialized workers and "people with propensities for military service, sports, science, or administration" (*ibid.*, p. 260). These experiments, however, are only mentioned in passing, by way of establishing the dystopian context. Voinovich focuses much more satirical attention on Edison Ksenofontovich's successful creation of a "superman." This was "an absolutely universal genius" (*ibid.*, p. 261), gifted and strong both mentally and physically. When this specimen was shown to the Editorial Commission (whose approval is required on every achievement), its members voiced various objections, could not agree, and finally insisted that he be "edited" (castrated). Voinovich's choice of verb in this case is very significant, for through his satire of Edik's experiments in eugenics, he indicts the process of editing and censorship of all creative art in the Soviet Union as one of emasculation and destruction.

Many writers of both utopias and dystopias devote considerable attention to the regulation of marriage, sex and childbearing. Wells, for example, in *Anticipations*, advocates the strict regulation of marriage and sexual relations by psychologists and physicians. Babies are decanted in Huxley's *Brave New World*, marriage is strictly for the purpose of procreation in Orwell's *1984* and sex is regulated by the pink-ticket system in

Zamiatin's *We*. Sexuality is regarded as a destabilizing force related to the knowledge of good and evil in this literary tradition (Rabkin, "Atavism and Utopia," p. 3). Therefore sex is either carefully controlled or replaced with casual lust and thus rendered meaningless.

Voinovich acknowledges his literary debt to his predecessors but parodically transcends these generic conventions in his own dystopia. Kartsev is provided with a mate upon his arrival in Moscowrep and she explains the scientific regulation of marriage that is the norm in this communist state. However, Voinovich provides only a cursory survey of this topic and focuses instead on the sexual debasement and nastiness engendered by the realization of communism in one city. Kartsev's first encounter with matters sexual occurs in a bathhouse, where two truck drivers offer to include him in a deal by which they will swap soap with a girl for her sexual favors. Even lust, it appears, is affected by material shortages and inflation; one of the drivers answers Kartsev's disgusted admonitions:

"Hey, listen, Pop!" cried the bandaged one chasing after me. "Why are you blowing your top! Are you a nut or something? It's not us who's corrupt, it's the girls. They used to take half a glass of soap," he said, indicating the glass in his hand. "That was no problem. You could satisfy your need and still get a good wash. But now they won't take less than three and that's why we need three people to chip in." (*Moskva 2042*, p. 136)

His adventures in the "Palace of Love," an institution where clients are allowed to masturbate, are equally vulgar and unsatisfying. Although Voinovich's "palace" is not as frightening a fictional creation as Orwell's "Ministry of Love" (a nominal parallel which is certainly not coincidental), it is thoroughly revolting, with its oilcloth, plastic pails and rude orderlies.

Marriage is based solely on practical considerations in *Moscow 2042*. It is a temporary, contractual arrangement subject to approval by the local "pentagons." Minimum and maximum ages for marriage coincide with productivity; when citizens are no longer capable of procreation, their marriages are automatically dissolved. Radical interference with marital privacy is almost always a feature of dystopia, but Voinovich particularizes his version to reflect contemporary problems in the Soviet Union. In cases where marriage partners want to keep living together after the mandated dissolution of their union, they are allowed to "If they have a place. And, if they don't, there are always bushes and doorways" (*ibid.*, p. 187). The dehumanizing effects of the Soviet housing shortage are underscored through *ostranenie* when Voinovich shifts the problem from the beginning of married life to the end.

Kartsev provides little information about the regulation of childbearing in *Moscow 2042*, but suggests that this aspect of life is controlled as well. Rather than giving a programmatic explanation, he details one particularly egregious example. Soviet cosmonauts have conceived a child in space under the supervision of scientific authorities: "They now had reached their due date, and, in Doctor Pirozhkov's opinion, the child would be a boy. They were hoping the child would be born by the Sixty-seventh KPGB Party Congress and had already named it Congress" (*ibid.*, p. 111).[50] Voinovich exaggerates just enough to make his futuristic vision ridiculous rather than frightening. The satirical denouement of this situation occurs when the cosmonauts land and seek asylum in the West. Their fleeing is a recontextualization of O-90's escape in Zamiatin's *We*; it is rendered banal in Voinovich's parodic version, for the motivation of these characters is material rather than spiritual.

Moscow 2042 offers what M. D. Fletcher calls "a consumer's view of the failings of the Soviet system."[51] Dystopian writing often describes poverty and shabbiness as a counterpoint to the material abundance promised in utopian works; in this respect, Voinovich's novel challenges *1984*. Martin Kessler notes that in the dystopian tradition, "stability and satisfaction can be obtained only through deliberate standardization of demand" ("Power and the Perfect State," 571). Sacrifice of personal comfort and convenience must be made on the part of the citizenry for the general good of the state. The irony of Voinovich's vision is that individual sacrifices are indeed made in Moscowrep (as in Soviet society), but little general good results. Moreover, the needs of the Communites are standardized in principle, but not in fact. Needs are actually defined as a function of ideological conformity and correctness, a situation that Smerchev explains in the euphemism-laden cant of the "secondary" language:

> "Before determining what a person's needs are, you must first learn his physical and moral characteristics – his weight, height, ideological views, his attitude toward work, and the extent of his involvement with the community. Naturally, a person who is a good worker – who fulfills his production assignments, takes part in community affairs, and studies the Genialissimo's works diligently – has much greater needs than someone who is lazy or violates social discipline." (*Moskva 2042*, p. 123)

As in its Soviet interpretation, the Marxist principle of "from each according to his ability, to each according to his needs" has been distorted until it has become unrecognizable.

Voinovich follows the dystopian models of Zamiatin, Huxley and Orwell in reducing art, music and literature in *Moscow 2042* to mechanical functions. Most of his attention – quite naturally – is focused on literature. The individuality of the creative process has been obviated; teams of writers collaborate to produce works on the Genialissimo. Communites do not read books, they "study" them. Literary criticism has been completely subsumed by the security organs. The dogma of socialist realism has been superceded by "communist realism." "Paperless literature" has solved the problem of potentially subversive art, since only high-ranking writers are entrusted with paper on which to record their words.

Much of Voinovich's satire is specific to the Soviet literary milieu. His indictment of the role played by the Writers' Union, his condemnation of the sycophancy of his fellow writers and his exposé of the use of threats and blandishments in the literary world have direct parallels in Soviet reality. Placing the institutions he portrays in the futuristic state of Moscowrep allows him to intensify his satirical attack. The technology applied in the control of art, for example, is ironically primitive. "Paperless literature" is as much an answer to the paper shortage (a perennial problem in the Soviet Union) as a result of ideological safeguards. Computers are not menacing in the sense that they monitor every word written for possible subversive tendencies; in fact, they are just a facade to placate graphomaniacs. Thus Voinovich parodies the motifs of the dystopian model to particularize his satirical attack on Soviet literature. He indicts the inefficiency, the injustice and the destructive effect on creativity of the Soviet literary bureaucracy.

Creativity seems to breed rebellion and dissidence in classical dystopian works and an intellectual elite often constitutes a vanguard in dystopian writing (Walsh, *From Utopia to Nightmare*, p. 164). *Moscow 2042* responds to this tradition with the discouraging premise that art can be utterly tamed and manipulated. Okhlamanov, a writer who initially seems to be a potential revolutionary, turns out to be a fanatical disciple of Karnavalov; his art too is ultimately subordinated to ideology. Nevertheless, Voinovich would seem to support the notion recognized by utopian and dystopian writers since Plato that the *genuine* poet is dangerous. In *Moscow 2042*, the unlikely figure of Kartsev turns out to fulfill this function, for he helps to bring about the destruction of one dystopian state (Moscowrep) and is exiled from a second (Karnavalov's monarchy).

In considering *Moscow 2042* and its relationship to the dystopian tradition, it is important to keep in mind that the expectations that we bring to this genre are different from those we bring to a novel. The poetics of dystopia differ radically from those of the novel, and an even-handed evaluation of narration, characterization and description must take this into account. Indeed, the collocation "dystopian novel" is misleading, for the dystopia is not simply a subset of the novelistic genre.[52] Of course, the size of the novel is appropriate to the dystopia; as John Glad notes, "in the creation of complex depiction of a future world, the shorter prose genres are not adequate to encompassing demands of plot and the socio-technical detail being predicted/illustrated."[53] The situation is complicated by the fact that the dystopia is often conflated with other forms, such as adventure novels, travelogues and fantastic voyages.

What distinguishes the dystopia from the novel and from

related prose genres is its ideational bent; *Moscow 2042*, like all dystopias, is a *roman à thèse*. That the sociopolitical element predominates and aesthetic considerations are secondary is therefore not an artistic failing, but a consistent feature of this genre. A moral concern to persuade the reader is more central than weaving a compelling fiction. Quite naturally, the question of the future relevance of both utopias and dystopias will arise: will a work become obsolete and outdated when the issues it explores are no longer current? It would seem that longevity is possible when the polemical element is not definitive. In the case of *Moscow 2042*, the ingredient of humor added to the formulae refined by Zamiatin, Orwell and others gives the work particular vitality.

The plot of literary dystopias tends to follow a prescriptive pattern. In general, writers of dystopia describe a sociopolitical situation that is despotic and oppressive. An attempt to subvert or destroy that system then provides the basis of an adventure plot. Voinovich makes use of the voyage device in structuring his dystopian parody. Traveling with the aid of a time machine and falling asleep to wake in another time and place are variants of this convention and Voinovich combines them in *Moscow 2042*. Suffering from a hangover and having consumed several servings of vodka, Kartsev falls asleep during his voyage into the future on a Lufthansa jet. As a newcomer to Moscowrep, he is subsequently initiated into the customs and institutions of that society and subjects them to comparison and contrast. This exposition of dystopian life is an invariant element of the genre and often replaces suspense. The brief resolution of the plot usually consists of the narrator's exit from dystopia and return home. Kartsev is ejected from the new regime established by Karnavalov and returns to Germany of sixty years earlier.

This rather skeletal frame into which the plot of *Moscow 2042* is set is on one level a parody of utopian writers' practice of embedding their tales within frames of prefaces, postscripts and various addenda (Morson, *Boundaries of Genre*, p. 138). Another layer of complexity (and parody) is added by Voinovich's interweaving references to his novel in the text. The simple frame given to the story is thus made labyrinthine, for Kartsev

Dystopia redux 229

gradually becomes aware that the Communites know of him through the novel that he will write upon returning home to Germany. Kartsev's confusion and suspicion of the sinister, telepathic powers of the secret police dissolve in anticlimax when he realizes that they have merely read his book. This is not, however, just narrative acrobatics on Voinovich's part. The satirical point of his embedding the frame device is to expose the ubiquitous quality of Soviet censorship. Kartsev is pressured to delete references to Karnavalov from his novel by the Communites in order to prevent the actualization of the future he has predicted; his reply is a stinging indictment of Soviet censorship:

"But don't you understand, there'll be nothing left of the novel. All that will be left is meaningless nonsense. And you simply fail to understand me. If I had been able to correct my novels that way, I would not have had any reason to come here. What a career I could have had back then in the days of socialism, under the Cultists, Volunteerists, Corruptionists and Reformists! I would already have been the secretary of the Writers' Union, a Hero of Labor, a Deputy to the Supreme Soviet and a Lenin-Prize laureate. I would have had royalties by the sackload. But I was incapable of that then and I am incapable of it now." (*Moskva 2042*, pp. 285–86)[54]

Reading a forbidden work of literature is a common subversive act in dystopian writing. That the work in this case is Kartsev's own future novel is a parodic twist of the device. The apparent absurdity of the situation echoes an actual event in Voinovich's experience:

During the discussion of how the manuscript [of *Chonkin*] got out of the country, he [Viktor Tel'pugov, a censor] said: "It is not really important how it got out of the country; it is not important how it came to be published there. What is important is that it was written. If I learned that it merely had been written – or not even written, but merely conceived by the author – then I would feel that the author deserved a prison term or even to be shot. I myself would petition the appropriate authorities to punish the author accordingly."[55]

The narrative technique that Voinovich uses in *Moscow 2042* to satirize the debilitating power of censorship reflects the convoluted rationale that supported strict control of actions, words and even thoughts in Soviet culture.

A common strategy of the dystopia entails introducing a narrator from outside the society who carries on a dialogue with insiders, thereby revealing and explicating the workings of the state. The dialogue probably owes its conventional status within the genre to Plato's model of utopia; this narrative device is combined with the topos of the voyage to produce a kind of fantastic guided tour. As Juan López-Morillas puts it, "Doctrine is the stuff of the dialogue and imagination that of the voyage" ("From 'Dreams of Reason'," 53). Both aspects of this narrative technique support *ostranenie*, for they facilitate an examination of the author's own society (or another society familiar to him and to the reader) from an objective viewpoint. Kartsev, as an émigré from the past, is simultaneously insider and outsider. He knows all about Moscow and the Soviet Union, but is baffled by Moscowrep, the futuristic state that has resulted from political metamorphosis.

Conflict is generally provided in utopias and dystopias by the narrator's doubt about the efficacy or ethics of the new society he describes. The work is given shape by the story of the hero's struggle with ideological uncertainty. Often this struggle culminates in a rejection of the basic tenets of the utopian or dystopian state. Voinovich toys with this formula, making Kartsev a skeptic at the outset. It is significant that he is willing, even eager to be convinced of the correctness of the communist vision; upon arriving in Moscowrep, he is thrilled to hear that the dream has been achieved:

"In other words," I said, returning to the previous subject, "you're saying that you have built communism, is that right? I confess that I never expected it, never saw it coming. The thing is I was always on the weak side as far as having a progressive worldview goes. I never had much of a head for school, and I always got poor grades in Marxist theory. But don't think I'm not very happy that things have turned out differently from what I'd imagined. Thank God I was wrong." (*Moskva 2042*, p. 104)

The twist Voinovich gives to the generic convention in this case is that his narrator only gradually comes to realize what the achievement of communism has meant. It is this process of discovery that the reader experiences through Kartsev's dialogues with Iskrina and with others. Because we already have certain expectations of what this utopia will look like (from Marxist theory), the disparity between the ideal and Voinovich's "reality" is much more stark.

Since it is important that the reader be able to identify and sympathize with the dystopian narrator, he is usually a positive character who reacts to his new surroundings in predictable, understandable ways. Kartsev is somewhat problematic when examined in this light. Like Chonkin, he is not a character who inspires emulation; he drinks heavily, cheats on his wife and eventually capitulates to moral pressure. Yet his ironic self-deprecation and humor directed at his own shortcomings help to establish his credibility and humanness. It is interesting that Voinovich creates a middle-aged hero in *Moscow 2042*; his earlier heroes are young and many of their weaknesses can be chalked up to youthful inexperience or naiveté. Daniel Rancour-Laferriere suggests that Kartsev is a thinly disguised autobiographical narrator[56] and there are in fact many parallels between author and narrator.[57] Kartsev's emigration from the Soviet Union, his identity as a writer, his residence in Germany and many other aspects of his character are certainly autobiographical. Yet Vitalii Kartsev is clearly a caricature of Voinovich, a distorted self-portrait. Voinovich undercuts Kartsev's heroism as he inverts Bulgakov:

"Manuscripts don't burn!" my devil maliciously reminded me, referring to a certain preliminary writer. "Get thee behind me!" I said with a wave of my hand. "Of course they burn poorly if you throw a whole manuscript in all at once, but if you ball up each page and throw them in one at a time, they'll burn perfectly well and there'll be nothing left." (*Moskva 2042*, p. 301)

Voinovich himself displayed integrity and firm conviction when pressured and harrassed by Soviet authorities. The difference in character, then, is a telling one. In contrast to the self-righteous figure of Karnavalov/Solzhenitsyn, Kartsev embodies the more banal truth that most human beings, when tormented enough, will compromise their principles, and that this is understandable and forgivable.

As the bearer of the authorial message, the dystopian narrator is usually described in terms of his psychology and emotions. Kartsev, a garrulous and confiding first-person narrator, is fully characterized internally by Voinovich, but he is alone in this respect. Most of the other characters in *Moscow 2042*, as in most dystopias, act chiefly as mouthpieces for ideas. That they are stylized, somewhat mechanical and flat – a frequent criticism of characterization in both utopia and dystopia (Elliott, *The Shape of Utopia*, p. 121) – is quite true. Indeed the reader can discern little psychological nuance in characters such as Starskii, Siromakhin and Smerchev. Focusing exclusively on their actions and speech is a means of satirically reducing them.

In describing Moscowrep and its institutions, Voinovich makes ample use of the grotesque, a *sine qua non* of dystopian literature. As Northrop Frye has insightfully noted, behavior in literary utopia and dystopia is described ritually ("Varieties of Literary Utopias," 26). Thus Kartsev is initially baffled by the incomprehensible actions of the Communites: "'Thank Genialissimo, thank Genialissimo,' he mumbled like a madman, making strange motions with his right hand. It looked like he was crossing himself but in some new way. Using all five fingers he touched himself in the following places and the following order: forehead, left knee, right shoulder, left shoulder, right knee, forehead" (*Moskva 2042*, p. 105). Rituals that seem irrational typically become rational when they are explained by insiders, members of the dystopian society. In *Moscow 2042*, however, explication of behavior does not necessarily make it reasonable. Indeed, Voinovich is intent on exposing the absurdity of Soviet life and to this end, the Communites' explanations consist of paradoxical rationalizations. This ritual of "starring" oneself, for example, is based on the Communites' simultaneous worship of the Genialissimo as god and atheism.

Scatological imagery pervades *Moscow 2042* and all of the details Voinovich provides have the effect of diminishing and debasing the society he describes. The chronic shortage of toilet paper has been solved by printing *Pravda* in rolls ready for use; a statue of Karl Marx has been virtually covered in pigeon dung; citizens are required to turn in "secondary matter" (excrement) in order to receive "primary matter" (food).

Voinovich is to some extent indebted to Orwell, whose dystopian vision in *1984* is characterized by filth and stench. And he may, like Orwell, be responding parodically to Wells' utopian enthusiasm for hygiene and cleanliness. Moreover, Voinovich combines the scatological element with the dystopian motif of the obliteration of privacy. Here, however, frightening prophecy turns to farce when he shifts the focus from intimate sexual relations (as in Zamiatin or Huxley) to excretion. The Communites utilize public toilets, where they defecate while being observed by orderlies. The only explanation given for the great value placed on "secondary matter" – that the Communites must supply it to the Outer Rings of Hostility to fulfill the terms of a contract – renders the whole issue still more repugnant.

The bathroom humor of *Moscow 2042* may be partially explained by the effectiveness of scatological imagery in "presenting an evaluation of the entire Soviet experience" (Fletcher, "Voinovich's 'Consumer' Satire," 108). As in *Chonkin*, extended realization of the metaphor makes Voinovich's satire visceral and intense. Furthermore, a reading of the text as a parodic treatment of the dystopian tradition suggests that it may represent an end point in a process of debasement and vulgarization of imagery that occurs with the concretization of utopia in modern literature. Kenneth Burke has called this process "transcendence downward"[58] and in Voinovich's work, we seem to have reached the nadir.

Another function of scatological imagery, and especially excrement, is relevant to *Moscow 2042* as a parodic dystopia. In psychoanalytical terms, anality and a preoccupation with the feces (connected with the infantile stage of anal eroticism) is not suppressed in the Golden Age or the age of innocence.[59] If utopia is related to the myth of the Golden Age, then Voinovich's dystopic vision is the inversion of this myth. True, anality is not repressed in this society; it is, however, rigidly controlled and directed. Feces are property not in the figurative sense understood by infant developmental psychologists, but in the most direct, literal sense. The Freudian symbolic equation of feces and money is actualized, as the Communites barter excrement for other goods. Like Swift, Voinovich revels in the scatological at least in part as a rejection of the rule of logic, civilization and restraint.

The debasement of language is a canonical feature of literary dystopia and Voinovich too creates a kind of "newspeak" for his fictive society. As in his dystopian models, the official, "secondary" language of Moscowrep is simplified and standardized to reflect ideological conformity. Chopped up and recombined to suit the new needs of the state, this language is lifeless and unnatural. Terming this language "secondary" (*vtorichnyi*) (ostensibly more advanced) echoes the recurring phrase "secondary matter" (*vtorichnyi produkt*) and creates a semantic association of the Communites' language with excrement. The terms Voinovich coins as representative of the secondary language are indeed exceedingly ugly: the Communites eat at *prekompity* or *predpriiatiia kommunisticheskogo pitaniia* (*comfoodests* or *Communist Food Establishments*); they gather in *meobskopy* or *mesta obshchestvennogo skopleniia* (*locpubasses* or *Locations of Public Assembly*); they receive supplies at *pukomrasy* or *punkty kommunisticheskogo raspredeleniia* (*comdispoints* or *Communist Distribution Points*); they relieve themselves in *kabesoty* or *kabinety estestvennykh otpravlenii* (*natfunctburs* or *Bureaus of Natural Functions*). Even the name of this state, Moscowrep, is a coinage recalling Orwell's Ingsoc. Earlier dystopias are not, of course, the only source of Voinovich's distortion of language; he is satirizing actual Soviet linguistic practice as well, with its *sovnarkhozy* (*sovet narodnogo khoziaistva*; *regional economic council*), its *minzdravy* (*ministerstvo zdravookhraneniia*; *ministry of public health*), its *raikomy* (*raionnyi komitet*; *district committee*).

Names are often replaced with numbers or otherwise made impersonal in the dystopian tradition. In Moscowrep, citizens are given "startismal" names that reflect their basic activity upon their full enfranchisement in the society.[60] These names are generic and impersonal in their hyperbolic quality. Voinovich's satiric innovation in this respect is to make them awkward and cumbersome rather than simple and bland. All the Communites have names ironically full of revolutionary significance: Dzerzhin Gavrilovich Siromakhin, Propaganda Parmonovna Bovinak, Iskrina Romanovna Poliakov, Kommunii Ivanovich Smerchev. Kartsev too is renamed when he arrives in Moscowrep; he is called Classic by the Communites and – rather absurdly – Klasha by his mistress.

Kartsev is initially befuddled by the secondary language and his difficulties understanding his hosts echo his problems with German in the frame chapters. That is, he is as much an outsider in Moscow of 2042 as he is in Munich of 1982. Here, however, he is assigned an interpreter who helps him with unfamiliar terminology and he is soon fluent himself. Voinovich exaggerates the difference between the preliminary and secondary languages to satirize the distortion of Russian in Soviet officialese and journalese:

> Usually Iskrina tried to speak with me in the preliminary language, which she had learned not from literature, but from precommunist *Pravda* editorials. I have to admit that my knowledge of that particular language was rather shaky too. And, for that reason, I proposed that we try to communicate in the communist language, in which I had already made a little progress. (*Moskva 2042*, p. 184)

The preliminary language, where it survives, provides an antidote to the stilted, awkward speech of the Communites. Voinovich is at pains, on the other hand, to make Karnavalov's exclusive preference for Russian root words seem silly. His devotion to reading Dal' and his substituting *gliadelka* ("looker") for *televizor* ("television") and *chitalka* ("reader") for *gazeta* ("newspaper") are spurious. Plain, colloquial Russian, including the rich lexicon of curses, is characteristic of Kartsev's speech and that of positive (if imperfect) characters. Kuzia, the mechanic who pops up to help Kartsev at several junctures speaks ordinary, earthy Russian. Part of the joy of Kartsev's recognition of his old friend Edik in the person of Edison Ksenofontovich is conversing naturally: "'You're bullshitting me,' I cried out in the preliminary language. 'I should drop dead,' replied Edik with a smile, in that same language" (*ibid.*, pp. 270–71).

In the Communites' secondary language, Voinovich has created a speech system based entirely on ideological considerations. This language supports and codifies the illusions and distortions of reality upon which the legitimacy of Moscowrep depends. Numerous dystopian models posit language as a means of indoctrination and coercion. At least in part, Voinovich's satiric treatment of euphemisms derives from the paradigms of Zamiatin and Orwell. An unneeded scientific subject will be "recycled" (*ibid.*, p. 265), a superman created through eugenic experiments has been "edited" (*ibid.*, p. 266), torture is "testing the firmness of various people's beliefs" (*ibid.*, p. 263). Voinovich also comments satirically on the specifically Soviet application of euphemisms to replace direct language in the signs Kartsev encounters: "The need for hot water is temporarily not being satisfied" and "The need to descend in elevators is temporarily not being satisfied" (*ibid.*, p. 147).

In *Moscow 2042*, Orwell's "doublethink," or the ability to believe in two contradictory ideas simultaneously, has been perfected. Yet the Communites' verbal sleight of hand is only a short step away from that of Soviet jargon. Voinovich draws on dystopian models, but makes his linguistic satire wickedly close to familiar Soviet cant. Equality (the ideal) and rigid hierarchy (the reality) are reconciled effortlessly by Iskrina:

"Oh, how backward you are!" she exclaimed heatedly. "What does that mean – to be like everyone else? And to what inequalities are you referring? We are all equal here. Every Communite is born with general needs. But if he develops and improves himself, fulfills his production assignments, maintains discipline, broadens his horizon, then of course his needs also increase, and we take that into account." (*Ibid.*, p. 169)

Official tolerance of – indeed veneration of – religion in the avowedly atheistic Moscowrep presents another conundrum to the uninitiated narrator. Voinovich briefly treats the paradoxical coexistence of official freedom and rigid constraint in Kartsev's dialogue with customs officials. He is told that he is free to photograph absolutely anything and anyone in Moscowrep; the only restriction is that he is forbidden to have film in his camera.

Aside from the coinages of the secondary language and illustrations of "doublethink," Voinovich utilizes a rather neutral style in *Moscow 2042*. Like his earlier works, this text is characterized by the narrator's chatty, colloquial speech. A common and effective feature of Voinovich's satire that is retained here is the use of lexicon slightly too pretentious for the subject to which it refers (Hosking, *Beyond Socialist Realism*, pp. 136–37). This is particularly true of Kartsev's ironic use of Soviet slogans and propaganda clichés in reference to quite ordinary matters. Considering whether to pack chewing gum as a gift before his departure for the future, he muses:

> I had heard that Soviet-made chewing gum had already appeared in the Soviet Union. Of course, it had to take second place to Western chewing gum, but I didn't have the slightest doubt that in the span of sixty years, as a result of the technological revolution, historic party and government decrees, and the masses' enthusiasm for labor, the production of chewing articles and their distribution to broad segments of the population would probably have undergone radical change for the better. (*Moskva 2042*, p. 22)

Within a single long sentence, Voinovich moves from standard Russian to the language of Soviet newspapers and speeches, incrementally intensifying the disparity between the topic discussed and the style employed.

If *Moscow 2042* were only about Soviet totalitarianism or even communism, it would already be an obsolete satire in light of the events of recent years. As a parody of literary dystopia, however, it has considerably more significance. Voinovich alludes to other utopias beyond the world he describes in this text and he suggests that they too are illusory, even threatening. The very idea of a chiliastic, utopian future, it would seem, is repugnant to the author. A utopia – any utopia – realized must become a totalitarian state. Life probably can be rendered rational and harmonious and everyone's needs probably can be met, but achieving this would mean sacrificing freedom and altering human nature. The first is undesirable, the second impossible. The image of Edison Ksenofontovich's distillation machine, in which he separates the elixir of life and the fluid of death, is a potent symbol of man's propensity to interfere with natural processes in the name of utopia. Kartsev realizes that the machine should be destroyed, that the fluids must literally "run together." When they do, "the puddles formed a combustible combination...and immediately blazed up, in a column of unbearably white flame which struck the ceiling and set it on fire like a sheet of paper" (*ibid.*, p. 319). This white flame is a cleansing, creative force and the image of a sheet of paper, a writer's raw material, is most apropos. For Voinovich, irrationality, individualism and imagination are powerful sources of resistance to utopian and dystopian schemes.

Conclusion

No single study could encompass the full range of contemporary Russian satire exhaustively, for satire is woven into the textual fabric of most of modern Russian literature. We do not think of Tolstaia, Bitov, Petrushevskaia, Aksenov or Makanin primarily as satirists, yet satire is a significant feature of their diverse styles. In limiting the scope of the present study, I have chosen to examine a few representative works intensively with the intention of demonstrating a common rhetorical procedure that may help us to describe contemporary Russian satire as a whole. Parody of the features associated with specific literary genres advances thematic satire in each of the seminal works I have considered. Rarely is the genre itself the target of satire; it is not the conventions of allegory or autobiography that satirists find objectionable or absurd. Rather generic parody provides a vehicle of exposing, mocking or condemning aspects of contemporary Russian/Soviet society which an author considers pernicious or ridiculous. The sophisticated use of parody makes all of these works densely referential and a full appreciation of the texts' satiric import is conditional on the reader's knowledge not only of contemporary Russian culture but also of the literary traditions that support it. In the Russian context, satire is not a liminal or "low" form of literary art. On the contrary, as this study shows, the best examples of modern satire are among the most complex, powerful and profound works of contemporary literature.

Rabbits and Boa Constrictors, a "philosophical fairy tale" by the author's own definition, is not a typical or representative work for Iskander. Using animal characters exclusively (with the exception of some natives whom we never see directly), he parodies the conventions of allegory in order to examine the debilitating ethical malaise affecting his homeland. Allegory is a most appropriate mode because Iskander is concerned above all with moral issues. Tracing the dynamics between the tyrannical boas and the seemingly docile rabbits, he condemns the "submission reflex" that leads the latter to submit to hypnotism. His chief satirical target is his compatriots' readiness to denounce and betray one another, a behavior that grows out of fear and hypocrisy. Iskander's parodic satire does offer a positive antidote to the evil he exposes; he advocates the rabbits' struggling to free themselves by rejecting complicity. He warns that this freedom will cost the rabbits their comfortable lifestyle, but counsels that you must stand up – even within the belly of the boa constrictor which is digesting you – and speak the truth. The sunny, optimistic mood of Iskander's earlier tales (especially of the early *Sandro* stories) has given way to a rather melancholy key in this work. While this change may reflect the growth and development of an individual writer, it may also be emblematic of the often violent political and social change to which Iskander has borne witness.

Erofeev's *Moscow–Petushki* has justly achieved the status of a modern classic; perhaps no other single work so eloquently expresses the essence of the *zastoi* period. The parodic basis of this satiric *tour de force* is the picaresque novel and Erofeev deftly adapts its structure and thematic conventions to expose the spiritual void of Soviet culture. Venia's alcoholic stupor, his inconsolable grief and his final descent into oblivion are all reactions to the bleak emptiness of life without God, without faith and without beauty. When he embarks upon a quest to rediscover Eden, innocence and purity – symbolized by Petushki and his loved ones who reside there – Venia discovers that the nasty, brutal world of the commuter train is inescapable. In a reversal of picaresque convention, his trip turns out to be circular and ends in the picaro's death. Densely polysemic, *Moscow–Petushki* includes parodic echoes of biblical, medieval, classical and modern texts. In a culture where individualism is suspect, no unique creation is possible and on one level, this text is a pastiche of borrowed (and parodied) ideas and styles. Philosophically and artistically, Erofeev's work is a brilliant satiric indictment of Soviet society.

While Iskander's and Erofeev's satires were both written within the Soviet milieu, Limonov's *It's Me, Eddie* is a product of the third wave of emigration. Indeed, Limonov posits the phenomenon of emigration as one of his satirical targets. The double vision of the text is one of its strongest qualities; Limonov's autobiographical narrator has been a social outcast both in the Soviet Union and in America and he trains his satirical lens on both societies. By way of reminiscence, Edichka ridicules Russian culture (especially Russian literature) and debunks the very notion of homeland; in the present of the text, he satirizes American mores, in particular what he perceives as spiritual stinginess, excessive materialism and banality. Limonov parodies the conventions of childhood autobiography to express forcefully the loss, rage and bitterness of the émigré experience. This procedure is particularly effective because the childhood autobiography has been closely connected with the pastoral in Russian literary tradition and Edichka's life in New York – his suffering, poverty and largely self-imposed degradation – represents the antipode of pastoral. *It's Me, Eddie* was Limonov's first prose work and it remains his best work; he has been prolific and successful, but nothing he has written since has matched the eloquent and searing satire of this parodic autobiography.

Ours is one of Dovlatov's last works and is representative of his *œuvre* in several ways: its satirical tenor is gentle, it is written from the distanced perspective of life in emigration, and it expresses bemused awe at the absurdity of life (especially of Soviet life). Dovlatov has chosen the genre of the family chronicle as a basis of parody to express the fate of the Russian intelligentsia in the twentieth century. His family, like many others, is maimed and partially destroyed, compelled to make ethical compromises, exposed to bigotry and ultimately driven out in the course of the Soviet era. At the same time, *Ours* is a very funny portrait gallery of disparate individuals – many eccentric and odd – who come alive under Dovlatov's pen.

They are an object of his satire, but more central to his satiric vision are the political and social conditions that shaped their lives. A truly Horatian satirist, Dovlatov exposes both the particular injustices and cruelties of Soviet society and the general absurdities of the human condition.

Voinovich's *Moscow 2042*, the subject of the final chapter of this study, is a parody of the dystopia (which is itself a parodic response to utopian literature). Here we are granted access to the foreseeable future to witness how Soviet society plays itself out in a political, economic and cultural endgame. Duplicity, illogicality and sycophancy — all fixed features of Soviet culture as Voinovich presents it — are taken to their logical extremes in this futuristic nightmare. Although the *ad hominem* attack on Solzhenitsyn included in *Moscow 2042* has drawn criticism, it is an integral part of Voinovich's satirical examination of totalitarianism. The cult of personality, he suggests, is not limited to the past (Stalinism) or the present (the Genialissimo); Solzhenitsyn's views represent for him the same kind of intolerance and dogmatism and thus present a commensurate threat. Through his alternate dystopias — Moscow under the Genialissimo and Moscow under Karnavalov/Solzhenitsyn — Voinovich targets any belief system that denies the preeminence of the individual. Dystopia is an effective medium for Voinovich's parodic satire because Russian history has, he suggests, already presented us with the ultimate dystopian state. Written on the cusp of *glasnost'*, this work remains timely and relevant, for Voinovich is interested in the mindset that gives rise to totalitarianism, a specter that has not disappeared from Russia today. *Moscow 2042* is formally very different from Voinovich's other works, but the themes that inform this text are constant in his œuvre.

Satire in all its varied forms is a pervasive element in Russia's literature both past and present. It is difficult to say whether this is so in spite of or because of the particular conditions that shaped its traditions; there are persuasive advocates of both points of view. In any case, the works examined here demonstrate that satire is not only alive and well, but evolving and expanding in most interesting directions. Satirists are utilizing a variety of genres, engaging in intertextual discourse and parody to enrich and revitalize the satirical mode. A common thread in all of the diverse texts included in this study is a focus on the particular conditions of Soviet society in the modern period, i.e. its material privations and inconveniences, political repression and institutionalized hypocrisy. And like all truly great satirical works, these transcend immediate circumstances to examine the human sources of the malady that crippled and ultimately destroyed the great Soviet experiment: mutual distrust, perfidy, lack of respect for the individual, greed and brutality. Moreover, for all of the bleakness of these visions of *homo Sovieticus* and *homo sapiens*, one can clearly discern the satirist's paradoxical conviction that life can be saner, that wisdom and compassion might prevail after all.

Notes

INTRODUCTION

1 Kenneth Burke, *The Philosophy of Literary Form. Studies in Symbolic Action* (Berkeley: University of California Press, 1973), pp. 231–32; Lev Loseff, *On the Beneficence of Censorship. Aesopian Language in Modern Russian Literature* (München: Verlag Otto Sagner, 1984).
2 Robert C. Elliott, *The Power of Satire: Magic, Ritual, Art* (Princeton: Princeton University Press, 1960); M. M. Bakhtin, *Rabelais and His World*, trans. Helene Iswolsky (Cambridge, MA: The MIT Press, 1968).
3 Ronald Paulson, *The Fictions of Satire* (Baltimore: The Johns Hopkins Press, 1967), pp. 72–73.
4 Joseph A. Dane, "Parody and Satire: A Theoretical Model," *Genre* 13 (1980), 154.
5 Linda Hutcheon, *A Theory of Parody. The Teachings of Twentieth-Century Art Forms* (London: Methuen, 1985), p. 43.
6 Gilbert Highet, *The Anatomy of Satire* (Princeton: Princeton University Press, 1962), p. 69.
7 Fred W. Householder, Jr., "Parody," *Classical Philology* 39 (1944), 1.
8 John D. Jump, *Burlesque* (London: Methuen, 1972), p. 18.
9 Dwight Macdonald, *Parodies. An Anthology from Chaucer to Beerbohm – and After* (New York: Random House, 1960), p. 557.
10 Iu. N. Tynianov, *Poetika. Istoriia literatury. Kino* (Moskva: Nauka, 1977), p. 310.
11 Gary Saul Morson, *The Boundaries of Genre. Dostoevsky's* Diary of a Writer *and the Traditions of Literary Utopia* (Evanston: Northwestern University Press, 1981), p. 108.
12 I. R. Titunik, "The Formal Method and the Sociological Method (M. M. Bakhtin, P. N. Medvedev, V. N. Voloshinov) in Russian Theory and Study of Literature," in *Marxism and the Philosophy of Language*, by V. N. Voloshinov (Cambridge, MA: Harvard University Press, 1986), p. 196.

This work is widely attributed to Bakhtin himself. This view is not unanimous, however, and several critics have argued convincingly for Voloshinov's authorship. For an overview of this debate, see Gary Saul Morson and Caryl Emerson, eds., *Rethinking Bakhtin. Extensions and Challenges* (Evanston: Northwestern University Press, 1989), pp. 31–49.

13 O. M. Freidenberg, "The Origin of Parody," in *Semiotics and Structuralism. Readings from the Soviet Union*, ed. Henryk Baran (White Plains: International Arts and Sciences Press, 1976), pp. 278–79.

14 Margaret A. Rose, *Parody//Meta-Fiction. An Analysis of Parody as a Critical Mirror to the Writing and Perception of Fiction* (London: Croom Helm, 1979), p. 185.

15 G. D. Kiremidjian, "The Aesthetics of Parody," *The Journal of Aesthetics and Art Criticism* 28 (1969), 231.

16 J. G. Riewald, "Parody as Criticism," *Neophilologus* 50 (1966), 132.

17 Wayne Booth, *A Rhetoric of Irony* (Chicago: University of Chicago Press, 1974), p. 126. Hutcheon (*Theory of Parody*, pp. 84–85) suggests a narratological compromise to avoid the problem of authorial intentionality. She speculates that the term "inferred encoder" may be more appropriate to discussions of parody that treat it as a process of encoding and decoding.

1 ISKANDER'S TRANSPARENT ALLEGORY

1 Natal'ia Ivanova, "Smekh protiv strakha," in *Kroliki i udavy. Proza poslednikh let*, by Fazil' Iskander (Moskva: Knizhnaia palata, 1988), p. 4.

2 Petr Vail' and Aleksandr Genis, "Beseda s Fazilem Iskanderom," *Al'manakh Panorama* (18–25 Dec. 1987), 20.

3 Grigorii Anisimov and Marina Bondariuk, "Korotko, no ne koroche istiny," *Literaturnoe obozrenie*, 11 (1985), 38–39.

4 For a more detailed discussion of the influence of classical Russian literature on Iskander's prose, see Benedikt Sarnov, "Mir Fazilia Iskandera," in *Fazil' Iskander. Bibliograficheskii uzakatel'*, by Z. B. Mikhailova (Ul'ianovsk: Oblastnoi sovet profsoiuzov, 1982), p. 15. See also Karen Ryan-Hayes, "Iskander and Tolstoj: The Parodical Implications of the Beast Narrator," *Slavic and East European Journal* 32 (1988), 225–36.

5 Natal'ia Ivanova (*Smekh protiv strakha, ili Fazil' Iskander* [Moskva: Sovetskii pisatel', 1990], p. 278) finds support for her classification of *Rabbits and Boa Constrictors* as an anti-utopia in its similarity with Dombrovskii's work: "In my opinion, in this philosophical fairy

tale of Iskander there glimmers an internal spiritual connection with Iurii Dombrovskii's novel *The Department of Unnecessary Things*, which relates an experience of realizing utopia. Iskander was friends with Dombrovskii, and in such generically diverse works it is possible to find spiritual resonance, to discover a clear unity of convictions."

6 *Kroliki i udavy* was previously published serially in the émigré journal *Kontinent* (22 and 23) in 1980.
7 In a personal interview with Iskander in 1988, the present author broached this subject; Iskander firmly declined to talk about the circumstances surrounding the publication of *Rabbits and Boa Constrictors* in the West.
8 Ivanova's explanation does not seem to account satisfactorily for all of the works Iskander published abroad. Although much of *Sandro of Chegem* is not satirical, some of the tales which comprise the epic (e.g. "The Feasts of Belshazzar") are very caustic. *Rabbits and Boa Constrictors* is also overtly critical of the Soviet system and its satirical tone is far from "gentle."
9 A. Lebedev, "... I smekh, i slezy, i liubov'," in *Izbrannoe. Rasskazy. Povest'*, by Fazil' Iskander (Moskva: Sovetskii pisatel', 1988), p. 5.
10 This story was published in the journal *Znamia* (7 [1987]) under the title "Staryi dom pod kiparisom." It was published as "Shkol'nyi val's, ili energiia styda" in Iskander's 1988 collection *Kroliki i udavy. Proza poslednikh let*.
11 Later stories include "Barmen Adgur" and "Chegemskaia Karmen," published together as "Dva rasskaza" (*Znamia* 12 [1986]); and "Dudka starogo Khasana" (*Oktiabr'* 4 [1987]). Some critics believe that Chegem has been exhausted as an artistic resource. Vladimir Solov'ev, for example, asserts that "he has dragged it out a bit with Sandro... you have to know how to stop in time, you must not exploit a successful hero, for he won't stand it" ("Fazil' Iskander v okruzhenii svoikh geroev," *Literaturnaia ucheba* 5 [1990], 110).
12 Sergei Chuprinin, "Pokhvala zlosloviiu," *Literaturnaia gazeta* (28 Oct. 1987), 5.
13 Aleksandr Kazintsev, "Ochishchenie ili zloslovie?" *Nash sovremennik* 2 (1988), 188–89.
14 Angus Fletcher, *Allegory. The Theory of a Symbolic Mode* (Ithaca: Cornell University Press, 1964), p. 3.
15 For a concise historical survey of allegory, see Edward A. Bloom, "The Allegorical Principle," *English Literary History* 18 (1951), 163–90.
16 Morton W. Bloomfield, "Allegory as Interpretation," *New Literary History* 3 (1972), 301.

Notes to pages 18–21

17 Northrop Frye, *Anatomy of Criticism. Four Essays* (Princeton: Princeton University Press, 1957), p. 89.
18 William Empson, *Seven Types of Ambiguity* (New York: New Directions, 1947), p. 111.
19 Bloom ("The Allegorical Principle," 174–75) concedes that some degree of obscurity is to be expected in allegory, but "If the secondary meaning consistently eludes apprehension, then it may be said that the allegorist has failed to integrate the various layers of intention and that he is justifiably censurable on the grounds of unnecessary obscurity or inept allegory." Fletcher (*Allegory*, p. 310) identifies a subclass of allegory in which the author deliberately tries to be obscure to arouse the reader's curiosity. Motivated by mystical or doctrinal concerns, the allegorist may purposefully "shroud abstract ideas under a cover of dimly understandable imagery."
20 A classificatory distinction may be made on the basis of personification. "Symbol-allegories" present characters and events that have a second, transcendent meaning (e.g. *The Divine Comedy*); "personification-allegories" rely on characters and events that are themselves abstract and have only a single meaning (e.g. *Piers Plowman*). Some allegories (such as Iskander's *Rabbits and Boa Constrictors*) combine these traditional approaches. These terms and examples are from Robert Worth Frank, Jr., "The Art of Reading Medieval Personification-Allegory," *English Literary History* 20 (1953), pp. 237–38. C. S. Lewis, in his influential work *The Allegory of Love* ([Oxford: Clarendon, 1936], pp. 44–111), treats this distinction and reserves the term "allegory" for the second type delineated by Frank, personification-allegory.
21 Gay Clifford, *The Transformations of Allegory* (London: Routledge, 1974), p. 7. A case can be made, as it is by Frye (*Anatomy of Criticism*, pp. 90–91), that only naive allegory is disguised discursive writing; sophisticated allegory, on the other hand, involves an aesthetic interplay of fictional means and didactic intention.
22 Ellen Douglass Leyburn, *Satiric Allegory: Mirror of Man* (New Haven: Yale University Press, 1956), pp. 7–8.
23 Wyndham Lewis, "The Greatest Satire is Nonmoral," in *Satire. Modern Essays in Criticism*, ed. Ronald Paulson (Englewood Cliffs: Prentice-Hall, 1971), pp. 70–71.
24 Bloom ("The Allegorical Principle," 164) asserts that the operative principle of allegory is "delighting while teaching." The inverse of this formula is apropos to Russian satire in general and Russian allegory in particular.
25 Evg. Shklovskii, "Potrebnost' ochishcheniia," *Literaturnoe obozrenie* 7 (1987), 32.

26 For a brief history of the allegorical *skazka* in Russian literature, see V. F. Osmolovskii, "Zhanr sotsial'no-didakticheskoi skazki v russkoi literature. Puti razvitiia," *Voprosy russkoi literatury* 51 (1988), 68–74.
27 The allegorical *skazka* has seen a limited revival in the contemporary period. Vasilii Shukshin's story "Do tret'ikh petukhov" (1975) is a notable example of extended use of fairy-tale conventions to allegorical purpose. *Skazki* have also been written by Kaverin, Belov, Ustinov, Abramov, Mikhalkov and Iskander in recent decades. See Osmolovskii, "Zhanr sotsial'no-didakticheskoi skazki," 72–73.
28 A. Kviatkovskii, *Poeticheskii slovar'* (Moskva: Sovetskaia entsiklopediia, 1966), p. 348.
29 Deming Brown, *The Last Years of Soviet Russian Literature. Prose Fiction 1975–1991* (Cambridge: Cambridge University Press, 1993), pp. 59–60.
30 Mark Lipovetskii, "Usloviia igry," *Literaturnoe obozrenie* 7 (1988), 47; Ivanova, *Smekh protiv strakha*, p. 272.
31 Sergei Ivanov, "O 'maloi proze' Iskandera, ili chto mozhno sdelat' iz nastoiashchei mukhi," *Novyi mir* 1 (1989), 255.
32 I have adopted the terminology used by Lev Loseff in his discussion of Aesopian art in his book *On the Beneficence of Censorship. Aesopian Language in Modern Russian Literature*.
33 Laura Beraha, "Compilation in the Art of Fazil' Iskander and as a Key to *Sandro iz Chegema*," (Ph.D thesis, McGill University, 1990), pp. 216–17.
34 Iuliia Troll', "*Kroliki i udavy* Fazilia Iskandera," *Novyi zhurnal* 151 (1983), 301.
35 This passage is quoted at length by Sarnov ("Mir Fazilia Iskandera," pp. 20–21). It is not included, however, in the version of "Shkol'nyi val's, ili energiia styda" included in the collection *Kroliki i udavy. Proza poslednikh let*.
36 Edwin Honig, *Dark Conceit. The Making of Allegory* (New York: Oxford University Press, 1966), p. 12.
37 Fazil' Iskander, *Kroliki i udavy* (Ann Arbor: Ardis, 1982), p. 1. The expansive, fairy-tale quality of the first sentence contrasts sharply with the terseness of the second in the Russian original: "Eto sluchilos' v dalekie-predalekie vremena v odnoi iuzhnoi-preiuzhnoi strane. Koroche govoria, v Afrike."
38 Especially famous are the lines: "A v Afrike,|A v Afrike,|Na chernoi|Limpopó|Sidit i plachet|frike|Pechal'nyi Gipopo" (*Sobranie sochinenii*, vol. 1 [Moskva: Khudozhestvennaia literatura, 1965], p. 259).

39 Natal'ia Ivanova, "Bestiarii Fazilia Iskandera," *Literaturnaia Armeniia* 5 (1989).
40 Richard Chapple, "Fazil Iskander's *Rabbits and Boa Constrictors*: A Soviet Version of George Orwell's *Animal Farm*," *Germano-Slavica* 5 (1985), 39.
41 The last sentence of the Russian original is very abstract, including only pronouns that have multiple referents in an allegorical interpretation: "Inache govoria, my – eto byvshie oni, a oni – eto budushchie my."
42 Mark Musa, *Dante's Inferno* (Bloomington: Indiana University Press, 1971), p. 207.
43 Ivanova (*Smekh protiv strakha*, p. 284) suggests that the symbiotic relationship of the boas and the rabbits alludes to the interdependence of the Soviet Writers' Union and the Stalinist regime. This interpretation is, I think, too particularized.
44 The Russian original is very concise: "– Poriadok byl." Indeed this phrase, rich with the complex political associations of the word "order," is emblematic of neo-Stalinism.
45 Elena Veselaia, "Esli ostanovimsia, nas poneset nazad," *Moskovskie novosti* (Mar. 12, 1989), 16.
46 The word Iskander uses, *strakh*, has the primary meaning of "fear," but also is widely used to refer to the "terror" brought about by Stalin.
47 Irina Vasiuchenko, "Dom nad propast'iu," *Oktiabr'* 3 (1988), 202.
48 Ivanova (*Smekh protiv strakha*, p. 286) asserts that the marmosets' caution is just as reprehensible as treachery: "But even behind disgust at betrayal in a society where perverted rabbit and boa constrictor principles hold sway, there lurks caution, which is in itself betrayal."
49 Chapple ("Fazil Iskander's *Rabbits and Boa Constrictors*," 35–36) interprets the natives in this work as representatives of international powers *vis-à-vis* the Soviet Union: "Iskander's pen exposes by implication the West, the East, and the Third World in their alliances and political behavior."
50 Fazil' Iskander, "Forbidden Fruit," in *The Thirteenth Labor of Hercules*, trans. Robert Daglish (Moscow: Progress, 1978), p. 61. This same incident is included in the tale "Shkol'nyi val's, ili energiia styda."
51 Fazil' Iskander, *Put'. Stikhi* (Moskva: Sovetskii pisatel', 1987), p. 176.
52 Chapple ("Fazil Iskander's *Rabbits and Boa Constrictors*," 45) traces these biblical parallels in some detail: "Much of the theological load of the novel is centered in Meditator [i.e. Ponderer]. His

ascent onto the Green Hill to meditate and to teach his disciple Seeker [i.e. Yearner] is an analogue of the Sermon on the Mount. While on the hill pondering, he observes to Seeker that it has come time to sacrifice his life while Seeker, like Peter of old, tries to dissuade him. Meditator's love for his brother rabbits is combined with a feeling of distress over being betrayed by the King and Resourceful [i.e. Sharpie], whose roles as Herod and Judas figures respectively parallel Meditator's as a Christ-figure."

53 It is significant that the Royal Guard uses an impersonal construction in his reply, eliding the pronoun *mne* that would make him the agent of the action: "– Tak bylo nado." Thus he abdicates responsibility linguistically as well as morally.

54 Compare Dostoevskii's tale *The Crocodile*, in which swallowing is used as an analogue of imprisonment for satirical effect as well. In Dostoevskii's work, a character much resembling Nikolai Chernyshevskii is swallowed by a crocodile that is part of a public exhibit; he nevertheless continues to expound – grotesquely and at great length – upon his philosophy of utopian socialism from within the belly of the crocodile.

55 The Russian original depends partly on onomatopoeia for its satirical effect: "– Tishe... shipite shepotom, ne zabyvaite, chto vrag vnutri nas..."

56 Ivanova (*Smekh protiv strakha*, p. 281) asserts that the Great Python's speech resembles Stalin's *Short Course*.

2 BEYOND PICARESQUE

1 Erofeev's sister, Nina Frolova, recalls in her reminiscences of him: "...his first-grade teacher complained about him. When the children were becoming Octobrists, he told her that he didn't want to. The teacher was beside herself: 'What do you mean, all the children are Octobrists!' 'I don't want to be like all the children'. And so he didn't become an Octobrist. And he was not a Pioneer or a member of the Komsomol. And this was in the forties and fifties" (Nina Frolova *et al.*, "Neskol′ko monologov o Venedikte Erofeeve," *Teatr* 9 [1991], 74).

2 The reason for his arrest, according to Frolova, was probably his penchant for relating anecdotes (Frolova *et al.*, "Neskol′ko monologov," 76).

3 These two versions of Erofeev's expulsion from MGU are told respectively by Svetlana Gaiser-Shnitman (*Venedikt Erofeev: "Moskva–Petushki" ili "The Rest is Silence"* [Bern: Peter Lang,

1989], p. 23) and Vladimir Murav'ev (Frolova *et al.*, "Neskol'ko monologov," 90).
4 These accounts of Erofeev's expulsion from the Vladimir Pedagogical Institute are given by Ol'ga Sedakova (Frolova *et al.*, "Neskol'ko monologov," 101) and by Erofeev himself in an interview with Irina Tosunian ("Ot Moskvy do samykh Petushkov," *Literaturnaia gazeta* [Jan. 3, 1990], 5).
5 The official reason for his being denied permission was a gap in his work record of four months. Erofeev gives an account of this incident in an interview with Igor' Bolychev ("Venedikt Erofeev: 'Umru, no nikogda ne poimu...'," *Moskovskie novosti* [Dec. 10, 1989], 13).
6 Gaiser-Shnitman (*Venedikt Erofeev*, p. 22) cites a letter from Erofeev in which he wrote that *Moscow–Petushki* was composed originally for a small circle of intimates. Igor' Avdiev recalls Erofeev saying that nothing in the text is invented and that he wrote it largely to entertain his friends (Frolova *et al.*, "Neskol'ko monologov," 115). Several sources place the writing of the text in the late sixties; all of the dates suggested differ substantially from Erofeev's own account. See Wolfgang Kasack, *A Dictionary of Russian Literature Since 1917,* trans. Maria Carlson and Jane T. Hedges (New York: Columbia University Press, 1988), p. 471; Sidney Monas, rev. of *Moscow to the End of the Line*, by Venedikt Erofeev, *Slavic Review* 40 (1981), 509; Vera S. Dunham, "Introduction," in *Moscow to the End of the Line*, by Venedikt Erofeev, trans. H. W. Tjalsma (New York: Taplinger, 1980), p. 8. Lidiia Liubchikova includes in her reminiscences of Erofeev a curious account of his attempt, together with his friend Vadim Tikhonov, to sell the manuscript of *Moscow–Petushki* (Frolova *et al.*, "Neskol'ko monologov," 86).
7 There is a second English translation entitled *Moscow Circles* (trans. J. R. Dorrell [London: Writers and Readers Publishing Cooperative, 1981]).
8 Murav'ev gives a slightly different account of the loss of this manuscript. According to his reminiscences, one of Erofeev's friends left it in a phone booth (Frolova *et al.*, "Neskol'ko monologov," 95). The hero of this non-extant work was not the composer Dmitrii Shostakovich, but a glassware inspector by the same name (Gaiser-Shnitman, *Venedikt Erofeev*, p. 23).
9 Fragments of *Fanni Kaplan* were published in *Moskovskii nabliudatel'* 2 (1991), 58–64. According to Alla Mikhaleva's foreword, this play was to be the "gayest and most disastrous for all its characters."

10 Edited excerpts from Erofeev's notebooks have been published in *Teatr* 9 (1991), 117–18; and in *Teatral'naia zhizn'* 20 (1991), 16–18.
11 On Erofeev's conversion to Catholicism, see Frolova *et al.*, "Neskol'ko monologov," especially Murav'ev (90), Sedakova (100) and Galina Erofeeva, the writer's widow (89). In a conversation with the present author in May 1992, Erofeeva suggested that her husband chose to be baptized in Catholicism because he believed that Russian Orthodoxy posed a threat of totalitarianism and rigid dogmatism that would rival communism.
12 On the question of Erofeev's alcoholism, see also Murav'ev (90) and Sedakova (100) in Frolova *et al.*, "Neskol'ko monologov" and Tosunian, "Ot Moskvy," 5.
13 N. Tomashevskii, *Plutovskoi roman* (Moskva: Khudozhestvennaia literatura, 1975), p. 9.
14 Claudio Guillén, "Toward a Definition of the Picaresque," in *Literature as System. Essays Toward the Theory of Literary History* (Princeton: Princeton University Press, 1971), p. 105.
15 Petr Vail' and Aleksandr Genis, "Literaturnye mechtaniia. Ocherk russkoi prozy s kartinkami," *Chast' rechi* 1 (1980), 221–22.
16 Andrei Zorin, "Prigorodnyi poezd dal'nego sledovaniia," *Novyi mir* 5 (1989), 256.
17 For treatment of the "picaresque myth," see Alexander Blackburn, *The Myth of the Picaro. Continuity and Transformation of the Picaresque Novel 1554–1954* (Chapel Hill: University of North Carolina Press, 1979), pp. 7–8.
18 Mikhail Bakhtin, *Problems of Dostoevsky's Poetics*, trans. R. W. Rotsel (Ann Arbor: Ardis, 1973), pp. 112, 122; Bakhtin, *Rabelais*, p. 11; Helen H. Reed, *The Reader in the Picaresque Novel* (London: Tamesis, 1984), p. 21; Zorin, "Prigorodnyi poezd," 257.
19 See also R. W. B. Lewis, *The Picaresque Saint. Representative Figures in Contemporary Fiction* (London: Victor Gollancz, 1960), pp. 18–19.
20 For treatment of the development of the picaresque in Russian literature, see Jurij Striedter, *Der Schelmenroman in Russland. Ein Beitrag zur Geschichte des Russischen Romans vor Gogol'* (Berlin: Otto Harrassowitz, 1961); John Leslie Wright, "Il'f and Petrov's *The Twelve Chairs* and *The Golden Calf* and the Picaresque Tradition" (Ph.D thesis, University of Wisconsin, 1980); Ronald D. LeBlanc, *The Russianization of Gil Blas: A Study in Literary Appropriation* (Columbus: Slavica, 1986).
21 The interpretation of *Dead Souls* as a picaresque novel is a controversial issue in Russian literary scholarship. See William Mills Todd III, *Fiction and Society in the Age of Pushkin. Ideology*,

Institutions, and Narrative (Cambridge, MA: Harvard University Press, 1986), pp. 177–86; T. E. Little, "*Dead Souls*," in *Knaves and Swindlers. Essays on the Picaresque Novel in Europe*, ed. Christine J. Whitbourn (London: Oxford University Press, 1974), pp. 112–38; Guillén, "Toward a Definition," 95; Tomashevskii, *Plutovskoi roman*, p. 5.

22 Ulrich Wicks, *Picaresque Narrative, Picaresque Fictions. A Theory and Research Guide* (New York: Greenwood Press, 1989), p. 62.

23 This urge to parody is observable already at the beginning of the seventeenth century with Ubeda's *La pícara Justina* and Quevedo's *El Buscón*. See Wicks, *Picaresque Narrative*, pp. 10–12.

24 Barbara A. Babcock, "'Liberty's a Whore': Inversions, Marginalia, and Picaresque," in *The Reversible World. Symbolic Inversion in Art and Society*, ed. Barbara A. Babcock (Ithaca: Cornell University Press, 1978), p. 99.

25 See, for example, Gaiser-Shnitman, *Venedikt Erofeev*; I. A. Paperno and B. M. Gasparov, "'Vstan' i idi'," *Slavica Hierosolymitana* 5–6 (1981), 387–400; E. A. Smirnova, "Venedikt Erofeev glazami gogoleveda," *Russkaia literatura* 3 (1990), 58–66.

26 Julia Kristeva, *Le texte du roman. Approche semiologique d'une structure dicursive transformationnelle* (The Hague: Mouton, 1970).

27 Anna Katona, "Picaresque Satires in Modern American Fiction," *Acta Litteraria Academiae Scientiarum Hungaricae* 12 (1970), 114.

28 See also M. Al'tshuller, "'Moskva–Petushki' Venedikta Erofeeva i traditsii klassicheskoi poemy," *Novyi zhurnal* 146 (1982), 75–85.

29 Venedikt Erofeev, *Moskva–Petushki* (Moskva: Prometei, 1989), p. 56.

30 The terms Erofeev uses – *detstvo, otrochestvo, iunost'* – are the titles of the three volumes of Tolstoi's pseudo-autobiography.

31 Venichka does not refer to Peter by name, but rather calls him "the Apostle." His formula for betrayal, "seven times seventy," is ironically that suggested by Christ to Peter for forgiveness.

32 The terms in the Russian original are, respectively, *milaia strannitsa* and *prokhodimets*. Venichka takes strong exception to the first appellation at least in part because of its feminine form; he has been stripped of even a gender identity by his interlocutor. The second term may also be translated as "rogue" or "rascal."

33 For treatment of the relationship between the trickster and the picaro, see C. G. Jung, "On the Psychology of the Trickster Figure," in *The Trickster. A Study in American Indian Mythology*, ed. R. F. C. Hull (New York: Greenwood Press, 1956), p. 200; Reed, *The Reader*, p. 23; Blackburn, "Myth of the Picaro," 6.

34 For an examination of the modern picaro as saint, see Lewis, *The Picaresque Saint*.
35 Joel I. Feldman, "First-Person Narrative Technique in the Picaresque Novel," *Scripta Hierosolymitana* 26 (1974), 163–64.
36 Paperno and Gasparov ("'Vstan' i idi'," 396) interpret the splitting of the narrative "I" as a "realization of the idea of the Trinity."
37 Venichka's internal dialogues contribute to what Gaiser-Shnitman (*Venedikt Erofeev*, pp. 246–47) calls the "theatricalization" of the text of *Moscow–Petushki*.
38 The version of *Moscow–Petushki* published in the almanac *Vest'* bore the subtitle *povest'* instead of *poema*. Several critics (Smirnova, "Venedikt Erofeev," 66; Al'tshuller, "'Moskva–Petushki'," 75) have noted the arbitrariness of this change. In subsequent editions the work has had its original subtitle restored.
39 Stuart Miller, *The Picaresque Novel* (Cleveland: Case Western Reserve University Press, 1967), p. 13.
40 Maiia Maravnik, "Ispoved' rossiianina tret'ei chetverti XX veka," *Tret'ia volna* 6 (1979), 104.
41 Grigorii Pomerants ("Sny zemli," *Poiski* 7–8 [1984], 153) actually refers to Erofeev's work as *Puteshestvie iz Moskvy v Petushki*.
42 This is a technique Erofeev shares with Dostoevskii, as has been pointed out by Paperno and Gasparov ("'Vstan' i idi'," 392).
43 Muravnik ("Ispoved' rossiianina," 104) points out that the etymology of the name Esino is satirically apt: "It is thought that Esino, or in the old style Estino, means 'prosperous.' After the Revolution they forgot to change the name. Well, for a train with Soviet passengers, what kind of stop can there be there?"
44 According to Frederick Monteser (*The Picaresque Element in Western Literature* [University, AL: University of Alabama Press, 1975], p. 7), interpolated sermons or philosophical digressions may contribute to the satirical effect of the picaresque narrative by emphasizing the contrast between words and reality.
45 Petr Vail' i Aleksandr Genis, *Sovremennaia russkaia proza* (Ann Arbor: Hermitage, 1982), p. 45.
46 V. S. Murav'ev, "Predislovie," in *Moskva–Petushki*, by Venedikt Erofeev (Moskva: Interbuk, 1990), p. 4.
47 From an anonymous review of *Moscow to the End of the Line*, by Venedikt Erofeev, *Russian Literature Triquarterly* 17 (1980), 266.
48 Cynthia Simmons, "An Alcoholic Narrative as 'Time Out' and the Double in *Moskva–Petushki*," *Canadian-American Slavic Studies* 24 (1990), 167.
49 Muravnik ("Ispoved' rossiianina," 103) takes this line of in-

terpretation further and suggests that we can easily decode the identity of the remaining three bandits once the allusion to Stalin is grasped. Presumably she has in mind Marx, Engels and Lenin.

50 Liubchikova, in her reminiscences of Erofeev (Frolova *et al.*, "Neskol′ko monologov," 81), suggests that the *iu* is an allusion to Iulia, the name of the author's lover at the time when *Moscow–Petushki* was written.

51 While Erofeev's use of imagery connected with crucifixion would seem to be strongly reminiscent of Bulgakov (a point noted by Paperno and Gasparov ["'Vstan′ i idi'," 393]), Erofeev himself denied any links between his work and *Master and Margarita*. Murav′ev recalls his distaste for Bulgakov: "He didn't find a kindred spirit in Bulgakov. He hated *Master and Margarita* so much that he would shake. Many people have written that he has connections with this book, but he himself would say 'Gasparov is a fool. I didn't even read *Master*, I couldn't read more than fifteen pages!'" (Frolova *et al.*, "Neskol′ko monologov," 93).

52 Jung ("On the Psychology," 211) connects the shadow figure with the Sphinx: "A minatory and ridiculous figure, he stands at the very beginning of the way of individuation, posing the deceptively easy riddle of the Sphinx or grimly demanding answer to a 'quaestio crocodilina'."

53 Maiia Kaganskaia ("Shutovskoi khorovod," *Sintaksis* 13 [1984], 181) refers to Erofeev's work by this title.

54 Lewis (*The Picaresque Saint*, p. 29) defines "symposium" in its original meaning as drinking together in a celebration of companionship.

55 Sedakova (Frolova *et al.*, "Neskol′ko monologov," 101) recalls Erofeev's attitude toward valor and its converse, faint-heartedness: "He often said that faint-heartedness is not only pardonable, but normal, even praiseworthy, that a person should not be put to the test by extreme experiences. Was this rebellion against communist socialism, against valor and the 'insanity of the brave' for which not only the brave and the insane, but also millions of reasonable and timid people had to pay?... Or were valor and sacrifice in their pure aspect unbearable for Venia? I myself don't know."

56 Erofeev himself objected to the suggestion that his literary language was stylized, insisting that it was an accurate approximation of contemporary Russian. In an interview (Tosunian, "Ot Moskvy," 5) he said: "They are always looking for anti-language, allegory, allusion... Is it really impossible to express oneself in a human way? When are we going to remind them what simply good Russian is?"

57 Smirnova ("Venedikt Erofeev," 64–65) suggests that Erofeev had "absolute pitch" for street language and vulgarisms.
58 Gaiser-Shnitman (*Venedikt Erofeev*, p. 254) demonstrates that Erofeev sometimes employs poetic meters in his prose.
59 Petr Vail' and Aleksandr Genis, "Vo chreve machekhi. Vozvrashchaias' k Erofeevu," *Moskovskii nabliudatel'* 2 (1992), 22.
60 The term is Gaiser-Shnitman's (*Venedikt Erofeev*, p. 268) and she traces the technique to Gogol'.
61 What Little ("*Dead Souls*," p. 126) writes about Gogol''s use of the mirror technique in "The Story of How Ivan Ivanovich Quarrelled with Ivan Nikiforich" is most apropos to Erofeev's use of the device in *Moscow–Petushki*:

> There is doubtless a technical term to express the geometrical distortion of the two Ivans, but all these characters are the products of minds which delight in the rearrangement of objects and concepts to conform with a private relish for topsy turvydom. This is amusing if such humour is to one's taste, but a joke founded on geometrical devices and given a touch of the grotesque by unexpected vegetable imagery is in no way serious literary characterisation of human beings.

See also Paperno and Gasparov, "'Vstan' i idi'," 391.
62 The term Erofeev uses for "jacket" refers to a piece of women's clothing, making the description even blurrier in terms of the characters' gender.
63 Simmons ("An Alcoholic Narrative," 163–65) suggests that Erofeev's system of doubles is related to Venichka's dual motives of escape and quest. Venichka, in her view, identifies with those characters who represent quest, but is frightened and repelled by those who represent cruelty or banality.

3 SATIRE AND THE AUTOBIOGRAPHICAL MODE

1 Patricia Carden, "Edward Limonov's Coming Out," in *The Third Wave: Russian Literature in Emigration*, ed. Olga Matich and Michael Heim (Ann Arbor: Ardis, 1984), p. 221.
2 Dmitrii Iakushkin, "Eto on, Edichka," *Moskovskie novosti* (Aug. 6, 1989), 16.
3 Aleksandr Maliugin, "Eduard Limonov: 'V etom byl kakoi-to azart'," *Iunost'* 2 (1991), 37.
4 Limonov pointedly terms his emigration a forced departure in his answer to a questionnaire sent to émigré Russian writers by Olga Matich ("Voprosy k vystupaiushchim," in Matich and Heim, *The Third Wave, p.* 228).

5 V. Shokhina, Afterword to "... U nas byla velikaia epokha," by Eduard Limonov, *Znamia* 11 (1989), 76.
6 Eduard Limonov, "Razocharovanie," *Novoe russkoe slovo* (Nov. 21, 1975), 3.
7 Eduard Limonov, *Eto ia – Edichka* (New York: Index, 1982), p. 47.
8 Eduard Limonov, "Limonov o sebe," in Matich and Heim, *The Third Wave*, p. 220. See also Limonov's remarks about the publication of *It's Me, Eddie* in Matich, "Voprosy k vystupaiushchim."
9 A. Kron, "Pro babochku poetinogo serdtsa," *Kovcheg* 3 (1979), 89–96. See also Aleksandr Donde, "Eduard, Edik i Edichka," *Al'manakh Panorama* (Jan. 21–28, 1983, 16–17; Jan. 28–Feb. 4, 1983, 12–13). Of interest in this regard is Edward Brown's assertion ("Russian Literature Beyond the Pale," *Slavic and East European Journal* 30 [1986], 381) that after the publication of *It's Me, Eddie*, "a commission was formed (I assume on paper only) 'for the annihilation of Limonov' (*po unichtozheniiu Limonova*)."
10 Leonid Pochivalov, "Chelovek na dne. Pokinuvshii rodinu – o sebe," *Literaturnaia gazeta* (Sept. 10, 1980), 14.
11 Nikolai Bokov, "Vokrug Limonova," *Dvadtsat' dva* 8 (1979), 176. A similar defense of publishing Limonov's work was offered by Kron ("Pro babochku," 89): "... the Russian and especially the Soviet reader has the right to be acquainted with the entire contemporary political spectrum, from extreme leftists and communists to fascists. We will always polemicize with them, but will never censor or distort their views."
12 Olga Matich, "The Moral Immoralist: Edward Limonov's *Eto ja – Edichka*," *Slavic and East European Journal* 30 (1986), 526–40.
13 Anatolii Karpov, "Po techeniiu... Chitaia povesti E. Limonova '... U nas byla velikaia epokha' i S. Dovlatova 'Filial'," *Literaturnaia gazeta* (Dec. 20, 1989), 4.
14 See also Limonov's remarks in John Glad, *Literature in Exile* (Durham: Duke University Press, 1990).
15 Olga Matich, "Russian Writers on Literature and Society," *Humanities in Society* 3–4 (1984), 229–30.
16 Examples are legion, but see especially Matich, "Voprosy k vystupaiushchim," 221–31; also of note is his scathing dismissal of Iosif Brodskii published as "Poet-bukhgalter," in *Muleta A* (Paris: Vivrisme, 1984), pp. 132–35.
17 Several critics have remarked upon Limonov's habit of obscuring the distinction between himself as author and his created autobiographical persona, Edichka. Brown ("Russian Literature," 383) notes that "the real man tends to confuse himself with that totally nihilistic other ego, Edichka." While Donde ("Eduard,

Edik i Edichka," 12) is careful to establish that Eduard Limonov and Edichka are quite distinct, he makes the intriguing suggestion that the essence of the relationship between the author and his narrative persona is the desire on Limonov's part to "merge with his hero" (*slit' sia s geroem*).

Georges Gusdorf ("Conditions and Limits of Autobiography," in *Autobiography: Essays Theoretical and Critical*, ed. James Olney [Princeton: Princeton University Press, 1980], p. 47), writing about autobiography's potential to affect the life of the autobiographer, has the following to say: "... every work is autobiographical insofar as being registered in the life it alters the life to come. Better still, it is the peculiar nature of the literary calling that the work, even before it has been realized, can have an effect on being. The autobiography is lived, played, before being written; it fixes a kind of retrospective mark on the event even as it occurs."

18 James Olney, "Autobiography and the Cultural Moment: A Thematic, Historical, and Bibliographical Introduction," in Olney, *Autobiography*, p. 4.
19 Roy Pascal, *Design and Truth in Autobiography* (Cambridge, MA: Harvard University Press, 1960), p. 160. See also Michael Sprinker, "Fictions of the Self: The End of Autobiography," in Olney, *Autobiography*, pp. 321–42.
20 Jane Gary Harris, "Diversity of Discourse: Autobiographical Statements in Theory and Praxis," in *Autobiographical Statements in Twentieth-Century Russian Literature*, ed. Jane Gary Harris (Princeton: Princeton University Press, 1990), p. 13.
21 Philippe Lejeune, *Le pacte autobiographique* (Paris: Editions du Seuil, 1975), p. 14.
22 Elizabeth W. Bruss, *Autobiographical Acts. The Changing Situation of a Literary Genre* (Baltimore: The Johns Hopkins University Press, 1976), pp. 10–11.
23 To S. L. Campbell's English translation of the Russian title *Eto ia – Edichka* as *It's Me, Eddie* is added the curious subtitle "a fictional memoir." Also interesting in this respect is the English rendering of *Podrostok Savenko* (literally "Adolescent Savenko") as *Memoirs of a Russian Punk*.
24 Olga Matich, "Unofficial Russian Fiction and Its Politics," *Humanities in Society* 7 (1984), 120.
25 Richard N. Coe, *When the Grass Was Taller. Autobiography and the Experience of Childhood* (New Haven: Yale University Press, 1984), pp. 230–31.
26 Estelle C. Jelinek, *Women's Autobiography. Essays in Criticism* (Bloomington: Indiana University Press, 1980), p. 13.

27 Patricia Carden, "The New Russian Literature," in *Russian Literature and American Critics. In Honor of Deming B. Brown*, ed. Kenneth N. Brostrom (Ann Arbor: University of Michigan Department of Slavic Languages and Literatures, 1984), p. 20.
28 Viktor Perel'man, "Vremia svobody," *Novoe russkoe slovo* (May 3, 1979), 3.
29 Barrett J. Mandel, "Full of Life Now," in Olney, *Autobiography*, p. 64.
30 Ann Shukman ("Taboos, Splits and Signifiers: Limonov's *Eto ya – Edichka*," *Essays in Poetics* 8 [1983], 7) suggests "indeed the writing [of *It's Me, Eddie*] can be looked on as a kind of therapy which explains the greater optimism of the latter chapters."
31 Leonid Geller ("Prigotovitel'nye zametki k teorii skandalov, avandarda i erotiki v literature na materiale sochineniia E. Limonova 'Eto ia – Edichka'," *Kovcheg* 5 [1980], 86), for example, indicts Edichka for what he perceives as his utter lack of self-directed irony: "Edichka is devoid of the most important quality – humor, irony, self-irony – that can render digestible sentimental gutter literature written seventy years too late." I. R. Titunik ("Vasilii Trediakovskii and Eduard Limonov: Erotic Reverberations in the History of Russian Literature," in Brostrom, *Russian Literature and American Critics*, pp. 397–98) compares Limonov to Trediakovskii in that "Limonov is perfectly serious: there is nothing 'mock,' nothing literary-parodic about *Eto ia – Edichka*."
32 In the course of a 1988 roundtable discussion on Nabokov's works that had recently appeared in the Soviet press, Ol'ga Matich ("Vladimir Nabokov: mezh dvukh beregov," *Literaturnaia gazeta* [Aug. 17, 1988], 5) suggested that *It's Me, Eddie* can be regarded as "a post-Soviet or émigré *Lolita*" in its treatment of the hero's search for lost love and lost paradise.
33 Nataliia Gross, "Shramy rossiiskogo Odisseia," *Vremia i my* 55 (1980), 192–96.
34 Olney ("Autobiography and the Cultural Moment," p. 13) suggests that typicality is one of the common features of the autobiographical mode: "... this special quality of autobiography – that is, that autobiography renders in a peculiarly direct and faithful way the experience and the vision of a people, which is the same experience and the same vision lying behind and informing all the literature of that people – is one of the reasons why autobiography has lately become such a popular, even fashionable, study in the academic world where traditional ways of organizing literature by period or school have tended to give way to a different sort of organization (or disorganization)."

35 For an analysis of the myth of happy childhood and its links to the pastoral tradition in Russian literature, see Andrew Baruch Wachtel, *The Battle for Childhood. Creation of a Russian Myth* (Stanford: Stanford University Press, 1990), pp. 88–92.
36 Stephen Spender, "Confessions and Autobiography," in Olney, *Autobiography*, p. 120.
37 For a characterization of Limonov's poetry, see Carden, "New Russian Literature," pp. 13–20.
38 Limonov's personification of New York in *It's Me, Eddie* parallels his characterization of the city as a primitive life force in his short story "Love, Love, Love" (trans. Judson Rosengrant, *Humanities in Society* 3–4 [Summer–Fall 1984], 183–94).
39 The fine sense of measure evident here is lost in *His Butler's Story*, where Limonov opts for gratuitous eroticism over the associations of children with natural innocence.
40 This is the point of departure adopted by Gross ("Shramy rossiiskogo Odisseia") for her analysis of Limonov's work.
41 Iakov Ashkenazi, "Edichka Limonov i drugie," *Dvadtsat' dva* 8 (1979), 197. On envy as Edichka's prime motivation, see also Kron, "Pro babochku," 94–95; Nina Voronel', "Pod sen'iu sinteticheskogo vibratora ili 'Tarakan ot detstva'," *Dvadtsat' dva* 8 (1979), 184.
42 Nikolai Bokov, "Nartsiss na asfal'te N'iu-Iorka," *Russkaia mysl'* (May 10, 1979), 12.
43 L. Kornilova, "Poslednii romantik Edichka," *Kovcheg* 5 (1980), 89–93.
44 For a more detailed treatment of the issue of Edichka's bisexuality, see Shukman, "Taboos, Splits and Signifiers," 8–9.
45 For an analysis of *It's Me, Eddie* as a parody of Norman Mailer's *An American Dream*, see Karen Ryan-Hayes, "Limonov's *Eto ia – Edichka* and the Failure of An American Dream," *Canadian Slavonic Papers* 30 (1988), 438–59.
46 Konstantin Kustanovich, "Golyi korol'. Edichka Limonov kak literaturnyi fenomen," *Novyi amerikanets* (Dec. 19–25, 1981), 33–34.
47 George Gibian, "'Russianness' and Twentieth-Century Emigres," in Matich and Heim, *The Third Wave*, p. 75.
48 Louis A. Renza, "The Veto of the Imagination: A Theory of Autobiography," in Olney, *Autobiography*, p. 279.
49 Philippe Lejeune, "Autobiography in the Third Person," *New Literary History* 9 (1977), 32.
50 This technique of shifting viewpoint has been used previously by Limonov in his verse, which is also essentially autobiographical. An instance examined by A. K. Zholkovskii ("Grafomanstvo kak

priem: Lebiadkin, Khlebnikov, Limonov i drugie," in *Amsterdam Symposium on the Centenary of Velimir Chlebnikov* (1985), ed. Willem G. Weststein [Amsterdam: Rodopi, 1986], 581–82) is the following stanza from a 1979 poem:

> Zato ia nikomu ne dolzhen
> Nikto poutru ne krichit
> I v dva chasa i v pol-drugogo
> Zaidet li kto a *ia – lezhit*.

In such extreme cases, Zholkovskii notes, grammatical lapsus occurs (the emphasis is Zholkovskii's). Mikh. Volin, in a review of a poetry reading by Limonov ("Na vechere Eduarda Limonova," *Novoe russkoe slovo* [Oct. 24, 1975], 3), cites the same example as evidence of "a certain free style, an original search for something new, where sometimes even grammar is purposely distorted."

51 William L. Howarth, "Some Principles of Autobiography," in Olney, *Autobiography*, p. 101.
52 The English translation has twelve chapters and an epilogue; the tenth chapter of the Russian version entitled "Leopol'd Sengor i Benzhamen" is omitted. A comparison of the Russian and English texts reveals numerous other cuts in the translated version, but this is the most substantial change. In all cases, the basis for these omissions would seem to be editorial rather than censorial.
53 Edward J. Brown, "The Exile Experience," in Matich and Heim, *The Third Wave*, p. 57.
54 Shukman ("Taboos, Splits and Signifiers," 5) notes that the epilogue appears to have been added precisely to subvert the linearity of the text. I. P. Smirnov ("O nartsissticheskom tekste (diakhroniia i psikhoanaliz)," *Wiener Slawistischer Almanach* 12 [1983], 21–46) suggests that *It's Me, Eddie* is structured as a narcissistic text, with the end mirroring the beginning in terms of the narrator's rage and frustration.
55 Janet Varner Gunn, *Autobiography. Toward a Poetics of Experience* (Philadelphia: University of Pennsylvania Press, 1982), p. 14.
56 Matich ("The Moral Immoralist," 536) writes that "Edichka speaks the newly formed language of the uncultured immigrant, whose Russian has been influenced by English on the lexical as well as the syntactic level." Il'ia Levin ("Ob evoliutsii literaturnogo iazyka v emigratsii," in Matich and Heim, *The Third Wave*, p. 266) is more specific in locating the dialect on which Limonov models Edichka's *Ich-Erzählung*: "The language of the novel *It's Me, Eddie* is oriented to the speech of new émigrés from the Soviet Union to New York."
57 Levin, "Ob evoliutsii"; Felix Dreizin, "Russian Style in Emi-

gration: Edward Limonov's Anglicisms," *Wiener Slawistischer Almanach* 22 (1988), 55–67.

58 Matich ("Unofficial Russian Fiction," 120) takes the opposite point of view, suggesting that Limonov's language is characterized by "the absence of political resonance." It is, she writes, the language of people losing touch with the Soviet Union and its peculiarly politicized brand of Russian. Dreizin ("Russian Style," 56) finds Limonov's language very political, but locates the source of his subversion of literary Russian (which would, it seem, include his occasional employment of journalese and propagandistic clichés) in his extreme individualism. Thus his language is a kind of bohemian expression of anti-anti-Soviet sentiment: "[Limonov] is hostile not so much to the Soviet authorities, as to the elitist Soviet anti-establishment and its taboos. Traditionally, a Russian writer is a public figure, a teacher of life, and above all an embodiment of national values and ideals. Edward Limonov is this image's antipode, an individualistic fighter against the primacy of social values and norms."

4 THE FAMILY CHRONICLE REVISITED

1 Il'ia Serman ("Teatr Sergeia Dovlatova," *Grani* 136 [1985], 145) emphasizes the importance of translations of Western works by these and other writers in Russian literary life of the sixties. Lev Loseff ("Sergei Dovlatov," in *Modern Encyclopedia of Russian and Soviet Literatures*, ed. Harry B. Weber [Gulf Breeze: Academic International Press, 1977], p. 241) notes that Dovlatov "named the unlikely trio of William Faulkner, John Dos Passos and Aleksandr Ivanovich Kuprin as primary literary influences in his writing."

2 *Filial* was first published in the émigré newspaper *Al'manakh Panorama* 350 (Dec. 25, 1987–Jan. 1, 1988). It was subsequently published in the Soviet Union in *Zvezda* 10 (1989), 21–88.

3 Sergei Dovlatov, *The Invisible Book*, trans. Katherine O'Connor and Diana L. Burgin (Ann Arbor: Ardis, 1979), p. 26.

4 A. Zverev, "Zapiski sluchainogo postoial'tsa," *Literaturnoe obozrenie* 4 (1991), 69.

5 Seth Mydans, "Writing Without Roots," *New York Times Book Review* (Sept. 23, 1984), 38.

6 Dovlatov's story "Lishnii," published in the 1987 collection *Predstavlenie i drugie rasskazy* (New York: Russica) also treats his life in Tallinn.

7 Sergei Dovlatov, *Remeslo* (Ann Arbor: Ardis, 1985), p. 108.

8 Sergei Dovlatov, *Nashi* in *Remeslo* (N.p.: Zvezdy, n.d.), p. 213. This edition is a reprint of the 1983 edition published by Ardis.
9 *Nevidimaia gazeta* comprises the second part of *Remeslo* (1985).
10 Mikhail Taranov, "Vyzhivanie," *Kontinent* 36 (1983), 402.
11 For a detailed treatment of depictions of America in Russian literature, see Alayne P. Reilly, *America in Contemporary Soviet Literature* (New York: New York University Press, 1971).
12 Dovlatov is not entirely unique in this regard. An important predecessor is Vladimir Nabokov, whose *Lolita* relies on a similar simultaneous insider/outsider viewpoint for its satirical efficacy. Nabokov, however, spoke English from childhood and was exposed to Western culture very early. Dovlatov is of a much later, purely Soviet generation of émigrés.
13 Sergei Dovlatov, *Marsh odinokikh* (Holyoke: New England Publishing Co., 1983), p. 98.
14 Andrei Ar'ev, "Teatralizovannyi realizm. O povesti Sergeia Dovlatova *Filial*," *Zvezda* 10 (1989), 19.
15 Iunna Morits, "Rasskazy iz knigi *Chemodan*," *Oktiabr'* 7 (1989), 119.
16 A fragment of *Kholodil'nik* is included in *Chemodan* (Leningrad: Sovetskii pisatel', 1991).
17 Viacheslav Kuritsyn, "Vesti iz filiala, ili duratskaia retsenziia na prozu Sergeia Dovlatova," *Literaturnoe obozrenie* 12 (1990), 41–42; Alla Marchenko, "...Obratitsia v pechal'noe...," *Literaturnaia gazeta* (May 16, 1990), 4.
18 Iurii Karabchievskii, "Pamiati Sergeia Dovlatova," *Literaturnaia gazeta* (Aug. 29, 1990), 7.
19 Kenneth Clifton Mason, "The Family Chronicle and Modern America" (Ph.D thesis, University of Nebraska-Lincoln, 1981), p. 2.
20 I. P. Viduetskaia, "*Poshekhonskaia starina* v riadu semeinykh khronik russkoi literatury," in *Saltykov-Shchedrin 1826–1976*, ed. A. S. Bushmin (Leningrad: Nauka, 1976), p. 207.
21 In the Russian original, the chapters are not individually titled; chapter titles are provided by Anne Frydman in her translation (*Ours. A Russian Family Album* [New York: Weidenfeld and Nicolson, 1989]).
22 In the Russian original, Dovlatov uses a third-person impersonal verb: "Kogda tetka zabolela i umerla, v ee bumagakh nashli portret seroglazogo obaiatel'nogo muzhchiny."
23 S. Mashinskii, "O memuarno-avtobiograficheskom zhanre," *Voprosy literatury* 6 (1960), 137.
24 Richard Freeborn, *The Rise of the Russian Novel. Studies in the Russian*

novel from Eugene Onegin to War and Peace (Cambridge: Cambridge University Press, 1973), pp. 123–24.
25 This passage is included in several paragraphs which are in Frydman's English translation (p. 26) but are not in the Russian original. There are numerous such discrepancies; in every case, the translation offers a fuller, more expanded account. We must presume that the translator was working from a later version of *Nashi* that has never been published in Russian.
26 This is not to say that all family chroniclers consign large-scale historical events to the periphery and focus on private family history. Salient examples of the opposite trend include Aleksandr Herzen's *My Past and Thoughts* and Vladimir Korolenko's *The History of My Contemporary*.
27 S. Mashinskii, *S. T. Aksakov. Zhizn' i tvorchestvo* (Moskva: Khudozhestvennaia literatura, 1961), p. 362.
28 A. M. Gracheva, "'Semeinye khroniki' nachala XX veka," *Russkaia literatura* 1 (1982), 64–75.
29 Andrew R. Durkin, *Sergei Aksakov and Russian Pastoral* (New Brunswick: Rutgers University Press, 1983), p. 98.
30 According to Freeborn (*Rise of the Russian Novel*, p. 123), this is characteristic of the Russian novel as a whole in this period of the nineteenth century.
31 S. T. Aksakov, *Izbrannye sochineniia* (Moskva: Sovremennik, 1982), p. 217.
32 Serman ("Teatr Sergeia Dovlatova," 139) sees this intention clearly written into *Ours*: "The author wanted to look back at the past in order to understand himself and how he is indebted to his ancestors, 'ours' as Dovlatov calls them."
33 Sergei Dovlatov, *A Foreign Woman*, trans. Antonina W. Bouis (New York: Grove Weidenfeld, 1991), p. 111.
34 Morits, "Rasskazy," 118; Karen Rosenberg, "Of Compromise and Corruption," *The Nation* (Nov. 5, 1983), 437.
35 Sergei Dovlatov, "Filial," *Zvezda* 10 (1989), 21.
36 *Ours*, p. 133; this sentence is not in the Russian original.
37 Ar'ev's comment pertains to "The Subsidiary," but is just as applicable to the structural characteristics of *Ours*.
38 Dovlatov employs a similar structural principle in *The Compromise* and *The Suitcase*.
39 Marchenko ("...Obratitsia v pechal'noe...," 4) discusses Dovlatov's use of the *povest'* and deems it the most appropriate genre to reflect contemporary reality.
40 Carol Luplow, *Isaac Babel's* Red Cavalry (Ann Arbor: Ardis, 1982), p. 110. Patricia Carden's analysis of the cycle form (*The Art*

of Isaac Babel [Ithaca: Cornell University Press, 1972], p. 50) is also pertinent to Dovlatov's structural praxis: "The cycle as a form is something more than a series of stories and something less than a novel. In the novel the elementary structure is A leads to B leads to C. In the cycle (if it is more than a mere stringing together of a number of stories) the elementary structure is A equals B equals C. The separate episodes have a weight that is determined outside their places in the cycle, by their own qualities and interest. The episodes determine the cycle rather than the cycle the episodes."

41 Frydman distinguishes between "Grandpa" Isaak and "Grandfather" Stepan in her translation; both characters are referred to as *ded* in the Russian text.

42 *Ours*, p. 98; the last two sentences of this passage are not in the Russian original.

43 E. Tudorovskaia, "Russkii pisatel' v Amerike," *Grani* 140 (1986), 304.

44 Michael West, "Homer's *Iliad* and the Genesis of Mock-Heroic," *Cithara* 21 (1981), 4, 9.

45 Ar'ev ("Teatralizovannyi realizm," 19) claims that "One of the most important motifs of his artistic ethic is an ineradicable, defiant attraction to *déclassé* people, to plebs." Loseff ("Sergei Dovlatov," p. 240) suggests that Dovlatov's focus on "nonconformist writers and artists, contemporary 'superfluous people,' prostitutes and drunks" was the source of his initial (unofficial) popularity in the Soviet Union.

46 A. Zverev, "Sovetuiu prochitat'," *Znamia* 6 (1990), 236.

47 *Ours*, p. 108; this sentence is part of a long concluding section to the chapter "Glasha" that is not included in the Russian original.

48 Donald M. Fiene (Review of *Zona*, by Sergei Dovlatov, *Slavic and East European Journal* 27 [1983], 273) suggests "In his laconic, economical style and expert rendering of the speech of the *narod*, Dovlatov belongs in the company of Babel', Voinovich, and Vasilii Shukshin..."; Ar'ev ("Teatralizovannyi realizm," 20) writes that "His prose has an additional dimension, an oral equivalent. It is senseless to see each of its fragments only in a subordinate context, necessary and sufficient for elucidation of the general idea of the work. His verbal arrangement, its concrete phonation is very entertaining."

49 Mydans ("Writing Without Roots," 38) notes that in emigration, Dovlatov wrote with the translator and the English-speaking reader in mind. It is also noteworthy in this regard that Dovlatov never mastered English as a second language.

50 *Ours*, p. 28; this paragraph is not in the Russian original.

51 Serman ("Teatr Sergeia Dovlatova," 143–44) also notes that Dovlatov's attitude toward the Soviet system was probably affected by his entering the prison camps as a guard in the relatively liberal period of the sixties rather than under Stalin.
52 *A Foreign Woman*, which is set in New York and includes characters from a variety of ethnic groups, represents an important experiment in Dovlatov's broadening his scope of interest.
53 In *Craft, A Foreign Woman* and *The Subsidiary*, Russian émigrés are primary objects of Dovlatov's satire.
54 *Ours*, p. 109; this passage is not in the Russian original.
55 *Ours*, p. 109; this passage is not in the Russian original.
56 *Ours*, p. 110; this passage is not in the Russian original.
57 "For most 'serious' writers, whether poets, novelists, or dramatists, irony is now much less often a rhetorical or dramatic strategy which they may or may not decide to employ, and much more often a mode of thought silently imposed upon them by the general tendency of the times" (D. C. Muecke, *The Compass of Irony* [London: Methuen, 1969], p. 10).
58 George A. Test, *Satire. Spirit and Art* (Tampa: University of South Florida Press, 1991), p. 251.
59 In other works Dovlatov includes "documents" to enhance the effect of verisimilitude. In *The Invisible Book*, for example, he reproduces numerous letters, declarations, official papers and so on to emphasize the absurdity of the actual events he relates.
60 Max Eastman, *Enjoyment of Laughter* (New York: Simon and Schuster, 1937), p. 272.
61 Franz Stanzel's treatment of the authorial narrator (*Narrative Situations in the Novel. Tom Jones, Moby Dick, The Ambassadors, Ulysses*, trans. James P. Pusack [Bloomington: Indiana University Press, 1971], pp. 23–24) is relevant to Dovlatov's narrative procedure in *Ours*, but the text represents an extreme case in Stanzel's classificatory system. He suggests that as a rule, "The authorial narrator strives for sovereign independence from his fictional world and for temporal, spatial, and psychological distance from it. This narrative distance is an important characteristic of the authorial narrative situation." Dovlatov reduces this distance to the point that it is negligible and establishes near-unity of authorial narrator and protagonist.
62 "The source of a narrative text's whole structure of meaning – not only of its assertion and denotation but also of its implication, connotation, and ideological nexus – is the implied author" (Seymour Chatman, *Coming to Terms. The Rhetoric of Narrative in Fiction and Film* [Ithaca: Cornell University Press, 1990], p. 75).

63 Sergei Dovlatov, *The Compromise*, trans. Anne Frydman (New York: Knopf, 1983), p. 11.
64 Such rogue narrators are quite common in Western first-person novels (see Bertil Romberg, *Studies in the Narrative Technique of the First-Person Novel* [Stockholm: Almqvist and Wiksell, 1962], p. 40). However, in the Soviet literary context, first-person rogue heroes are rare. A comparison of Dovlatov's narrator to the figure of Il'f and Petrov's Ostap Bender is useful in this regard. *The Twelve Chairs* and *The Golden Calf* are not first-person novels, of course, but the fate of the rogue hero Ostap Bender is exemplary of Soviet satirical treatment of the character type.
65 *Ours*, p. 108; this passage is not in the Russian original.
66 Dovlatov also satirizes Soviet vestiges in the Russian émigrés who people his works. In *Remeslo*, for example, he writes: "... Soviet power is not a Tatar-Mongol yoke. It lives in each of us. In our habits and our tendencies. In our predilections and our antipathies. In our consciousness and in our soul. Soviet power is us" (pp. 150–51).

5 DYSTOPIA REDUX

1 Tat'iana Bek, "Iz russkoi literatury ia ne uezzhal nikuda," *Druzhba narodov* 12 (1991), 247.
2 Vladimir Voinovich, "Korotko o sebe," in *Antisovetskii Sovetskii Soiuz* (Ann Arbor: Ardis, 1985), p. 5.
3 Vladimir Voinovich, "Voinovich o sebe," in Matich and Heim, *The Third Wave*, p. 144. The phrase Voinovich uses is "vlasti... protianuli mne vmesto knuta prianik." Since his works have begun to be republished in Russia under *glasnost'*, Voinovich has been accused of hypocrisy by conservative critics. Evgenii Ovanesian ("Gde ishchet pochestei glumlivoe pero? O 'pokhozhdeniiakh' soldata Chonkina v SSSR," *Molodaia gvardiia* 5 [1990], 274), for example, suggests that *A Degree of Trust* is evidence of Voinovich's willingness to compromise with the regime. Gennadii Murikov ("... Bez slez, bez zhizni, bez liubvi (O segodniashnem literaturnom bezvremen'e)," *Sever* 8 [1991], 153–59) has likewise criticized Voinovich harshly. In considering the place of *A Degree of Trust* in Voinovich's *œuvre*, however, it is worthwhile noting that such eminent liberal figures as Bulat Okudzhava, Vasilii Aksenov, Anatolii Gladilin, Mark Popovskii and Natan Eidel'man also published books in the "Ardent Revolutionaries" series.
4 I. Kruglianskaia, "Voskresnye zagadki dlia Vladimira Voinovicha," *Izvestiia* (Dec. 27, 1991), 5.
5 *Ivan Chonkin*, which remains Voinovich's *magnum opus*, was written

1963–70. Although its publication was announced by *Novyi mir* in 1963, it did not appear as scheduled. The first two parts, entitled *The Life and Extraordinary Adventures of Private Ivan Chonkin*, were published as a separate edition in Paris in 1975. A fifth and final part to complement *Pretender to the Throne* has long been anticipated. Robert Porter (*Four Contemporary Russian Writers* [Oxford: Berg, 1989], p. 114) suggests that *Ivan Chonkin* is a picaresque work and like many other picaresques, may be ultimately unfinishable.

6 Vladimir Voinovich, *The Anti-Soviet Soviet Union*, trans. Richard Lourie (San Diego: Harcourt Brace Jovanovich, 1986), pp. 307–14; Bek, "Iz russkoi literatury," 249–53.
7 The two editions of *Moskva 2042* published in Russia are in *Utopiia i antiutopiia XX veka. Vecher v 2217 godu. Russkaia literaturnaia utopiia* (Moskva: Progress, 1990), pp. 387–716; and *Moskva 2042* (Moskva: Vsia Moskva, 1990).
8 Vladimir Voinovich, "Where Glasnost Has Its Limits," *New York Times Magazine* (July 19, 1987), 30–31; Malcolm Bradbury, "Cosmic Misunderstandings," *New York Times Book Review* (June 7, 1987), 1, 36–37.
9 El'dar Riazanov, "Proshchai, Chonkin," *Al'manakh Panorama* (Sept. 29–Oct. 6, 1989), 26–29.
10 G. Vasil'eva, "Ia dushevno pripisan k Rossii," *Izvestiia* (June 8, 1990), 7.
11 Darko Suvin, "Defining the Literary Genre of Utopia: Some Historical Semantics, Some Genology, A Proposal and a Plea," *Studies in the Literary Imagination* 6 (1973), 132.
12 S. K. Vohra, *Negative Utopian Fiction (Aldous Huxley and George Orwell: Commitment and Fabulation)* (Shastrinagar, Meerut: Shalabh Prakashan, 1987), pp. 6–7.
13 As Northrop Frye ("Varieties of Literary Utopias," in *Utopias and Utopian Thought*, ed. Frank E. Manuel [Boston: Houghton Miflin, 1965], p. 36) writes of More's *Utopia*, "It does not lead to a desire to abolish sixteenth-century Europe and replace it with Utopia, but it enables one to see Europe, and to work within it, more clearly."
14 Eduard Gevorkian, "Chem vymoshchena doroga v rai? Antipredislovie," in *Antiutopii XX veka* (Moskva: Knizhnaia palata, 1989), p. 11.
15 Robert C. Elliott, *The Shape of Utopia. Studies in a Literary Genre* (Chicago: University of Chicago Press, 1970), pp. 3–24.
16 Juan López-Morillas, "From 'Dreams of Reason' to 'Dreams of Unreason'," *Survey* 18 (1972), 53.

17 Suvin ("Defining the Literary Genre," 138) takes this distinction further in his theoretical opposition of the two modes: "the explicit utopian construction is the logically necessary obverse of any satire. Utopia explicates what satire implicates, and vice versa."
18 Alexandra Aldridge, *The Scientific World View in Dystopia* (Ann Arbor: UMI Research Press, 1984), p. 16.
19 Chad Walsh, *From Utopia to Nightmare* (New York: Harper and Row, 1962), p. 117.
20 Dragan Klaic, *The Plot of the Future. Utopia and Dystopia in Modern Drama* (Ann Arbor: The University of Michigan Press, 1991), p. 60.
21 López-Morillas uses *anti-Utopia* as a synonym of *dystopia* in the sense that I have adopted the latter term.
22 Philip Stevick, "The Limits of Anti-Utopia," *Criticism* 6 (1964), 234–35; Walsh, *From Utopia to Nightmare*, p. 26.
23 Arthur O. Lewis, Jr., "The Anti-Utopian Novel: Preliminary Notes and Checklist," *Extrapolation* 2 (1961), 27–32.
24 Viacheslav Shestakov, "Evoliutsiia russkoi literaturnoi utopii," in *Utopiia i antiutopiia XX veka* (Moskva: Progress, 1990), p. 12.
25 Richard Stites, "Fantasy and Revolution: Alexander Bogdanov and the Origins of Bolshevik Science Fiction," in *Red Star. The First Bolshevik Utopia*, by Alexander Bogdanov (Bloomington: Indiana University Press, 1984), p. 4.
26 Helen S. Reeve, "Utopian Socialism in Russian Literature: 1840s–1860s," *American Slavic and East European Review* 43 (1959), 374–93.
27 Gevorkian ("Chem vymoshchena doroga," 6) makes the analogy that "utopian socialism is a forerunner of scientific communism ... to the same extent that alchemy preceded and gave rise to chemistry." Shestakov too ("Evoliutsiia," p. 7) states that utopian socialism was one of the sources of Marxism.
28 Fyodor Dostoevsky, *The Brothers Karamazov*, trans. Constance Garnett (New York: Norton, 1976), p. 240.
29 Evgenii Pavlovich Brandis and Vladimir Ivanovich Dmitrevskii, *Zerkalo trevog i somnenii* (Moskva: 1967), p. 17.
30 Irina Ryshina, "Ia vernulsia by..." *Literaturnaia gazeta* (June 20, 1990), 8.
31 Vladimir Voinovich, *Moskva 2042* (Moskva: Vsia Moskva, 1990), p. 29.
32 Vladimir Voinovich, *Stepen' doveriia. Povest' o Vere Figner* (Moskva: Izdatel'stvo politicheskoi literatury, 1972), pp. 199–200.
33 Porter suggests that this sort of gentle satire directed at the notions espoused by the early revolutionaries was encouraged under

Brezhnev. It was, in his view, a means of discrediting both Khrushchev's claims and the "embarrassing orthodoxy of Stalinist die-hard writers."

34 Vladimir Voinovich, "Dva tovarishcha," *Novyi mir* 1 (1967), 89.
35 Voinovich's use of the phrase *shtokdorfskii supermarket* gives the Russian original a curiously foreign quality. His frame of reference for verbal *ostranenie* is the émigré milieu.
36 Stevick ("The Limits of Anti-Utopia") suggests that neither Huxley nor Orwell presents a completely closed vision. There are, he maintains, at least implicit alternatives in these texts.
37 Even the best-intentioned planners of utopias, Voinovich suggests (Bek, "Iz russkoi literatury," 254), inevitably resort to coercion to actualize their visions: "Those trying to realize [utopia] run up against the impossibility of doing this – and invariably apply force. So if the key doesn't go into the lock and doesn't open the door, they begin to press it, to turn it and so on and as a result break it. When they want to join utopia with life, I repeat, they apply force and thus separate reality from the programmatic ideal."
38 Nikolas Berdyaev, *The End of Our Time*, trans. Donald Atwater (New York: Sheed and Ward, 1933), p. 188. Aldous Huxley cites this passage as an epigraph to *Brave New World*.
39 Serge Schmemann, "Satirist Paints Soviet Future," *New York Times* (July 11, 1987), 13.
40 Irving Howe, "The Fiction of Anti-Utopia," in *A World More Attractive. A View of Modern Literature and Politics* (New York: Horizon, 1963), pp. 225–26.
41 Eric S. Rabkin, "Atavism and Utopia," in *No Place Else. Explorations in Utopian and Dystopian Fiction*, ed. Eric S. Rabkin *et al.* (Carbondale: Southern Illinois University Press, 1983), p. 4.
42 Ivan Shukhov, "Korabl' 'izmofrenikov'," *Moskovskii komsomolets* (Dec. 7, 1990), 4.
43 While this is true of utopian works in the Russian tradition, notably Radishchev's and Chernyshevskii's dream utopias, it is less so of classical Western utopias. In fact, hierarchy is characteristic of many Western utopias from Plato to More. As Suvin ("Defining the Literary Genre," 134) writes, "there are authoritarian and libertarian, class and classless utopias, but no unorganized ones."
44 Mary A. Weinkauf, "Five Spokesmen for Dystopia," *The Midwest Quarterly* 16 (1975), 184.
45 This motif itself is parodical of the conventional exchange in utopia in which a ruler or "delineator" reveals the truth to an outsider or skeptic. See Morson, *Boundaries of Genre*, p. 126.

46 Kartsev's comment that the last time he saw such writing implements was at Beskudnikovo, seventy-five years ago is not incidental. This aside strengthens the parallel between the dystopian state of Moscowrep described in parts two through six of the novel and the equally horrific regime established by Karnavalov in part seven.
47 Geoffrey Hosking, *Beyond Socialist Realism. Soviet Fiction since Ivan Denisovich* (New York: Holmes and Meier, 1980), p. 152.
48 Martin Kessler, "Power and the Perfect State. A Study in Disillusionment as Reflected in Orwell's *Nineteen Eighty-Four* and Huxley's *Brave New World*," *Political Science Quarterly* 72 (1957), 566–67.
49 The freezing and thawing of Sim Simych Karnavalov may also be an allusion to Maiakovskii's play *The Bedbug*. Like Prisypkin/Skripkin, Karnavalov returns to a futuristic world that has changed radically. While Prisypkin/Skripkin experiences extreme alienation and withdraws from this world, Karnavalov forcibly imposes his reforms upon Moscowrep and effects a revolution. In Voinovich's satirical scenario, the individual drives the collective for better or worse.
50 The name of the child is *S″ezdii*, which is not identical to the Russian word for "congress" (*s″ezd*). The form resembles many names given to males (e.g. Evgenii, Arkadii, Vasilii), but nevertheless sounds very strange.
51 M. D. Fletcher, "Voinovich's 'Consumer' Satire in *2042*," *The International Fiction Review* 16 (1989), 106.
52 Frye (*Anatomy of Criticism*, pp. 308–312) suggests that the negative utopia is best thought of not as a type of novel, but as a variety of Menippean satire or anatomy.
53 John Glad, *Extrapolations From Dystopia. A Critical Study of Soviet Science Fiction* (Princeton: Kingston Press, 1982), p. 108.
54 The verb that I have translated "correct" is *korezhit'*, a colloquial word meaning to bend or warp, hence to distort.
55 Marianna Tax Choldin and Maurice Friedberg, eds., *The Red Pencil. Artists, Scholars, and Censors in the USSR* (Boston: Unwin Hyman, 1989), p. 93.
56 Daniel Rancour-Laferriere, "Castratory Imagery in Vladimir Voinovich's *Moscow 2042*," unpublished manuscript.
57 It is noteworthy that travelling fifty years into the future, as Kartsev originally wanted – to 2032 – would have placed the novel in the year of the centennial jubilee of Voinovich himself.
58 George Knox, "Apocalypse and Sour Utopias," *Western Humanities Review* 16 (1962), 12.

59 Norman O. Brown, "The Excremental Vision," in *Life Against Death. The Psychoanalytical Meaning of History* (Middletown: Wesleyan University Press, 1959), pp. 179–201.
60 The term "startismal" is derived from "star," the gesture that the Communites make to symbolize the Supreme Pentagon.

Select bibliography

Aldridge, Alexandra, *The Scientific World View in Dystopia*, Ann Arbor: UMI Research Press, 1984.
Al'tshuller, M., "'Moskva-Petushki' Venedikta Erofeeva i traditsii klassicheskoi poemy," *Novyi zhurnal* 146 (1982), 75–85.
Anisimov, Grigorii and Bondariuk, Marina, "Korotko, no ne koroche istiny," *Literaturnoe obozrenie* 11 (1985), 38–39.
Ar'ev, Andrei, "Teatralizovannyi realizm. O povesti Sergeia Dovlatova *Filial*," *Zvezda* 10 (1989), 19–20.
Ashkenazi, Iakov, "Edichka Limonov i drugie," *Dvadtsat' dva* 8 (1979), 195–97.
Babcock, Barbara A., "'Liberty's a Whore': Inversions, Marginalia, and Picaresque Narrative," in *The Reversible World. Symbolic Inversion in Art and Society*, ed. Barbara A. Babcock, Ithaca: Cornell University Press, 1978, pp. 95–116.
Bakhtin, M. M., *Rabelais and His World*, trans. Helene Iswolsky, Cambridge, MA: MIT Press, 1968.
  Problems of Dostoevsky's Poetics, trans. R. W. Rotsel, Ann Arbor: Ardis, 1973.
Bek, Tat'iana, "Iz russkoi literatury ia ne uezzhal nikuda," *Druzhba narodov* 12 (1991), 245–61.
Beraha, Laura, "Compilation in the Art of Fazil' Iskander and as a Key to *Sandro iz Chegema*," Diss. McGill University, 1990.
Blackburn, Alexander, *The Myth of the Picaro. Continuity and Transformation of the Picaresque Novel 1554–1954*, Chapel Hill: University of North Carolina Press, 1979.
Bloom, Edward A., "The Allegorical Principle," *English Literary History* 18 (1951), 163–90.
Bloomfield, Morton W., "Allegory as Interpretation," *New Literary History* 3 (1972), 301–17.
Bokov, Nikolai, "Nartsiss na asfal'te N'iu-Iorka," *Russkaia mysl'* (May 10, 1979), 12–13.
  "Vokrug Limonova," *Dvadtsat' dva* 8 (1979), 175–76.

Bolychev, Igor', "Venedikt Erofeev: 'Umru, no nikogda ne poimu...'," *Moskovskie novosti* (Dec. 10, 1989), 13.
Booth, Wayne, *A Rhetoric of Irony*, Chicago: University of Chicago Press, 1974.
Bradbury, Malcolm, "Cosmic Misunderstandings," *New York Times Book Review* (June 7, 1987), 1, 36–37.
Brostrom, Kenneth N., ed., *Russian Literature and American Critics. In Honor of Deming B. Brown*, Ann Arbor: University of Michigan Department of Slavic Languages and Literatures, 1984.
Brown, Deming, *The Last Years of Soviet Russian Literature. Prose Fiction 1975–1991*, Cambridge: Cambridge University Press, 1993.
Brown, Edward J., "Russian Literature Beyond the Pale," *Slavic and East European Journal* 30 (1986), 380–88.
Brown, Norman O., "The Excremental Vision," in *Life Against Death. The Psychoanalytical Meaning of History*, Middletown: Wesleyan University Press, 1959, pp. 179–201.
Bruss, Elizabeth W., *Autobiographical Acts. The Changing Situation of a Literary Genre*, Baltimore: The Johns Hopkins University Press, 1976.
Burke, Kenneth, *The Philosophy of Literary Form. Studies in Symbolic Action*, Berkeley: University of California Press, 1973.
Chapple, Richard, "Fazil Iskander's *Rabbits and Boa Constrictors*: A Soviet Version of George Orwell's *Animal Farm*," *Germano-Slavica* 5 (1985), 33–47.
Chatman, Seymour, *Coming to Terms. The Rhetoric of Narrative in Fiction and Film*, Ithaca: Cornell University Press, 1990.
Choldin, Marianna Tax and Friedberg, Maurice, eds., *The Red Pencil. Artists, Scholars, and Censors in the USSR*, Boston: Unwin Hyman, 1989.
Chuprinin, Sergei, "Pokhvala zlosloviiu," *Literaturnaia gazeta* (Oct. 28, 1987), 5.
Clifford, Gay, *The Transformations of Allegory*, London: Routledge, 1974.
Coe, Richard N., *When the Grass Was Taller. Autobiography and the Experience of Childhood*, New Haven: Yale University Press, 1984.
Dane, Joseph A., "Parody and Satire: A Theoretical Model," *Genre* 13 (1980), 145–59.
Donde, Aleksandr, "Eduard, Edik i Edichka," *Al'manakh Panorama* (Jan. 21–28, 1983), 16–17; (Jan. 28–Feb. 4, 1983), 12–13.
Dovlatov, Sergei, *The Invisible Book*, trans. Katherine O'Connor and Diana L. Burgin, Ann Arbor: Ardis, 1979.
  The Compromise, trans. Anne Frydman, New York: Knopf, 1983.
  Marsh odinokikh, Holyoke: New England Publishing Co., 1983.

Nashi, in *Remeslo*, N.p.: Zvezdy, n.d., pp. 143–220 [Reprint of *Nashi*, Ann Arbor: Ardis, 1983].
Remeslo, Ann Arbor: Ardis, 1985.
Ours. A Russian Family Album, trans. Anne Frydman, New York: Weidenfeld and Nicolson, 1989.
"Filial," *Zvezda* 10 (1989), 21–88.
A Foreign Woman, trans. Antonina W. Bouis, New York: Grove Weidenfeld, 1991.
Dreizin, Felix, "Russian Style in Emigration: Edward Limonov's Anglicisms," *Wiener Slawistischer Almanach* 22 (1988), 55–67.
Durkin, Andrew R., *Sergei Aksakov and Russian Pastoral*, New Brunswick: Rutgers University Press, 1983.
Eastman, Max, *Enjoyment of Laughter*, New York: Simon and Schuster, 1937.
Elliott, Robert C., *The Power of Satire: Magic, Ritual, Art*, Princeton: Princeton University Press, 1960.
The Shape of Utopia. Studies in a Literary Genre, Chicago: University of Chicago Press, 1970.
Empson, William, *Seven Types of Ambiguity*, New York: New Directions, 1947.
Erofeev, Venedikt, *Moscow to the End of the Line*, trans. H. W. Tjalsma, New York: Taplinger, 1980.
Moskva-Petushki, Moskva: Prometei, 1989.
Feldman, Joel I., "First-Person Narrative Technique in the Picaresque Novel," *Scripta Hierosolymitana* 26 (1974), 160–73.
Fiene, Donald M., Rev. of *Zona*, by Sergei Dovlatov, *Slavic and East European Journal* 27 (1983), 272–73.
Fletcher, Angus, *Allegory. The Theory of a Symbolic Mode*, Ithaca: Cornell University Press, 1964.
Fletcher, M. D., "Voinovich's 'Consumer' Satire in *2042*," *The International Fiction Review* 16 (1989), 106–108.
Frank, Robert Worth Jr., "The Art of Reading Medieval Personification-Allegory," *English Literary History* 20 (1953), 237–50.
Freeborn, Richard, *The Rise of the Russian Novel. Studies in the Russian novel from* Eugene Onegin *to* War and Peace, Cambridge: Cambridge University Press, 1973.
Freidenberg, O. M., "The Origin of Parody," in *Semiotics and Structuralism. Readings from the Soviet Union*, ed. Henryk Baran, White Plains: International Arts and Sciences Press, pp. 269–83.
Frolova, Nina *et al.*, "Neskol'ko monologov o Venedikte Erofeeve," *Teatr* 9 (1991), 74–116.
Frye, Northrop, *Anatomy of Criticism. Four Essays*, Princeton: Princeton University Press, 1957.

"Varieties of Literary Utopias," in *Utopias and Utopian Thought*, ed. Frank E. Manuel, Boston: Houghton Miflin, 1965, pp. 25–49.

Gaiser-Shnitman, Svetlana, *Venedikt Erofeev: "Moskva–Petushki" ili "The Rest is Silence,"* Bern: Peter Lang, 1989.

Geller, Leonid, "Prigotovitel′nye zametki k teorii skandalov, avangarda i erotiki v literature na materiale sochineniia E. Limonova 'Eto ia – Edichka'," *Kovcheg* 5 (1980), 84–88.

Gevorkian, Eduard, "Chem vymoshchena doroga v rai? Antipredislovie," in *Antiutopii XX veka*, Moskva: Knizhnaia palata, pp. 5–12.

Glad, John, *Extrapolations From Dystopia. A Critical Study of Soviet Science Fiction*, Princeton: Kingston Press, 1982.

Literature in Exile, Durham: Duke University Press, 1990.

Gracheva, A. M., "'Semeinye khroniki' nachala XX veka," *Russkaia literatura* 1 (1982), 64–75.

Gross, Nataliia, "Shramy rossiiskogo Odisseia," *Vremia i my* 55 (1980), 192–208.

Guillén, Claudio, "Toward a Definition of the Picaresque," in *Literature as System. Essays Toward the Theory of Literary History*, Princeton: Princeton University Press, 1971, pp. 71–106.

Gunn, Janet Varner, *Autobiography. Toward a Poetics of Experience*, Philadelphia: University of Pennsylvania Press, 1982.

Harris, Jane Gary, "Diversity of Discourse: Autobiographical Statements in Theory and Praxis," in *Autobiographical Statements in Twentieth-Century Russian Literature*, ed. Jane Gary Harris, Princeton: Princeton University Press, 1990, pp. 3–35.

Highet, Gilbert, *The Anatomy of Satire*, Princeton: Princeton University Press, 1962.

Honig, Edwin, *Dark Conceit. The Making of Allegory*, New York: Oxford University Press, 1966.

Hosking, Geoffrey, *Beyond Socialist Realism. Soviet Fiction since* Ivan Denisovich, New York: Holmes and Meier, 1980.

Householder, Fred W. Jr., "Parody," *Classical Philology* 39 (1944), 1–9.

Howe, Irving, "The Fiction of Anti-Utopia," in *A World More Attractive. A View of Modern Literature and Politics*, New York: Horizon, 1963, pp. 216–26.

Hutcheon, Linda, *A Theory of Parody. The Teachings of Twentieth-Century Art Forms*, London: Methuen, 1985.

Iakushkin, Dmitrii, "Eto on, Edichka," *Moskovskie novosti* (Aug. 6, 1989), 16.

Iskander, Fazil′, *Kroliki i udavy*, Ann Arbor: Ardis, 1982.

Put′. Stikhi, Moskva: Sovetskii pisatel′, 1987.

Rabbits and Boa Constrictors, trans. Ronald E. Peterson, Ann Arbor: Ardis, 1989.
Ivanov, Sergei, "O 'maloi proze' Iskandera, ili chto mozhno sdelat' iz nastoiashchei mukhi," *Novyi mir* 1 (1989), 252–56.
Ivanova, Natal'ia, "Bestiarii Fazilia Iskandera," *Literaturnaia Armeniia* 5 (1989), 101–11.
Smekh protiv strakha, ili Fazil' Iskander, Moskva: Sovetskii pisatel', 1990.
Jelinek, Estelle C., *Women's Autobiography. Essays in Criticism*, Bloomington: Indiana University Press, 1980.
Jump, John D., *Burlesque*, London: Methuen, 1972.
Jung, C. G., "On the Psychology of the Trickster Figure," in *The Trickster. A Study in American Indian Mythology*, ed. R. F. C. Hull, New York: Greenwood Press, 1956.
Kaganskaia, Maiia, "Shutovskoi khorovod," *Sintaksis* 13 (1984), 139–90.
Karabchievskii, Iurii, "Pamiati Sergeia Dovlatova," *Literaturnaia gazeta* (Aug. 29, 1990), 7.
Karpov, Anatolii, "Po techeniiu... Chitaia povesti E. Limonova '... U nas byla velikaia epokha' i S. Dovlatova 'Filial'," *Literaturnaia gazeta* (Dec. 20, 1989), 4.
Kasack, Wolfgang, *A Dictionary of Russian Literature Since 1917*, trans. Maria Carlson and Jane T. Hedges, New York: Columbia University Press, 1988.
Katona, Anna, "Picaresque Satires in Modern American Fiction," *Acta Litteraria Academiae Scientiarum Hungaricae* 12 (1970), 105–20.
Kazintsev, Aleksandr, "Ochishchenie ili zloslovie?," *Nash sovremennik* 2 (1988), 186–89.
Kessler, Martin, "Power and the Perfect State. A Study in Disillusionment as Reflected in Orwell's *Nineteen Eighty-Four* and Huxley's *Brave New World*," *Political Science Quarterly* 72 (1957), 565–77.
Kiremidjian, G. D., "The Aesthetics of Parody," *The Journal of Aesthetics and Art Criticism* 28 (1969), 231–42.
Klaic, Dragan, *The Plot of the Future. Utopia and Dystopia in Modern Drama*, Ann Arbor: The University of Michigan Press, 1991.
Knox, George, "Apocalypse and Sour Utopias," *Western Humanities Review* 16 (1962), 11–22.
Kornilova, L., "Poslednii romantik Edichka," *Kovcheg* 5 (1980), 89–93.
Kristeva, Julia, *Le texte du roman. Approche semiologique d'une structure discursive transformationnelle*, The Hague: Mouton, 1970.

Kron, A., "Pro babochku poetinogo serdtsa," *Kovcheg* 3 (1979), 89–96.
Kruglianskaia, I., "Voskresnye zagadki dlia Vladimira Voinovicha," *Izvestiia* (Dec. 27, 1991), 5.
Kuritsyn, Viacheslav, "Vesti iz filiala, ili duratskaia retsenziia na prozu Sergeia Dovlatova," *Literaturnoe obozrenie* 12 (1990), 41–42.
Kustanovich, Konstantin, "Golyi korol'. Edichka Limonov kak literaturnyi fenomen," *Novyi amerikanets* (Dec. 19–25, 1981), 32–34.
Kviatkovskii, A., *Poeticheskii slovar'*, Moskva: Sovetskaia entsiklopediia, 1966.
Lebedev, A., "... I smekh, i slezy, i liubov'," in *Izbrannoe. Rasskazy. Povest'*, by Fazil' Iskander, Moskva: Sovetskii pisatel', 1988, pp. 3–18.
LeBlanc, Ronald D., *The Russianization of Gil Blas: A Study in Literary Appropriation*, Columbus: Slavica, 1986.
Lejeune, Philippe, *Le pacte autobiographique*, Paris: Editions du Seuil, 1975.
  "Autobiography in the Third Person," *New Literary History* 9 (1977), 27–50.
Lewis, Arthur O. Jr., "The Anti-Utopian Novel: Preliminary Notes and Checklist," *Extrapolation* 2 (1961), 27–32.
Lewis, C. S., *The Allegory of Love. A Study in Medieval Tradition*, Oxford: Clarendon, 1936.
Lewis, R. W. B., *The Picaresque Saint. Representative Figures in Contemporary Fiction*, London: Victor Gollancz, 1960.
Leyburn, Ellen Douglass, *Satiric Allegory: Mirror of Man*, New Haven: Yale University Press, 1956.
Limonov, Eduard, "Razocharovanie," *Novoe russkoe slovo* (Nov. 21, 1975), 3.
  Eto ia – Edichka, New York: Index, 1982.
  It's Me, Eddie, trans. S. L. Campbell, New York: Random House, 1983.
Lipovetskii, Mark, "Usloviia igry," *Literaturnoe obozrenie* 7 (1988), 46–49.
López-Morillas, Juan, "From 'Dreams of Reason' to 'Dreams of Unreason'," *Survey* 18 (1972), 47–62.
Loseff, Lev, "Sergei Dovlatov," in *Modern Encyclopedia of Russian and Soviet Literatures*, ed. Harry B. Weber, Gulf Breeze: Academic International Press, 1977, pp. 239–41.
  On the Beneficence of Censorship. Aesopian Language in Modern Russian Literature, München: Verlag Otto Sagner, 1984.

Macdonald, Dwight, *Parodies. An Anthology from Chaucer to Beerbohm – and After*, New York: Random House, 1960.
Maliugin, Aleksandr, "Eduard Limonov: 'V etom byl kakoi-to azart'," *Iunost'* 2 (1991), 36–37.
Marchenko, Alla, "... Obratitsia v pechal'noe ...," *Literaturnaia gazeta* (May 16, 1990), 4.
Mashinskii, S., "O memuarno-avtobiograficheskom zhanre," *Voprosy literatury* 6 (1960), 129–45.
S. T. Aksakov. Zhizn' i tvorchestvo, Moskva: Khudozhestvennaia literatura, 1961.
Mason, Kenneth Clifton, "The Family Chronicle and Modern America," Diss. University of Nebraska-Lincoln, 1981.
Matich, Olga, "Unofficial Russian Fiction and Its Politics," *Humanities in Society* 7 (1984), 109–22.
"The Moral Immoralist: Edward Limonov's *Eto ja – Edichka*," *Slavic and East European Journal* 30 (1986), 526–40.
Matich, Olga and Heim, Michael, eds., *The Third Wave: Russian Literature in Emigration*, Ann Arbor: Ardis, 1984.
Matich, Ol'ga *et al.*, "Vladimir Nabokov: mezh dvukh beregov," *Literaturnaia gazeta* (Aug. 17, 1988), 5.
Miller, Stuart, *The Picaresque Novel*, Cleveland: Case Western Reserve University Press, 1967.
Monas, Sidney, Rev. of *Moscow to the End of the Line*, by Venedikt Erofeev, *Slavic Review* 40 (1981), 509.
Monteser, Frederick, *The Picaresque Element in Western Literature*, University, AL: University of Alabama Press, 1975.
Morits, Iunna, "Rasskazy iz knigi *Chemodan*," *Oktiabr'* 7 (1989), 118–19.
Morson, Gary Saul, *The Boundaries of Genre. Dostoevsky's Diary of a Writer and the Traditions of Literary Utopia*, Evanston: Northwestern University Press, 1981.
Mueke, D. C., *The Compass of Irony*, London: Methuen, 1969.
Murav'ev, V. S., "Predislovie," in *Moskva-Petushki*, by Venedikt Erofeev, Moskva: Interbuk, 1990, pp. 3–12.
Muravnik, Maiia, "Ispoved' rossiianina tret'ei chetverti XX veka," *Tret'ia volna* 6 (1979), 99–105.
Murikov, Gennadii, "... Bez slez, bez zhizni, bez liubvi (O segodniashnem literaturnom bezvremen'e)," *Sever* 8 (1991), 143–49.
Mydans, Seth, "Writing Without Roots," *New York Times Book Review* (Sept. 23, 1984), 1, 38–39.
Olney, James, ed., *Autobiography: Essays Theoretical and Critical*, Princeton: Princeton University Press, 1980.

Osmolovskii, V. F., "Zhanr sotsial'no-didakticheskoi skazki v russkoi literature. Puti razvitiia," *Voprosy russkoi literatury* 51 (1988), 68–74.
Ovanesian, Evgenii, "Gde ishchet pochestei glumlivoe pero? O 'pokhozhdeniiakh' soldata Chonkina v SSSR," *Molodaia gvardiia* 5 (1990), 272–88.
Paperno, I. A. and Gasparov, B. M., "'Vstan' i idi'," *Slavica Hierosolymitana* 5–6 (1981), 387–400.
Pascal, Roy, *Design and Truth in Autobiography*, Cambridge, MA: Harvard University Press, 1960.
Paulson, Ronald, *The Fictions of Satire*, Baltimore: The Johns Hopkins Press, 1967.
Paulson, Ronald, ed., *Satire. Modern Essays in Criticism*, Englewood Cliffs: Prentice-Hall, 1971.
Perel'man, Viktor, "Vremia svobody," *Novoe russkoe slovo* (May 3, 1979), 3.
Pochivalov, Leonid, "Chelovek na dne. Pokinuvshii rodinu – o sebe," *Literaturnaia gazeta* (Sept. 10, 1980), 14.
Porter, Robert, *Four Contemporary Russian Writers*, Oxford: Berg, 1989.
Rabkin, Eric S., "Atavism and Utopia," in *No Place Else. Explorations in Utopian and Dystopian Fiction*, ed. Eric S. Rabkin *et al.*, Carbondale: Southern Illinois University Press, 1983, pp. 1–10.
Reed, Helen H., *The Reader in the Picaresque Novel*, London: Tamesis, 1984.
Reeve, Helen S., "Utopian Socialism in Russian Literature: 1840s – 1860s," *American Slavic and East European Review* 43 (1959), 374–93.
Riazanov, El'dar, "Proshchai, Chonkin," *Al'manakh Panorama* (Sept. 29 – Oct. 6, 1989), 26–29.
Riewald, J. G., "Parody as Criticism," *Neophilologus* 50 (1966), 125–48.
Romberg, Bertil, *Studies in the Narrative Technique of the First-Person Novel*, Stockholm: Almqvist and Wiksell, 1962.
Rose, Margaret A., *Parody//Meta-Fiction. An Analysis of Parody as a Critical Mirror to the Writing and Perception of Fiction*, London: Croom Helm, 1979.
Rosenberg, Karen, "Of Compromise and Corruption," *The Nation* (Nov. 5, 1983), 437–40.
Ryan-Hayes, Karen, "Iskander and Tolstoj: The Parodical Implications of the Beast Narrator," *Slavic and East European Journal* 32 (1988), 225–36.
  "Limonov's *Eto ia – Edichka* and the Failure of An American Dream," *Canadian Slavonic Papers* 30 (1988), 438–59.

Ryshina, Irina, "Ia vernulsia by...," *Literaturnaia gazeta* (June 20, 1990), 8.
Sarnov, Benedikt, "Mir Fazilia Iskandera," in *Fazil' Iskander. Bibliograficheskii ukazatel'*, by Z. B. Mikhailova, Ul'ianovsk: Oblastnoi sovet profsoiuzov, 1982, pp. 12–28.
Schmemann, Serge, "Satirist Paints Soviet Future," *New York Times* (July 11, 1987), 13.
Serman, Il'ia, "Teatr Sergeia Dovlatova," *Grani* 136 (1985), 138–62.
Shestakov, Viacheslav, "Evoliutsiia russkoi literaturnoi utopii," in *Utopiia i antiutopiia XX veka*, Moskva: Progress, 1990, pp. 5–21.
Shklovskii, Evg., "Potrebnost' ochishcheniia," *Literaturnoe obozrenie* 7 (1987), 32–34.
Shokhina, V., Afterword to "...U nas byla velikaia epokha," by Eduard Limonov, *Znamia* 11 (1989), 76–77.
Shukhov, Ivan, "Korabl' 'izmofrenikov'," *Moskovskii komsomolets* (Dec. 7, 1990), 4.
Shukman, Ann, "Taboos, Splits and Signifiers: Limonov's *Eto ya – Edichka*," *Essays in Poetics* 8 (1983), 1–18.
Simmons, Cynthia, "An Alcoholic Narrative as 'Time Out' and the Double in *Moskva-Petushki*," *Canadian-American Slavic Studies* 24 (1990), 155–68.
Smirnov, I. P., "O nartsissisticheskom tekste (diakhroniia i psikhoanaliz)," *Wiener Slawistischer Almanach* 12 (1983), 21–46.
Smirnova, E. A., "Venedikt Erofeev glazami gogoleveda," *Russkaia literatura* 3 (1990), 58–66.
Solov'ev, Vladimir, "Fazil' Iskander v okruzhenii svoikh geroev," *Literaturnaia ucheba* 5 (1990), 110.
Stanzel, Franz, *Narrative Situations in the Novel*. Tom Jones, Moby Dick, The Ambassadors, Ulysses, trans. James P. Pusack, Bloomington: Indiana University Press, 1971.
Stevick, Philip, "The Limits of Anti-Utopia," *Criticism* 6 (1964), 233–45.
Stites, Richard, "Fantasy and Revolution: Alexander Bogdanov and the Origins of Bolshevik Science Fiction," in *Red Star. The First Bolshevik Utopia*, by Alexander Bogdanov, Bloomington: Indiana University Press, 1984.
Striedter, Jurij, *Der Schelmenroman in Russland. Ein Beitrag zur Geschichte des Russischen Romans vor Gogol'*, Berlin: Otto Harrassowitz, 1961.
Suvin, Darko, "Defining the Literary Genre of Utopia: Some Historical Semantics, Some Genology, A Proposal and a Plea," *Studies in the Literary Imagination* 6 (1973), 121–45.
Taranov, Mikhail, "Vyzhivanie," *Kontinent* 36 (1983), 400–404.

Test, George A., *Satire. Spirit and Art*, Tampa: University of South Florida Press, 1991.
Titunik, I. R., "The Formal Method and the Sociological Method (M. M. Bakhtin, P. N. Medvedev, V. N. Voloshinov) in Russian Theory and Study of Literature," in *Marxism and the Philosophy of Language*, by V. N. Voloshinov, Cambridge, MA: Harvard University Press, 1986.
Tomashevskii, N., *Plutovskoi roman*, Moskva: Khudozhestvennaia literatura, 1975.
Tosunian, Irina, "Ot Moskvy do samykh Petushkov," *Literaturnaia gazeta* (Jan. 3, 1990), 5.
Troll', Iuliia, "*Kroliki i udavy* Fazilia Iskandera," *Novyi zhurnal* 151 (1983), 301–304.
Tudorovskaia, E., "Russkii pisatel' v Amerike," *Grani* 140 (1986), 303–309.
Tynianov, Iu. N., *Poetika. Istoriia literatury. Kino*, Moskva: Nauka, 1977.
Vail', Petr and Genis, Aleksandr, "Literaturnye mechtaniia. Ocherk russkoi prozy s kartinkami," *Chast' rechi* 1 (1980), 204–32.
  Sovremennaia russkaia proza, Ann Arbor: Hermitage, 1982.
  "Beseda s Fazilem Iskanderom," *Al'manakh Panorama* (Dec. 18–25, 1987), 20–22.
  "Vo chreve machekhi. Vozvrashchaias' k Erofeevu," *Moskovskii nabliudatel'* 2 (1992), 22–25.
Vasil'eva, G., "Ia dushevno pripisan k Rossii," *Izvestiia* (June 8, 1990), 7.
Vasiuchenko, Irina, "Dom nad propast'iu," *Oktiabr'* 3 (1988), 199–202.
Veselaia, Elena, "Esli ostanovimsia, nas poneset nazad," *Moskovskie novosti* (Mar. 12, 1989), 16.
Viduetskaia, I. P., "*Poshekhonskaia starina* v riadu semeinykh khronik russkoi literatury," in *Saltykov-Shchedrin 1826–1976*, ed. A. S. Bushmin, Leningrad: Nauka, 1976, pp. 206–19.
Vohra, S. K., *Negative Utopian Fiction (Aldous Huxley and George Orwell: Commitment and Fabulation)*, Shastrinagar, Meerut: Shalabh Prakashan, 1987.
Voinovich, Vladimir, "Dva tovarishcha," *Novyi mir* 1 (1967), 85–152.
  Stepen' doveriia. Povest' o Vere Figner, Moskva: Izdatel'stvo politicheskoi literatury, 1972.
  "Korotko o sebe," in *Antisovetskii Sovetskii Soiuz*, Ann Arbor: Ardis, 1985, pp. 5–8.
  The Anti-Soviet Soviet Union, trans. Richard Lourie, San Diego: Harcourt Brace Jovanovich, 1987.

Moscow 2042, trans. Richard Lourie, San Diego: Harcourt Brace Jovanovich, 1987.
"Where Glasnost Has Its Limits," *New York Times Magazine* (July 19, 1987), 30–31.
Moskva 2042, Moskva: Vsia Moskva, 1990.
Volin, Mikh., "Na vechere Eduarda Limonova," *Novoe russkoe slovo* (Oct. 24, 1975), 3.
Voronel', Nina, "Pod sen'iu sinteticheskogo vibratora ili 'Tarakan ot detstva'," *Dvadtsat' dva* 8(1979), 182–94.
Wachtel, Andrew Baruch, *The Battle for Childhood. Creation of a Russian Myth*, Stanford: Stanford University Press, 1990.
Walsh, Chad, *From Utopia to Nightmare*, New York: Harper and Row, 1962.
Weinkauf, Mary A., "Five Spokesmen for Dystopia," *The Midwest Quarterly* 16 (1975), 175–86.
Wicks, Ulrich, *Picaresque Narrative, Picaresque Fictions. A Theory and Research Guide*, New York: Greenwood Press, 1989.
Wright, John Leslie, "Il'f and Petrov's *The Twelve Chairs* and *The Golden Calf* and the Picaresque Tradition," Diss. University of Wisconsin, 1980.
Zholkovskii, A. K., "Grafomanstvo kak priem: Lebiadkin, Khebnikov, Limonov i drugie," in *Amsterdam Symposium on the Centenary of Velimir Chlebnikov (1985)*, ed. Willem G. Weststein, Amsterdam: Rodopi, 1986, pp. 573–93.
Zorin, Andrei, "Prigorodnyi poezd dal'nego sledovaniia," *Novyi mir* 5 (1989), 256–58.
Zverev, A., "Sovetuiu prochitat'," *Znamia* 6 (1990), 236.
  "Zapiski sluchainogo postoial'tsa," *Literaturnoe obozrenie* 4 (1991), 65–70.

Index

Abkhazia 11–15
absurd 2, 62, 74, 80, 87, 95, 97, 124, 139, 146, 151, 155, 169–70, 172, 175–76, 185, 188, 193, 216, 229, 232, 235, 239, 241–42
Aksakov, Sergei 118, 121–22, 158–62, 177, 184
   Childhood Years 158, 162
   Family Chronicle 158, 161–62
Aksenov, Vasilii 8, 13, 150, 191, 239
alcoholism 45, 61–62, 64, 67, 70–71, 80, 82–83, 88–90, 119, 123, 139, 174, 182–84, 240
Aleshkovskii, Iuz 8
allegory 10–11, 17–30, 33, 36, 38, 40–41, 45, 49, 51–52, 54–57, 239–40
Al'manakh Panorama 153
America 65, 102–04, 106, 108, 115, 117–21, 124–26, 130, 132, 134–35, 139–40, 143, 145–46, 149, 151–56, 163, 165, 168–69, 173, 182–86, 195, 197, 199, 241
anti-Semitism 165, 181–82
anti-utopia 200, 202, 206
Apollon 103
atheism 80, 91, 232, 236
autobiography 10, 104–49, 151, 153, 160–62, 170, 190, 231, 239, 241
   childhood 116–23, 126, 128, 131, 134–35, 141, 146–49, 241
   confession 73, 106, 109, 115, 118–19, 128, 130
   pseudo-autobiography 101, 108, 117, 130, 142, 144, 149, 160–61

Babel', Isaak 133, 163
   Red Cavalry 133

Bakhtin, Mikhail 5–6
beast fable (*basnia*) 21, 29, 38
Bednyi, Dem'ian 22
belles-lettres 26, 107, 160
bogatyr' 173
Bogdanov, Aleksandr 204
   Red Star 204
Brezhnev 2–3, 9, 11, 23, 26, 162, 176, 179
Brodskii, Iosif 111–12, 154–55
Bulgakov, Mikhail 2, 93, 231
Bunin, Ivan 159, 176
   "Sukhodol" 159, 176
bureaucracy 2, 62, 185, 227

carnival 4, 64, 89
censorship 2–4, 15, 19–20, 22, 24–27, 63, 80, 104, 106, 109, 204, 208–9, 223, 229
characterization 2, 5, 39, 45, 98, 113, 124, 138, 172–74, 206, 216, 227, 232
Chernyshevskii, Nikolai 203
   What Is To Be Done? 203
chiliasm 198, 201
Christ 17, 41, 45–47, 70, 72, 84–85, 174, 216, 221
Chukovskii, Kornei 29, 191, 195
City Folk (*Gorozhane*) 152
Civil War 165, 217
cliché 5, 34, 55–56, 74, 93, 95, 147–48, 179, 237
communism 34, 63, 189, 191, 204, 206–07, 209–14, 216–17, 220–21, 224, 226, 230, 234–35, 237
Communist Party 64, 92, 134, 188–91, 212, 215, 225, 237
Concrete 102

cycle   15–16, 101, 163, 166–67
Dal', Vladimir   21, 235
Dante   17, 33, 76
   Divine Comedy   76
dictatorship   23, 215
didacticism   3, 16, 18, 20–21, 33, 49, 51–52, 56, 66–67, 73, 80, 161, 163, 190
digression   48, 52, 68, 74, 79, 80, 142, 172
documentary prose   51, 110, 112, 142, 157, 160
Dombrovskii, Iurii   13, 163
Dostoevskii, Fedor   62, 93, 126, 139, 203, 205, 208–09, 216
   The Devils   205
   "The Legend of the Grand Inquisitor"   42, 205, 208, 210, 216
Dovlatov, Sergei   9–10, 150–92, 241–42
   The Compromise   152, 190
   Craft   153, 170
   A Foreign Woman   164, 189
   The Invisible Book   151, 153
   The Invisible Newspaper   154
   The March of the Lonely   154–55
   Ours   10, 150–92, 241–42
   The Refrigerator   156
   Solo on the Underwood   172
   "The Subsidiary"   151, 153, 164
   The Suitcase   174
   The Zone   151, 189
dream   34, 89, 117, 119, 127, 129, 133, 135, 141, 201, 203, 208, 210, 230
dystopia   10, 193–238, 242

education   58, 61, 134, 193, 221–22
Efimov, Igor'   152
Ekho   103, 153
emigration   9, 101–03, 110, 112, 116–17, 119, 123–24, 126, 131–33, 135, 137, 140, 142–43, 145, 147, 151–53, 155–57, 165, 168–69, 178, 181, 187, 190–91, 193, 196–97, 210, 231, 241
epic   13, 68, 94, 167, 172–74, 182
Erenburg, Il'ia   66, 191, 195
Erofeev, Venedikt   2, 9–10, 58–100, 240–41
   Dmitrii Shostakovich   61
   Fanni Kaplan (Dissidents)   61
   Good News   60
   Moscow–Petushki   2–3, 10, 58–100, 240–41
   Notes of a Psychopath   60
   Notes of a Happy Neurasthenic   60
   Valpurgis Night, or the Steps of the Commander   61
   "Vasilii Rozanov Through the Eyes of an Eccentric"   61
estrangement (*ostranenie*)   29, 74, 118, 131, 138, 145
ethnicity   31, 132–33, 150, 181–82, 212
euphemism   55–56, 176, 226, 236

fabula   28–29
fairy tale (*skazka*)   21–22, 24, 29, 47, 239
family chronicle   10, 150–92, 241
fantastic   2, 29, 88, 106, 128, 132, 184, 199, 206, 208–09, 222, 227, 230
farce   95, 176, 233
feuilleton   2–3, 14, 197
Figner, Vera   194, 207–08
film   1, 51, 130–31, 195, 197–98
Five-Year Plan   64
folklore   21, 72, 151
Formalists   5
Forster, E. M.   213
   The Machine Stops   213
Freud, Sigmund   201, 233
Frye, Northrop   18, 49, 232

glasnost'   11, 15–16, 58, 102, 105, 150, 152, 155, 194, 197, 206, 242
Gogol', Nikolai   1, 27, 56, 62, 66, 76, 86, 92–93, 96, 98, 112, 181, 191, 193
Golden Age   1, 122, 199, 233
Goncharov, Ivan   121
Gor'kii Institute of World Literature   12, 194
Gor'kii, Maksim   45, 93, 133
Grani   103, 195
grotesque   32, 98–100, 173, 193, 222, 232

Hemingway, Ernest   13, 150, 152, 178, 189
Herzen, Aleksandr   99, 161, 204
   My Past and Thoughts   161
Horatian satire   9, 16, 20, 164, 184, 242
humor   3, 7, 14, 16, 27, 34, 97, 136, 163–64, 174, 176, 206, 216, 228, 231, 233

Hutcheon, Linda 5–7
Huxley, Aldous 202–03, 209, 211, 213, 215, 223, 226, 233
 Brave New World 49, 202–03, 223
hyperbole 43, 52, 101, 170, 175, 188, 212, 214, 222, 234

Il'f, Il'ia and Petrov, Evgenii 2, 66, 92
imagery 19, 28, 32–33, 35, 37, 41–42, 54–55, 76, 82–86, 94, 98–99, 121, 130–31, 145, 149, 210, 232–33, 237–38
 apocalyptic 122, 210
 biblical 30, 71, 84, 240
 mirror 76, 98–99
 scatological 80, 86, 99, 176, 232–34
incongruity 7, 30, 84, 94–95, 97, 109, 172, 175–76, 179, 188
intelligentsia 25, 27–28, 35, 37–38, 40, 44–45, 64, 91, 102–3, 133, 147, 152, 165, 178, 180, 241
irony 1, 7–8, 16, 25, 27, 29, 32, 34–35, 37–38, 42, 47–48, 50, 52, 54, 63, 67, 69, 72, 75, 92, 112–13, 115–16, 119, 128–30, 132, 136, 145, 147, 163, 166, 168, 175, 177, 179, 185–88, 200, 216, 219–21, 225–26, 231, 234, 237
Iskander, Fazil' 2, 9–57, 239–40
 Forbidden Fruit 14
 The Goatibex Constellation 2, 14, 24
 Rabbits and Boa Constrictors 10–57, 239–40
 Sandro of Chegem 13, 15–16, 30, 240
Iunost' 13, 16, 22, 105, 152, 197
Ivanova, Natal'ia 12–15, 23, 33, 39–40

Jung, C. J. 72, 87
Juvenalian satire 9, 16, 20

KGB 62, 102–03, 168, 176, 196, 217
Khrushchev 13, 15, 34, 150, 180, 189, 194–95
Kontinent 61, 104, 153
Kovcheg 103–4, 111
Kremlin 79, 82, 89, 91–92
Krokodil 152

language 4, 12–13, 22, 25–29, 47, 55–56, 58, 60, 73, 78, 94–96, 114, 116, 122, 134, 145–49, 153, 177–79, 182, 184, 197, 212, 226, 234–37

Aesopian 22, 25–27, 47, 56
 barbarisms 144–45
 colloquial speech (*razgovornaia rech'*) 55, 177–78, 235, 237
 diminutives 138
 English 60, 65, 104, 118, 126, 134, 139, 146–47, 155–56, 184, 203, 209
 obscenity (*mat*) 78, 104, 144, 148–49, 178–79
 substandard 55, 96
Lenin 61, 91, 177, 188, 212, 221
Leningrad Prose 150, 156, 178, 189
Lesage, Alain-René 65
 Gil Blas 65
Leskov, Nikolai 125, 158, 160, 184
 A Decrepit Clan 158
 Old Times in the Village of Plodomasov 158, 160
Limonov, Eduard (Savenko) 9–10, 101–49, 184, 241
 "The Beautiful Woman Who Inspired the Poet" 105
 His Butler's Story 105
 It's Me, Eddie 10, 101–49, 241
 Limonov Against Zhirinovskii 105
 Memoir of a Russian Punk 105
 "Ours Was a Great Epoch" 105
 Russkoe 103
 Young Rascal 105
 "We Are the National Hero" 102
Literaturnaia gazeta 60, 103–5, 109, 156, 196
Loseff, Lev 3–4, 25–26
lyricism 60, 68, 97, 113, 145, 194

Maiakovskii, Vladimir 2, 22, 113, 204
Maksimov, Vladimir 104, 180
martyrdom 46, 84, 127
Marxism 32, 35, 79, 95, 204, 206, 226, 230–32
Menippean satire 68
metaphor 29, 42, 44, 64, 90, 116, 120, 122, 127, 145, 164, 166, 169, 184, 233
Metropole Affair 14
mise-en-abyme 25
mock-heroic 174
More, Thomas 198
Morson, Gary Saul 7–8, 200, 207
Moscow 2, 12, 14, 16, 58–59, 61–62, 77–78, 82, 91, 101–02, 105, 111, 113, 120, 127, 146, 194, 197–98,

208, 211, 213–15, 220, 230, 235, 242
Moscow State University 12, 58–59
Moskovskie novosti 105
Murav'ev, Vladimir 60, 62, 81

Nabokov, Vladimir 115, 118, 121
  Lolita 115
  Speak, Memory 121
names 54–55, 73, 77, 85, 101, 110, 112–13, 126, 138, 147, 170, 191, 215, 225, 234–35
narration 6, 10, 15, 27, 29–30, 39, 47–54, 63–66, 68, 71–80, 82–84, 88, 90, 92, 94, 97, 106, 108, 110–11, 115, 117–18, 126, 134–42, 144–45, 147, 151, 153, 157–60, 164, 166–71, 173–92, 207–08, 211, 214, 227–31, 237, 241
Natural School 159
Nedelia 103–04
Neizvestnyi, Ernst 111–12
Neva 152
New York 102, 104, 108, 110–11, 113, 118–20, 122–23, 125–26, 134, 142–43, 149, 153–54, 163, 169, 184, 241
The New Yorker 154, 186
nondisjunction 68
novel 2, 19, 60–61, 63, 77, 101, 105, 114, 116, 151, 158–60, 166, 194–95, 197, 199–200, 206–08, 210, 214, 219, 225, 227–29, 240
Novoe russkoe slovo 102, 112, 153–54
Novyi mir 15, 103, 194
Novyi amerikanets 154

Ogonek 197
Okudzhava, Bulat 195
Olesha, Iurii 126
Orwell, George 65, 193, 203–04, 209, 211, 213, 215, 217, 223–24, 226, 228, 233–34, 236
  1984 203, 223, 233

Panova, Vera 152, 191
parody 4–10, 25, 27–29, 32–33, 38, 41–45, 47, 49, 51–54, 57, 66–70, 72–74, 76–78, 80–82, 86, 90, 93–95, 99–100, 115–17, 121, 130–31, 135, 139, 148, 162, 167, 176–77, 179, 193, 200, 206–08, 210, 212, 220, 224–25, 227–29, 233, 237, 239–43

pastiche 67, 241
pastoral 97, 118, 121, 162, 213, 241
Pen Club 154
period of stagnation (*zastoi*) 2, 26, 63, 159, 212
personification 17–18
Petrashevskii Circle 204
Petrushevskaia, Liudmila 239
picaresque 10, 58–100, 240
picaro 64–66, 68–74, 76, 79, 82, 86–87, 92–93, 240
Plato 141, 198, 227, 230
plot 19, 38, 50, 52–53, 55, 76–77, 82, 166, 168, 172, 206, 209, 211, 215, 227–28
poema 76, 96
poetry 7, 11, 13–14, 17–19, 35, 40–41, 44–48, 50, 52, 59, 61–62, 101–03, 107, 113, 115, 117, 122, 126–28, 134–35, 140, 147, 161, 186–87, 194, 204
poliv 96
Posev 153
poshlost' 92–93
postmodernism 186
povest' 2, 14, 16, 23, 30, 39, 105, 151–52, 160, 166, 194, 196–97, 208
protreptic function 41, 52, 161, 163
Pushkin, Aleksandr 13, 21, 27

quasi-indirect discourse 37, 44

Rabelais, François 89, 93–94
Radio Liberty 153
Radishchev, Aleksandr 77–78, 203
  A Journey from St. Petersburg to Moscow 77–78, 203
realism 96–99, 122, 145, 159, 171
Red Army 165, 194, 217
religion 2, 13, 19, 22, 42, 62, 64, 84, 93, 133, 159, 165, 177, 179, 182, 201, 207, 209, 211–12, 214, 216, 220–22, 227, 234, 237
revolution 22, 79, 89, 92, 132–33, 152
  of 1905 22
  of 1917 2, 122, 159, 165, 177, 179, 182, 201, 212, 214
rhetorical figure 5, 7, 17, 28, 55, 69, 73, 94, 188, 239
rhetorical question 140, 163, 190
Riazanov, El'dar 1
romanticism 14, 18, 21, 134
Rousseau, Jean-Jacques 118, 126

Index

Rozanov, Vasilii 25, 61
Russian Orthodoxy 46, 102, 220
Russkaia mysl' 60

Sakharov, Andrei 103, 111, 133, 147
Salinger, J. D. 13, 150
Saltykov-Shchedrin, Mikhail 1, 22, 25, 27, 62, 158–59, 162, 166, 184
   Golovlev Family 158, 162, 184
   Old Days in Poshekhonie 158
samizdat 2, 26, 58, 60, 102, 152–53, 165, 195
Sapgir, Genrikh 102, 112
Satan 72, 75, 81, 85
satura 66
science 95, 207, 218–19, 223
science fiction 131, 199, 203, 205, 219
sexuality 90, 113, 118, 120, 123, 128–30, 132, 152, 223–24, 233
Shchapova, Elena 102, 104
short story 14, 105, 160, 166
Shvarts, Evgenii 43–44
simile 42, 90, 122, 145
Siniavskii, Andrei 8, 195
skaz 2
sketch 3, 12, 14, 110, 160, 166–68
Slavophilism 160
socialism 64, 68, 91, 204–06, 212–14, 229
socialist realism 2, 45, 150, 226
Sokolov, Sasha 8
Solzhenitsyn, Aleksandr 14, 25, 41, 103, 111–12, 133, 147, 151, 180, 192, 195–97, 231, 242
Soviet Writers' Union 13, 195, 226, 229
Soviet Union 2–4, 9, 11–12, 14–15, 26, 60–61, 69, 102, 105–06, 115, 119, 141, 148, 151–52, 156–57, 168–69, 180, 182–83, 194–95, 197, 204–05, 212, 216–17, 219–20, 223, 225–26, 230–31, 237, 241
Stalin 1–2, 16, 22, 31–32, 34–35, 37, 55, 64, 83, 150, 162, 165, 168, 172–75, 179–81, 187, 191, 204–05, 212, 221–22, 242
Sterne, Lawrence 48, 62, 78, 93
stranstvie 81
Strugatskii, Arkadii and Boris 205
stylistics 10, 54, 68, 94, 97, 144–45, 148, 166, 172, 177–79
surrealism 61, 100, 123, 129, 194

Swift, Jonathan 200–01, 234
   Gulliver's Travels 200
symbolism 13, 17–18, 24, 29–30, 34–35, 39, 42, 52, 54, 77, 81, 83–84, 87, 89, 91, 109, 184, 213, 233, 237, 240

tamizdat 2, 26, 60, 153, 165
Tarkovskii, Arsenii 102
technology 188, 199, 201, 203, 211, 213–14, 218–19, 226, 237
Thaw 2, 13, 63, 96, 150, 155, 158, 174, 180
Third Wave 101, 112, 114, 116, 119, 124, 135, 141, 143, 145–46, 153–54, 156, 196, 210, 241
Tolstaia, Tat'iana 239
Tolstoi, Lev 13, 22, 48, 99, 118, 121–23, 158, 160, 162, 175, 177
   Anna Karenina 100
   Childhood 158, 160, 162
   War and Peace 99
tone 8–9, 16, 19, 52, 56, 65, 68, 80, 83, 89, 101, 124, 136, 164, 170, 186–87, 190, 210
totalitarianism 50, 63, 179, 193, 201, 205, 237, 242
trickster 71–72
Turgenev, Ivan 80, 91
Tvardovskii, Aleksandr 14
Twentieth Party Congress 13

understatement 177, 189
utopia 10, 133, 197–211, 213–15, 219, 221–23, 225, 227–28, 230–33, 237–38, 242

Vail', Petr and Genis, Aleksandr 21, 63, 81, 97, 106, 154, 178
Vakhtin, Boris 152
velirechie 94
verisimilitude 73, 112, 139, 143, 146, 170
Voice of America 195, 197
Voinovich, Vladimir 9–10, 193–238, 242
   The Anti-Soviet Soviet Union 197
   "By Way of Mutual Correspondence" 196
   A Degree of Trust 194, 207
   "A Distance of Half a Kilometer" 194

"The Fur Hat"   197–98
"Incident at the Metropole"   196
"In the Sleeping Compartment"   194
The Ivankiad   196
"I Want to Be Honest"   194
The Life and Extraordinary Adventures of Private Ivan Chonkin   195–98
Moscow 2042   10, 193–238, 242
Pretender to the Throne   196
"The Sovereign"   194
"Two Comrades"   194, 208
"We Live Here"   194
Voltaire   56, 126, 200
Vremia i my   153

war   39, 133, 158, 164, 172, 211–12
Wells, H. G.   199, 203, 205, 218, 223, 233
Anticipations   223
A Story of the Days to Come   203
The Time Machine   203
When the Sleeper Wakes   203
West   3, 9–10, 13–15, 60–61, 64–66, 91, 102–04, 106, 112, 117, 124, 127, 130–31, 134, 139, 141, 143, 147, 150–53, 155–56, 159, 168, 172, 178, 186, 191, 195–99, 201, 203–6, 214, 225, 237
World War II   64, 92, 132, 150, 158–59, 172, 201

Youth Prose   13

Zamiatin, Evgenii   203–05, 209, 211, 213–15, 224–26, 228, 233, 236
"The Cave"   214
We   203, 205, 224–25
Zhirinovskii, Vladimir   105
Znamia   105
Zoshchenko, Mikhail   2, 157

CAMBRIDGE STUDIES IN RUSSIAN LITERATURE

General editor MALCOLM JONES

Editorial board: ANTHONY CROSS, CARYL EMERSON,
HENRY GIFFORD, BARBARA HELDT, G. S. SMITH,
VICTOR TERRAS

In the same series

Novy Mir
EDITH ROGOVIN FRANKEL

The enigma of Gogol
RICHARD PEACE

Three Russian writers and the irrational
T. R. N. EDWARDS

Words and music in the novels of Andrey Bely
ADA STEINBERG

The Russian revolutionary novel
RICHARD FREEBORN

Poets of modern Russia
PETER FRANCE

Andrey Bely
J. D. ELSWORTH

Nikolay Novikov
W. GARETH JONES

Vladimir Nabokov
DAVID RAMPTON

Portraits of early Russian liberals
DEREK OFFORD

Marina Tsvetaeva
SIMON KARLINSKY

Bulgakov's last decade
J. A. E. CURTIS

Velimir Khlebikov
RAYMOND COOKE

Dostoyevsky and the process of literary creation
JACQUES CATTEAU

The poetic imagination of Vyacheslav Ivanov
PAMELA DAVIDSON

Joseph Brodsky
VALENTINA POLUKHINA

Petrushka – the Russian carnival puppet theatre
CATRIONA KELLY

Turgenev
FRANK FRIEDEBERG SEELEY

From the idyll to the novel: Karamzin's sentimentalist prose
GITTA HAMMARBERG

The Brothers Karamazov *and the poetics of memory*
DIANE OENNING THOMPSON

Antrei Platonov
THOMAS SEIFRID

Nabokov's early fiction
JULIAN W. CONNOLLY

Iurii Trifonov
DAVID GILLESPIE

Mikhail Zoshchenko
LINDA HART SCATTON

Andrei Bitov
ELLEN CHANCES

Nikolai Zabolotsky
DARRA GOLDSTEIN

Nietzsche and Soviet Culture
edited by BERNICE GLATZER ROSENTHAL

Wagner and Russia
ROSAMUND BARTLETT

Russia literature and empire: Conquest of the Caucasus from Pushkin to Tolstoy
SUSAN LAYTON

Jews in Russian literature after the October Revolution: writers and artists between hope and apostasy
EFRAIM SICHER